✡ ✡ ✡
I AM MY BROTHER'S KEEPER

I AM MY BROTHER'S KEEPER

American Volunteers
in Israel's War
for Independence
1947-1949

Jeffrey Weiss & Craig Weiss

With a Foreword by
Prime Minister of Israel Benjamin Netanyahu

Schiffer Military History
Atglen, PA

Dedications:

*To my wife Leisha, for all of her love, support, and assistance,
and to my children Danny, Abby and Tali. Together, they gave this meaning.*
J.W.

*To my sweet Erica, whose enduring support and everlasting love
made this book a reality.*
C.W.

To all members of the Weiss family, for their love, support and encouragement.

Book Design by Robert Biondi.

We are interested in hearing from authors with book ideas on military topics.

Published by Schiffer Publishing Ltd.
4880 Lower Valley Road
Atglen, PA 19310
Phone: (610) 593-1777
FAX: (610) 593-2002
E-mail: Schifferbk@aol.com.
Please write for a free catalog.
This book may be purchased from the publisher.
Please include $3.95 postage.
Try your bookstore first.

FOREWORD
by Prime Minister of Israel Benjamin Netanyahu

*A*s time passes and the War of Independence becomes a subject for history books, the danger that the events of that period will be subjected to distortion and dissimilation grows. That is why it is of paramount importance to tell the story of that fateful struggle with precision, and to illuminate all its aspects with great care.

One of the lesser known parts of the liberation saga is the role played by American and Canadian volunteers. Their contribution to the struggle for liberation – which to most military experts in the world seemed doomed to failure – was crucial and effective. They brought with them World War II experience, Western efficiency, exemplary dedication and infinite courage.

Relating the story of these volunteers in fascinating detail and flowing prose, "I Am My Brother's Keeper" is as timely as it is riveting. To read it is to realize yet again that the secret of our survival lies in the fervor of our faith and in the feeling of oneness which unifies our people in times of crisis.

CONTENTS

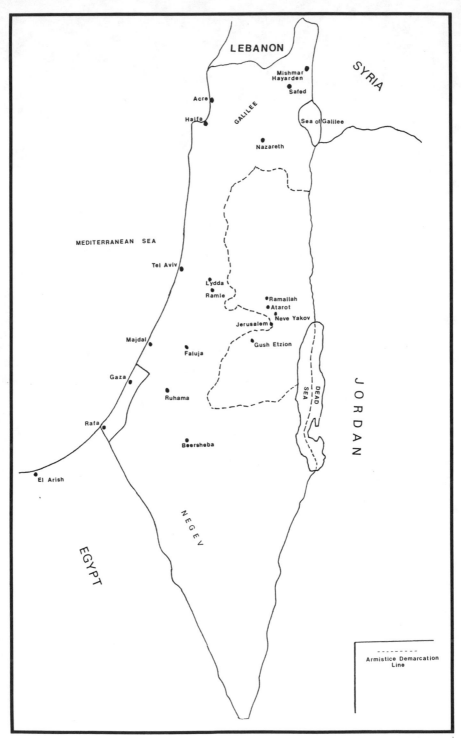

LEBANON

SYRIA

Mishmar
Hayarden

Safed

Acre

GALILEE

Haifa

Sea of Galilee

Nazareth

MEDITERRANEAN SEA

Tel Aviv

Lydda

Ramle

Ramallah

Atarot

Neve Yakov

Jerusalem

Majdal

Faluja

Gush Etzion

Gaza

DEAD SEA

JORDAN

Ruhama

Rafa

Beersheba

El Arish

N E G E V

EGYPT

- - - - - - - -
Armistice Demarcation
Line

(Map by Sherri Belassen)

ACKNOWLEDGMENTS AND SOURCES

We could not have written this book without the generous assistance of the following individuals: Ralph Lowenstein, Harold Livingston, Aaron "Red" Finkel, Eddy Kaplansky, Zipporah Porat, Sid Rabinovich, Smoky Simon, Avi Cohen, David Gen, Rudy Augarten, Gideon Lichtman, Natalie Chahine, Eli Mallus, Abraham Kenny, Dr. David Gutmann, Roanne Mokhtar, Al Ellis, and David Bar Ilan. We thank our agent David Hendin for his hard work, persistence, and belief in this project.

We are particularly grateful for the cooperation of the more than one hundred and ten volunteers who agreed to be personally interviewed. These included members of every branch of Israel's army, air force and navy. We interviewed American veterans of Israel's pre-state underground armies: the Haganah, the Irgun and the Stern Group. Our interview subjects included both men and women. We spoke to individuals who fought on each front and against all of Israel's Arab opponents. We have also benefited from more than one hundred additional volunteer interviews conducted by others over the years, and scattered among archives in Canada, the United States and Israel. We are particularly grateful to Dr. David Bercuson and Dan Kurzman, who granted us access to their interview notes and transcripts. Appendix A contains a complete list of all of the interviews upon which this book is based.

This book is also the product of extensive documentary research, in both English and Hebrew. Our research has been drawn from the following archives and libraries in Israel, Canada, and the U.S.: the Israeli Army's Military Archives (Givattayim, Israel); the Historical Branch of the Israeli Air Force (Tel Aviv, Israel); the Central Zionist Archives (Jerusalem, Israel); the Jerusalem Post archives (Jerusalem, Israel); the National Library at the Hebrew University (Jerusalem, Israel); the archives of Kibbutz Kfar Blum (Kfar Blum, Israel); the Diaspora Research Center (Tel Aviv, Israel); Tel Aviv University (Tel Aviv, Israel); the Maritime Museum (Haifa, Israel); Boston University (Boston, Massachusetts); the American Veterans of Israel Archives (Gainesville, Florida); the United States Military Academy (West Point, New York); the U.S. National Archive (College Park, Maryland); the U.S. National Archive (Laguna Niguel, California); the University of Judaism (Los Angeles, California); the Jewish Library of Montreal (Montreal, Canada); and the National Archives of Canada (Ontario, Canada). We are particularly indebted to Micha Kaufman of Israel's Military Archives. Mr. Kaufman arranged, at our request, the declassification of the official files on American and Canadian volunteers. These documents had remained secret from the War of Independence until our request.

1

SEVEN DAYS IN OCTOBER

American Rudy Augarten flew his Messerschmitt Me 109 toward the Egyptian coastal town of El Arish. Egypt's air base at El Arish had been one of the sites of the previous day's raid by Israel's only fighter squadron, the 101st. Augarten was on a photo-reconnaissance mission to determine what targets the air force had destroyed, and what it needed to finish off. Although his assignment was simple, he was happy for the chance to be flying at all. Israel was in short supply of almost everything, and with less than ten serviceable fighter planes in the entire country, the 101st was particularly afflicted. The fighter squadron didn't have enough planes for the two dozen pilots who were capable of flying them, and there was competition for each flight. On October 16, 1948, one day into the first major Israeli offensive against the Egyptians, Augarten's turn had finally arrived.

As he flew southwest toward the coast, Augarten passed over isolated tracts of green in the otherwise barren Negev desert, indicating the location of Israeli kibbutzes and towns. Suddenly, in the distance, he spotted two Spitfires flying in formation. Augarten could tell by their shape they were not Me 109s, like the plane he was flying. Augarten was too far away to make out their markings, but it didn't matter. Even though the Israeli Air Force had several Spitfires in its arsenal, he knew immediately that the two Spits were Egyptian. Because mechanical problems and fuel shortages limited the Israeli Air Force to only a few planes in the air at any one time, the pilots were always confident when they saw another plane that it was not one of their own.

Augarten, a veteran of ninety-three missions with the U.S. Air Force in World War II, didn't panic. He carefully got into position behind the two Egyptians, hoping they wouldn't detect his approach. Just then, fellow 101 pilot Leon Frankel, who was patrolling in the area, saw Augarten beginning to engage the Spits. Trying to come to Augarten's aid, Frankel rolled his plane over and dove toward the combatants. But before he reached the scene, Augarten lined up one of the Spits in his gunsight, and fired a burst from the Me 109's two 7.92 millimeter machine guns. Pieces of the Spitfire flew off as the bullets pierced its thin aluminum body. The Egyptian plane plummeted toward Israeli lines, leaving a trail of black smoke. The other Spit fled the battle scene. With no other enemy planes in sight, Frankel and Augarten fell into formation for the trip back to the base. A few days later, Augarten got a treat few fighter pilots ever receive. An army unit took him by jeep to see firsthand the wreckage of the plane he had downed. Smiling broadly, he posed for a photograph in front of what remained of the Spit.

With that victory, Augarten had experienced the Czech version of the Me 109 at its best. The Me 109 was the mainstay of the 101 Squadron, even though most of the pilots regarded it as a flying coffin because of its unusual and often deadly flight characteristics. The Me 109 that the Israeli Air Force flew was not the vaunted Messerschmitt that had struck fear into the hearts of Allied pilots during World War II. The Czech plane was fitted with an engine that was both heavier and weaker than the engines the Germans used during the war. That switch caused the plane to pull left on take-off and right on landing, sometimes so violently that the Me 109 actually flipped over. Yet the Me 109 had an even more deadly problem. Its two machine guns were mounted on the nose of the plane. They were supposed to be timed to the revolutions of the propeller, firing their bullets between the propeller's broad, paddle-type blades. In practice, the guns had a tendency to go out of synch, causing several pilots to literally shoot themselves down. But as Augarten's mission proved, even with all these problems, the Me 109 was still fighter plane enough for the veteran pilots of the new Israeli Air Force to hold their own against the superior Spitfires flown by the Egyptians.

Former U.S. Navy pilot Leon Frankel, though, was about to experience the Me 109 at its worst. As Frankel headed back to the air base at Herzliya with Augarten, Frankel's fuel gauge warning light began flashing, indicating fifteen minutes of fuel remaining. He was not sure he could make it back to the base, so he changed course and headed to the nearer airfield at Ekron for refueling. There he noticed his engine was leaking oil. He pointed out the leak to an Israeli mechanic, who, after a few twists of a wrench, pronounced the problem "fixed."

In the air, Frankel immediately knew he was in trouble. The engine started to run rough. Frankel checked his oil pressure gauge. He couldn't believe his eyes – the gauge read zero. Frankel rapped on the gauge, hoping it was only stuck. The needle stayed where it was. What Frankel couldn't know was that when he left Ekron, a giant black cloud had poured out of the bottom of the plane. He had lost every ounce of the plane's oil on takeoff. It was obvious he wouldn't make it to Herzliya, and Frankel looked for someplace else to land. He spotted the Lydda airfield, and tried to line up for a landing on its east-west runway.

With a crash landing imminent, Frankel tried to jettison the Messerschmitt's canopy, which would give him a better chance of jumping free if the plane caught fire on landing. The canopy was hinged on one side and locked down on the other. A lever in the cockpit was supposed to unlock the canopy and detach the hinges, but, like so many things with the Me 109, this feature was unreliable. Frankel yanked the lever and desperately pushed the canopy. The canopy unlocked, but the hinges didn't detach. The canopy flopped open, closed, open, closed as the wind buffeted the plane.

Compounding Frankel's problems, the Me 109 had no flaps, so he couldn't slow the plane as it plunged downward. Smoke poured into the cockpit, the canopy flopped back and forth, and the plane – with its wheels up – was coming in fast between two rows of orange trees. Just beyond the trees, Frankel could see a fifty-foot-deep gully filled with boulders. He barely cleared the gully and reached a grassy area just before the airfield, sliding the plane in on its belly. On impact, the rudder pedals jolted back, jamming Frankel's left leg so violently that, nearly fifty years later, it was still an inch shorter than the right. Otherwise, Frankel was unhurt. It was to be his last flight for Israel.

The Israeli offensive, code-named Operation Yoav, had begun only the day before with Israeli air raids on Egyptian air bases and troop concentrations. Israel launched Yoav to relieve the isolation of its Negev settlements and to drive Egyptian forces from the area. A mostly barren desert in the southern part of Israel, the Negev had a few scattered Jewish kibbutzes and a number of Arab towns. Although Israel occupied a large portion of the Negev, Egyptian troops entirely surrounded the Israeli settlements, cutting them off from the rest of the country. Before Operation Yoav, Israel had to supply the isolated settlements by air or by infiltrating across enemy lines at night. But it was not only the plight of the besieged residents of the Negev that spurred Israel's decision to launch Operation Yoav. Israel's leaders were well aware that the final contours of the new state were still to be decided, and that Israel could not claim territory it did not occupy.

While Augarten and Frankel were busy with the Egyptian Spits, the Israeli ground forces were in action as well. On October 16, the ground troops attacked Egyptian-occupied fortresses at the strategically located Negev villages of Iraq Suweidan and Iraq El Manshie, as well as Egyptian forces on a nearby hill known as "Hill 113." The attack on Hill 113 was successful, though the Egyptians rebuffed the other Israeli assaults. The towns of Iraq Suweidan and Iraq El Manshie would prove to be stubborn targets.

After Hill 113 was captured, the army ordered the Fourth Anti-Tank Squad, commanded by a former American infantry officer named Lester Gorn, to proceed to the top of the hill. The army hoped the Egyptians had left some anti-tank weapons, which the Fourth could put to immediate use in the fighting. Although the Fourth was an "anti-tank" unit, that designation reflected more the aspirations of the army's general staff than anything else. The unit's most powerful weapon was a single twenty-millimeter Hispano Suiza machine gun, a weapon whose bullets were more likely to bounce off the thick armor plating of an enemy tank than pierce its shell.

The Fourth was one of Israel's more unconventional units. Gorn modeled the Fourth on Carlson's Raiders, a World War II commando unit renowned for operating according to democratic principles. Like Carlson's Raiders, the Fourth's soldiers voted whether or not to participate in particular actions. They also met following each operation to discuss the squad's performance. The Fourth attracted more than twenty Americans to its ranks, including former U.S. Marine Jerry Balkin and Jesse Slade.

Balkin, known to everyone as "Tiny," stood six feet tall and weighed in at over two hundred pounds. Though he wasn't religious, the death of eighty-five members of his family during the Holocaust convinced Tiny of the need for a Jewish homeland. But that was not the only reason he decided to leave his Los Angeles home to fight for an independent Jewish state. Tiny was embarrassed to admit it, but he enjoyed the camaraderie he shared fighting with the marines in the Pacific, and he had trouble finding himself after the war. Israel's struggle for independence was his chance to recover the glory days of World War II.

Jesse Slade became one of Tiny's closest friends in the Fourth. Slade was an American Indian from Oklahoma. During World War II, his commanding officer had been a Jew, and the two men had gotten along well. Slade was unaccustomed to non-Indians treating him as an equal, and he appreciated his relationship with the Jewish officer. "He was the first guy to treat me like a white man," Slade told Tiny. When the War of Independence broke out, Slade made his way to Israel to join the fighting. He found his home in the Fourth.

When Margaret Bourke-White, the famous *Life Magazine* photographer, came to Israel to cover the war, she talked with Slade, who was wearing his trademark cowboy hat. She asked the obvious question: "What's an Indian doing here in a war between Arabs and Jews?" Slade paused for a moment, slid the hat back on his head, and answered: "Well ma'am, I reckoned it was the Christian thing to do."

When Tiny, Slade and the other members of the Fourth reached the top of Hill 113, they scoured the Egyptian positions. The battle had been fierce. Dead Egyptian bodies littered the makeshift encampment. Tiny and the others quickly crisscrossed the rocky slopes, but there were no anti-tank weapons to be found. As the men frantically searched, Egyptian reinforcements arriving at the base of the hill began to lob mortar shells at the Israeli positions. The Fourth's soldiers immediately dove for cover, and dug in for the night. The next morning, Tiny woke with a start – there was a strange hand on his face. His shock quickly turned to revulsion. His hastily chosen position had been right next to a dead Egyptian soldier. The force of the shelling had caused the body to shift during the night, until the dead soldier was laying with his hand on Tiny's face.

Later during the Negev fighting, the Fourth received orders to hold a newly-captured hilltop. The surrounding area was not secure, and an Egyptian sniper fired at the men from a nearby field. Tiny and Slade were standing together, taking cover behind one of several primitive huts the Egyptians had erected. Slade turned to Tiny: "I think I know where he is, but I gotta make sure. So you run between the huts, and when he shoots, I'll spot him."

Tiny hesitated. He knew it was crazy, but he couldn't let Slade down. "Okay," said Tiny, and away he went. The sniper fired, and bullets kicked up the dirt at Tiny's feet. Almost immediately, two shots rang out from Slade's position. "Okay, you can come back now," Slade called out. He handed Tiny his rifle and said, "I'll be right back." While Tiny watched dumbfounded, Slade walked down into the valley unarmed, found the body of the Egyptian sniper, and dragged him back up the hill. The sniper had two bullet holes in his head.

As the Negev fighting continued, Israeli intelligence intercepted a message that an Egyptian tanker was moving in to deliver fuel to Majdal, a coastal town where large numbers of Egyptian troops were concentrated. On October 19, four days into Operation Yoav, Israel's navy dispatched three ships to confront the Egyptian vessel. Those warships were not particularly intimidating. The *Hashomer* and the *Haganah* were small corvettes, and the third, the *Nogah*, was a minesweeper. Israel had purchased each as war surplus and, in the case of the two corvettes, had used them prior to Israel's Declaration of Independence to ferry thousands of Holocaust survivors and other Jewish refugees from Europe to Palestine. With the establishment of the state, the new Israeli Navy bolted a few machine guns to the ships' decks, and called them warships.

The fastest of the three ships, the *Nogah*, led the assault. As she approached the Egyptian vessel, the *Nogah's* crew immediately saw they were overmatched. The Egyptian "tanker" turned out to be the *Emir Farouk*, the flagship of the Egyptian navy. Armed with heavy guns and cannons, the *Farouk* had a crew of 1,100 sailors. The *Nogah* fell back, rejoining the *Hashomer* and the *Haganah*. Both sides called in air support. The Egyptian air force reached the scene first. Three Spitfires and a Sea Fury strafed and bombed the Israeli ships, killing one sailor and wounding four others. Then a lone Israeli plane appeared. It was a Bristol Beaufighter, a twin-engine, medium bomber. The pilot was Canadian Len Fitchett, one of several non-Jewish members of the air force's 103 Squadron.

The Egyptian fighters protecting the *Emir Farouk* spotted Fitchett's Beaufighter as soon as it entered the fray. The Egyptian Fury immediately turned to go after Fitchett's plane. The other planes, perhaps low on fuel, left the scene. The Fury was piloted by Squadron Leader Abu Zaid. A veteran of seventy-two missions, he was considered Egypt's finest pilot. Although Fitchett was flying a slow, difficult-to-maneuver bomber, he had flown nightfighters with the Royal Canadian Air Force during World War II and had not lost his fighter pilot's instincts. He jettisoned his bombs to increase maneuverability, and dove toward the water. The Fury was right on his tail. At the last possible moment, Fitchett pulled back on the stick, straightening his plane out just over the wave tops. The Egyptian could not turn quickly enough and didn't have enough time to bail out. The Fury and its pilot plunged into the Mediterranean.

2

I AM MY BROTHER'S KEEPER

Rudy Augarten, Leon Frankel, Tiny Balkin, Jesse Slade, and Len Fitchett were not the only North Americans to fight in Israel's War of Independence. More than one thousand men and women followed their same path, many leaving behind wives, children, university studies, and careers. They came for many different reasons, some ideological and some personal. But they came and they made a difference. This is their story.

Of all of Israel's wars, the War of Independence was the longest and the most costly. It officially began with Israel's Declaration of Independence on May 14, 1948, although the fighting actually started months earlier, with the passage on November 29, 1947, by the United Nations General Assembly of a resolution favoring the partition of Palestine into Jewish and Arab states. That vote, rejected by Palestine's Arab residents and all of its Arab neighbors, finally led the British rulers of Palestine to give up a Mandate they had held since the end of World War I – setting the stage for a confrontation between Jews and Arabs for the right to control the land. In the bloody, nearly year-long war between Israel and the Arabs, fully one percent of Israel's 600,000 Jewish residents would lose their lives.

Nearly a decade before the U.N. vote, Palestine's Jewish community began to mount an armed struggle against the British occupation. But most of Palestine's Jews believed that, by fighting the British, they were diverting England's resources away from the war against the Nazis. It was only in the years following World War II, after the defeat of the Nazis, that the Jews' armed struggle against the British reached its zenith. By 1947, there were three separate Jewish underground fighting forces: the Haganah, the Irgun, and the Stern Group. The Haganah was by far the largest, best-equipped, and most organized of the three, with some 30,000 full or part-time soldiers in its ranks. Its leaders set out to create the infrastructure of an army that could defend the future state from outside attack. The Haganah was also at the forefront of Aliyah Bet, the ship-born immigration of Jewish refugees into Palestine in defiance of Britain's naval blockade. The post-World War II Aliyah Bet voyages, which presented the world with dramatic confrontations between the pitiable remnant of European Jewry and the crushing might of Britain's Royal Navy, went a long way toward bringing about the end of Britain's Mandate over Palestine.

On May 14, 1948, Israeli independence, and war, became official. On that day the British finally departed the country, their twenty-eight years of rule at an end. In Tel Aviv, David Ben Gurion proudly proclaimed the independence of the State of Israel. Within hours, forces from all of Israel's Arab neighbors – Egypt, Jordan, Lebanon, and Syria – supported by troops from Iraq and Saudi Arabia, invaded the country. The Lebanese and Syrians attacked Israeli settlements in the north, the Jordanians moved against Jerusalem from the east, and the Egyptians sent their tanks into the Negev from the south. Most believed the new state's meager forces could not resist the massive Arab attack for long.

One of Ben Gurion's first official acts was to create the Israel Defense Forces (IDF), the army of the new state. As a practical matter, Ben Gurion turned the Haganah into the IDF, and members of the Irgun and the Stern Group joined its ranks. But the newly formed army was woefully underequipped. Its air force consisted of about two dozen light aircraft – single-engine Piper Cubs and Austers – which had been used primarily to resupply besieged settlements. The navy had fourteen ships, the legacy of Aliyah Bet. The armored corps had only one tank to its name – a broken-down M4 Sherman that the Haganah found in a scrap yard. The IDF had no fighter planes, no medium or heavy bombers, and no heavy artillery pieces. Israel lacked even the transport planes needed to quickly bring military supplies into the country. It desperately needed these weapons of war, as well as more light machine guns, ammunition, and military equipment of every other kind.

The Haganah's leaders saw the writing on the wall months before Ben Gurion's Declaration of Independence, and had started to take steps to address the severe equipment shortages. They sent emissaries all over the world to search for weapons, and to recruit veterans, particularly pilots, to join the new country's armed forces. Much of this activity took place in the United States, where a seemingly unlimited quantity of World War II surplus equipment was available for purchase. A clandestine network of offices sprang up in major cities throughout the U.S. The Haganah created two front organizations to assist in these tasks, each of which violated U.S. law. Land and Labor for Palestine masked the recruitment of soldiers, while Materials for Palestine shielded the purchase of arms. Ultimately, Israel would equip its entire heavy bomber and transport squadrons with World War II surplus planes purchased in the United States. Those planes would be crewed by American airmen located by the Haganah. North American servicemen of all kinds would make their way by boat from New York to France, through displaced persons camps in Europe, and on to Israel to join in the fighting.

The paucity of the Israeli forces and the inexperience of most of its fighters left a vacuum for foreign volunteers to fill. West Point graduate Mickey Marcus became Israel's first general. Annapolis graduate Paul Shulman became the first commander of the navy. Canadian Ben Dunkelman commanded one of Israel's twelve brigades. His fellow countryman Lionel Druker commanded the IDF's first tank. Pennsylvanian Marlin Levin, a code specialist, helped break the Jordanian army's code, and assisted in the establishment of security procedures for Haganah headquarters. U.S. Air Force veteran Nat Cohen was the first head of air force intelligence. Former X-1 test pilot Slick Goodlin became the first test pilot of the Israeli Air Force. Americans Arieh Jacoby and Les Goodwin created the air force's photographic-reconnaissance group. The list goes on.

The Americans and Canadians served in all branches of the Israel Defense Forces: the army, the air force, and the navy. The presence of volunteers was most significant in the air force, where a majority of the pilots came from the United States, Canada, and other English-speaking countries. Several of the air force's squadrons, including the fighter squadron, the transport squadron, and the heavy bomber squadron, were made up almost entirely of Americans and Canadians. The leading aces of the war, with four victories each, were American Rudy Augarten and Canadian Jack Doyle. American Bill Katz piloted a B-17 during a July 1948 raid on Cairo – the only assault on Egypt's capital during the war.

An obvious question is why these particular individuals interrupted their lives to travel halfway around the world so they could fight in another country's war of independence. Some had volunteered before. Americans Chris Magee and Slick Goodlin, who later became fighter pilots for Israel, began their aviation careers with the Royal Canadian Air Force, where they received their initial training. Pilot Martin Ribakoff flew supplies for the Loyalists during the Spanish Civil War.

Since Israel's War of Independence, many other countries have achieved independence, and there has been no shortage of regional conflicts. Yet, there has been no large-scale participation of non-mercenary Americans in any of these wars. In trying to determine why so many Americans were willing to travel to Israel to fight, the conclusion is inescapable that there was something special about this war. By 1948, everyone knew that six million Jews, one third of the world's Jewish population, had perished in the Holocaust. Hundreds of thousands of Holocaust survivors languished in European displaced persons camps, desperate to go to the only country that wanted them. Sympathy for the Jewish cause was never higher, and the need for a Jewish state as a guarantor of the Jewish people's physical survival was never more clear. The volunteers who fought for Israel, Jews and non-Jews alike, saw this as another "good" war, like World War II. For them, justice lay entirely on the side of the Jews who fought for the independence of their tiny state.

That is not to say that the volunteers were a homogeneous lot. While most of the volunteers were Jewish, many non-Jews also fought. Some of the volunteers, like pilot Jerry Renov, an observant Jew from Louisiana who became known in Israel as "The Flying Kippah," and Leonard Fitchett, a devout Christian from Canada, came from religious backgrounds, and saw themselves contributing to the fulfillment of the prophesied return of the Jewish people to their homeland. Most of the Americans who came to Israel, however, were not religious, and joined Israel's armed forces for other reasons. The Holocaust was a rallying point for many. One volunteer, Milton "Limey" Miller, still carries in his wallet pictures he took fifty years ago of a massacre site that his American army unit came across toward the end of World War II. For others, like Canada's leading World War II ace George "Buzz" Beurling, a pilot with thirty-one kills to his credit, it was the opportunity to recapture the glory and adventure of their previous war-time experiences that drew them to Israel.

Most of the volunteers were veterans of the American, Canadian, or even British armies, and had the military skills needed to make a contribution to a new state struggling for independence. There were exceptions. Eighteen-year-old Ralph Lowenstein from Danville, Virginia had just completed his freshman year at Columbia University when he traveled to Europe, walked into the new Israeli Embassy in Paris, and volunteered to join the Israeli Army. Of the overwhelming majority of the volunteers who were veterans, many had fought in World War II, with some compiling particularly noteworthy achievements. Canadian John McElroy, with ten kills, was one of Canada's top ten World War II aces. Rudy Augarten had been shot down over occupied France just after D-Day, and spent sixty-three days behind enemy lines. Air force pilot Chris Magee flew in Pappy Boyington's famed Black Sheep Squadron, where he recorded nine kills and won the coveted Navy Cross.

Those who came to fight for Israel faced many barriers when they arrived in the country: linguistic, cultural, and sometimes religious. While the volunteers were technically considered *"Machal"* – a Hebrew acronym meaning "Volunteers from Outside of the Land" – they joined regular army units. After an early experiment with an all-Canadian infantry platoon, the army quickly abandoned the idea of units comprised entirely of foreign nationals. While many of the Anglo-Saxons, as all of the native English speakers were known, congregated in a few different units, none of these were exclusively American or Canadian. One issue then that most of the volunteers had to struggle with was the language barrier. While many Israelis spoke English, the language of the British mandatory authorities, Hebrew was the country's official language and the language of its army. There was one notable exception. Air force operations were conducted in English, the language of nearly all of the pilots and air crews.

Otherwise, all of the foreign volunteers had to learn, or at least reach some accommodation with, the Hebrew language. American Paul Shulman, the commander of the navy, needed to bring an interpreter with him to meetings of the IDF's general staff. Few of the volunteers had extensive Hebrew backgrounds, and the language barrier often proved to be difficult, and occasionally deadly.

Adjusting to Israel and Israelis proved to be the source of the greatest frustration. Many of the North Americans felt unappreciated, if not resented, despite their having travelled thousands of miles to fight. Another source of friction was the general policy of the IDF to appoint Israelis to positions of command – particularly in the air force – even where foreign volunteers were clearly more qualified. On the other hand, a small minority of the North American volunteers exaggerated their military qualifications, or caused disciplinary problems. For all of these reasons, the assimilation of foreign volunteers into the Israeli Army was not smooth. The absorption of the North Americans into the country following the war was an almost complete failure. Less than ten percent of those who came for the fighting stayed on after the war was over.

In the final analysis, there is no question that the Americans and Canadians contributed way beyond their numbers to Israel's dramatic victory. The air force would not have been an effective fighting force without the North Americans. Had they stayed home, there would have been no transport squadron, no heavy bomber squadron, and not much of a fighter squadron. The navy, beginning with its commander Paul Shulman, was also heavily dependent on the volunteers. Colonel Mickey Marcus and Seventh Brigade Commander Ben Dunkelman made key contributions to the successes of the ground forces – including the lifting of the siege of Jerusalem and the clearing of the Galilee of all of its invaders. While we can never know how the war might have ended without the volunteers, Israel is fortunate that it did not have to find out.

3

ALIYAH BET

David Gutmann's eyesight had been too poor to qualify him for combat service in World War II. Determined not to miss out on the fighting entirely, he joined the merchant marine, which had less rigorous physical requirements than the other services. The merchant marine, Gutmann believed, would at least give him the opportunity to go to sea. He hoped there would be some action as well.

Like many of his generation, Gutmann enjoyed the war years. He liked being at sea, visiting exotic ports, learning a trade. Gutmann felt that he grew up during this period. With the war over, he wasn't excited about returning to what now seemed a dull, pre-war life in New York City, and he had difficulty adjusting. Not only did the slower pace of life "on the beach" gnaw at him, there was a lack of opportunity as well. Unlike their counterparts who had served in the regular military, veterans of the merchant marine did not qualify for educational benefits under the GI Bill of Rights. Like many others in his position, Gutmann felt crowded out by the returning GI's. With nothing better to do, he continued to sail on merchant ships, staying with family in the Bronx between jobs.

One day in 1946, Gutmann, who was between trips, saw an ad in the *New York Post*. Placed by the American League for a Free Palestine (ALFP), the ad attacked Great Britain for its continued refusal to allow Jews to freely enter Palestine. Throughout the war years, the British had steadfastly refused to allow more than a token number of Jews to trickle into Palestine. It was a policy that stranded untold numbers of Jews in Nazi-occupied Europe, and guaranteed that the ovens of Auschwitz would never be empty. Even after the war was over, when the extent of the destruction of the Jewish people became known, the British refused to alter their policy against free Jewish emigration into Palestine.

As David Gutmann sat in his apartment, reading the American League for a Free Palestine's advertisement, there were hundreds of thousands of Jewish refugees in displaced persons camps in the Allied zones of occupation in Europe. Most of these refugees had survived the Holocaust, and it was not an option for them to return to their pre-war homes in Europe. With the wounds of the Holocaust still fresh, the DP's wanted to leave the continent that had become a graveyard for the Jewish people. Many wanted to go to Palestine to start a new life in a land where Jews would be a majority. Their desires and British policy were on a collision course.

The American League for a Free Palestine was the American wing of the *Irgun Zvai Leumi,* one of three underground armies fighting against the British in Palestine for Jewish independence. More confrontational than the much larger Haganah, the Irgun believed that direct attacks against Britain's occupying forces represented the best hope for ending the Mandate. Led by Menachem Begin, its name had become synonymous with its most dramatic, and deadly, strike against British rule in Palestine – the July 22, 1946 bombing of British military headquarters in the King David Hotel in Jerusalem, an attack that left nearly one hundred fifty dead and wounded.

In the years following the Nazi ascent to power in Germany, and continuing throughout World War II, agents of the Haganah and Irgun were involved in desperate efforts to rescue the Jews of Europe. In the beginning of what would later become known as "Aliyah Bet" ("Immigration B"), European Jews were loaded onto small, broken-down ships and transported toward Palestine. (The name "Aliyah Bet" was intended to distinguish this unauthorized immigration from the legal entry of Jews into Palestine.) The goal of Aliyah Bet voyages was to evade the British blockade and to physically land the passengers on Palestine's shores. By the beginning of World War II in 1939, the Haganah alone had rescued some seven thousand refugees.

The character of Aliyah Bet changed with the end of World War II. Following Germany's defeat, the Jews of Europe no longer faced an imminent threat of physical annihilation. Although life in the displaced person's camps was hard, there was no meaningful comparison between life in those post-war detention centers and the concentration camps. There was, as a result, less of the desperation that had characterized Aliyah Bet during the war years. On the other hand, the struggle for Jewish independence in Palestine had intensified, and the transport of Jewish refugees now assumed a political, as well as humanitarian, dimension. By exposing to the world Britain's refusal to allow Holocaust survivors and other Jewish refugees to enter Palestine, the Jews believed they could pressure Britain to change its immigration policy. But more ambitiously, the effort to bring Jews to Palestine despite the blockade was part of a larger struggle to free Palestine from British rule.

Beginning in 1946, much of the Aliyah Bet operation shifted from Europe to the United States. In the post-war period, Aliyah Bet operatives found it difficult to acquire large, seaworthy vessels that could move refugees in sufficient numbers to pressure the British and attract the attention of the world press. The Haganah in particular, which by now had a virtual monopoly in Aliyah Bet trafficking, was attracted by the availability in the U.S. of war-surplus ships that were well-suited for illegal immigration.

As the *New York Post* ad that had attracted David Gutmann showed, the Irgun also looked to America as a base for launching Aliyah Bet ships. That ad was exactly what Gutmann had been looking for. The Holocaust had disturbed him deeply, and he was angered by Britain's determination to prevent the survivors from making their way to a new life in Palestine. He saw Aliyah Bet as another cause worth fighting for. Gutmann contacted the American League for a Free Palestine, and offered his services.

The Irgun's Aliyah Bet recruiters, like those of the Haganah, were particularly interested in men with seaman's papers. They preferred experienced sailors to those who believed fervently in the "cause," but had never put to sea. Still, the Irgun wanted to be sure that the volunteers were prepared for the challenges they might face as participants in an Irgun-style Aliyah Bet voyage. The Irgun had a different attitude toward Aliyah Bet than the Haganah. The Haganah believed that once the British captured an Aliyah Bet ship, the ship's crew had completed its mission and needed to be saved from British prisons. It would become standard Haganah policy to either hide crewmen aboard the captured vessel, to be removed later by Haganah agents, or to mix the crewmen with the passengers.

The Irgun saw things differently. It believed the crew could continue the battle even after the ship's capture. When Irgun members were charged in Palestine with attacks against the British, they used the trials to publicly challenge the legitimacy of British rule in the country. Irgun soldiers like Dov Gruner, although facing death sentences, would turn the tables on their accusers – refusing to defend themselves and instead speaking out defiantly against the British occupation. Those speeches were intended to rally public opinion against the British, in Palestine and outside of the country. Attempting to translate this practice into the world of Aliyah Bet, the Irgun wanted the American crewmen of their vessels to identify themselves to the British as Americans, be arrested, and then use the subsequent trials to attack Britain's Palestine policy.

The Irgun's plan carried obvious risks for the crewmen, most notably that of imprisonment. As Gutmann sat in the offices of the ALFP, the subject, not surprisingly, came up. Gutmann's interviewer that day was Abraham Stavsky, an Irgun veteran whose name would forever be linked with a tragic episode in Zionist history. In 1933, a prominent Labor Zionist named Chaim Arlosoroff was gunned down in Tel Aviv. The Jewish Agency immediately accused the right wing Revisionist Zionists – from whose ranks the Irgun would later grow – of being behind the killing. The British arrested Stavsky and another Palestinian Jew named Zvi Rosenblatt, both Revisionists, and tried them for Arlosoroff's murder. They were initially convicted, and sentenced to hang. But their convictions were overturned on appeal and they were released for a lack of evidence. They could not, however, remain in Palestine. Each took assumed names, Stavsky became "Palest" and Rosenblatt became "Stein" – together spelling their beloved homeland "Palestine" – and left the country. Stavsky ultimately became involved with the Irgun in the United States.

Stavsky made a lasting impression on Gutmann. A dark, heavy-set man, Stavsky dressed formally, but more like a gangster than a businessman. He talked tough, with a heavy European accent. To Gutmann, he seemed like a Jewish Mafioso. After going over Gutmann's credentials, Stavsky turned to the issue of imprisonment. "You know you could go to jail for this. Are you prepared to spend perhaps a year in jail?" Gutmann thought it over for a moment. "Well, the prospect doesn't make me happy, but if that's what it takes, that's what it takes." The answer satisfied Stavsky, who accepted Gutmann as a crewman.

The boat that Gutmann was to serve on was the S.S. *Abril*, a German-built yacht the American League for a Free Palestine had purchased for $38,000 at a government auction of surplus vessels. There was a rumor that the yacht had belonged to the Krupp family, wealthy German industrialists who had avidly supported the Nazi regime. Regardless of who had previously owned it, the ship was in poor condition and needed extensive refitting. The yacht's new owners found a novel way to pay for the refitting – they used the proceeds of a Broadway play.

The author of the play, *A Flag is Born*, was Ben Hecht, an early American recruit to the Irgun's American arm and a noted playwright. An Irgun sympathizer since 1941, Hecht wrote propaganda, gave speeches, and sought the sponsorship of noted public figures for various Irgun publicity campaigns. Hecht brought a special creativity to his work. Once, in 1942, he needed co-sponsors for a telegram supporting the creation of a Jewish army to fight against the Nazis. (One of Hecht's allies in this effort was a non-Jewish British colonel named John H. Patterson, a legendary soldier whose lion-hunting exploits were chronicled in the 1997 film *The Ghost and the Darkness*.) Hecht approached movie studio head David O. Selznick for his support. Selznick demurred, explaining that he was, first and foremost, an American, and therefore had no interest in Hecht's Jewish cause. "If I can prove you are a Jew, David, will you sign the telegram as a co-sponsor with me?" Hecht asked. "How are you going to prove it?" inquired Selznick. "I'll call up any three people you name, and ask them the following question: 'What would you call David O. Selznick, an American or a Jew?' If any of the three answers that he'd call you an American, you win. Otherwise, you sign the telegram," Hecht responded. Selznick chose the names, and Hecht made the calls, with Selznick eavesdropping on an extension. As Hecht had expected, each responded that Selznick was a Jew. The last person on Selznick's list, agent Leland Hayward, was emphatic: "For God's sake, what's the matter with David?

He's a Jew and he knows it." Selznick signed the telegram.

To help the Irgun raise funds, Hecht turned to the thing he knew best – writing plays. *A Flag is Born*, an unabashed piece of propaganda, opened on Broadway in 1946. Hecht was able to attract several talented artists for the production. Paul Muni and Marlon Brando starred as two Jewish men who wander among tombstones in Europe, recalling the horrors of the past and expressing despair over the future of the Jewish people. At the end, young Jewish soldiers appear, promising the men that they will "wrest our homeland out of British claws." The *London Evening Standard* called *A Flag is Born* "the most virulent anti-British play ever staged in the United States." In the end, it raised nearly one million dollars, much of which went to restoring the *Abril*.

Ultimately, some twenty Americans would form the crew of the *Abril*, together with two Norwegian engineers. Not all of the crewmen were Jewish. Like the Haganah, the Irgun accepted non-Jewish seamen on its boats. It would be difficult, though, to imagine a less likely fit than that between Walter "Heavy" Greaves and Aliyah Bet. Greaves, the ship's bosun, was a professional sailor who had survived three torpedoings during World War II. Heavy was in his late twenties, and had been at sea since the age of sixteen. In all respects, he looked the part of the well-travelled, carousing sailor. As his nickname suggested, Heavy was a large, overweight man. His upper body was covered with tattoos. Some of the tattoos, like "Mother" and "Sailor's Grave," were harmless enough, but others, like "Rape Before Jack-Off," gave testimony to Heavy's seedier side. The incongruity of Heavy's association with the cause of Jewish immigration was not lost on Heavy himself, who observed that it was to the Jews' credit that they were able to attract men like him to their ranks. In fact, the fit may not have been as odd as appearances suggested. Despite Heavy's rough exterior, Gutmann and the other *Abril* crewmen, Jews and non-Jews alike, soon came to appreciate Heavy as a consummate sailor and gifted storyteller with a wonderful sense of humor. Heavy and Gutmann were among the first crewmen to report to the *Abril*, and the two men shared cold night watches. The younger Gutmann would listen mesmerized as Heavy talked about his sea-going experiences.

The *Abril* sailed from New York on December 26, 1946. The small ship encountered fierce seas as it crossed the North Atlantic for Europe.

The ship nearly foundered as it was pounded from astern by strong winds and crashing waves. Much of the crew, including experienced seamen like Gutmann, became ill. During the worst of the storm, Heavy came upon two Orthodox sailors, huddled in the deckhouse. The men were wrapping their phylacteries as they prepared to pray. Heavy looked first at the menacing sea, before turning to the sailors: "That's right boys, give them beads a good working-over."

On January 10, 1947, after a brief refueling stop at the Azores, the *Abril* arrived at the French harbor of Port de Bouc. There, workers came on board to ready the *Abril* for its load of illegal immigrants. Wherever possible, they installed wooden bunks below decks in the yacht's six cabins, enough to provide sleeping accommodation for the more than six hundred expected passengers. The process took some six weeks, and the crew had little to occupy themselves while the ship was being readied.

Meanwhile, with the sailing of the *Abril* from New York, the ALFP had started up its publicity campaign in earnest. ALFP ads and press releases spoke of a "fleet" of blockade runners that the group was readying in France. Gutmann and the others were upset about the publicity, which they first learned about from reading *Time* magazine. They knew there was no fleet of ships, only the one small yacht that had barely made it across the Atlantic. The misleading nature of the stories wasn't all that bothered them. The publicity exposed the ship while it was still being refitted and before it loaded its passengers, a clear breach of security. Gutmann was a political novice when it came to Palestine. Before the voyage, he had no idea of the difference between the Haganah and the Irgun. Now he was beginning to regard the Irgun as amateurish. Worse, he felt as though he was being used by the organization solely for publicity purposes, and thought seriously of leaving the ship.

Abraham Stavsky, the man who had hired Gutmann for the voyage, was in France for the final preparations and visited the *Abril* regularly. On one occasion, the crew complained bitterly to Stavsky about the publicity. Stavsky listened patiently, a smile on his face. When they were done, he spoke: "You know who the security leak is – it's you. When I fuck I don't talk. When you fuck you talk." Unsatisfied, some of the other crewmen decided to take the drastic step of visiting the Haganah's office in Marseilles, to seek the Haganah's counsel. The advice of its French representative was simple and direct: "The best thing you can do for us is to get that fucking ship out of here and get yourselves fucking arrested as soon as possible."

Stavsky did tend to one matter to the crew's satisfaction. The crew believed the *Abril's* captain had proved himself incompetent during the stormy voyage across the Atlantic, and wanted him replaced for the run to Palestine. Stavsky decided to promote Bob Levitan, the ship's first-mate and navigator, to the position. Levitan would ultimately vindicate Stavsky's confidence in him.

On February 28 and March 1, 1947, the crew loaded more than six hundred refugees onto the *Abril*. The displaced persons, who had arrived by train and bus from Grenoble, were squeezed into the ship's six berthing spaces. That left little room for the crew, who would be forced to sleep in shifts. On March 1, fully loaded, the *Abril* sailed out of Port de Bouc bound for Palestine, ready at last to challenge the British blockade. Almost immediately, disaster struck. The *Abril's* port diesel engine broke down. When the ship's engineers got into the engine, they quickly realized it had been sabotaged, presumably by one of the French workers who had come aboard in Port de Bouc. Using a hacksaw, someone had sawed through an oil pump connecting rod to a point where the strain of engine operations would complete the act of cutting the rod. Once broken, it had whipped around and punched a hole in the bottom of the engine sump, where lubricating oil collected. The oil leaked through the hole and into the bilges, leaving the ship with two problems: replacing the rod and sealing the hole. Although the ship had a second engine, the two diesels had proved themselves unreliable on the voyage across the Atlantic, during which they had frequently broken down. If the second engine, which the crew feared might have been sabotaged as well, were to fail, the *Abril* would find itself floating out of control. The seas south of France were still filled with mines left over from the war, and the ship faced mortal danger if both of its engines became inoperable.

Faced with his first major challenge as ship's captain, Levitan originally favored returning to France. He delayed the return when the ship's two Norwegian engineers announced that they could fix the engine. Working without sleep over the next two and a half days, the engineers, assisted by crewman Lou Brettschneider, replaced the rod and repaired the hole, using hand tools to shape portions of the engine room deck plates to fit the contours of the torn sump. Back at full strength, the *Abril* continued her journey toward Palestine.

Meanwhile, in New York, the propaganda mill continued to turn. One of the important public relations tools used to bring attention to Aliyah Bet voyages was to change the names of Aliyah Bet ships to a Jewish or Hebrew name just as they approached Palestine. For security reasons, it was customary to maintain the ship's original name until it had cleared its final port before Palestine. Otherwise, a Jewish or Hebrew name would prematurely give away a ship's destination, something the Aliyah Bet operatives obviously wanted to avoid. On the final leg of the voyage, the crew for the first time would display the new name, hand-painting it on the side of the ship or unfurling a banner that had been brought on board in Europe. Previous U.S. Aliyah Bet ships had all undergone such transformations, with the *Norsyd* becoming the *Haganah*, the *Ulua* changing to the *Chaim Arlosoroff*, and the *Beauharnois* being replaced by the *Josiah Wedgewood*.[1] In New York, the ALFP announced the new name of the *Abril* – The *Ben Hecht* – to honor the playwright whose work had made the voyage possible. For whatever reason, though, the crewmen were never advised of the name change. For them, the *Abril* would forever remain the *Abril*.

As the ship drew nearer to its destination, a British patrol aircraft began circling overhead to monitor the *Abril's* progress. On March 8, one week after leaving France and less than a day away from Palestine, three British destroyers intercepted the *Abril*. The destroyers jockeyed for position alongside the *Abril*, preparing to send waves of British Royal Marines on board to overpower the crew and passengers and to seize control of the ship. The British clearly feared a major confrontation with the Irgun ship, and wanted to be certain to have sufficient forces to subdue it. The ultimate goal of all Aliyah Bet voyages was to run the British blockade and beach the ship, but the British were determined not to let this happen.

The Irgun was new to the post-war world of sailing into the British blockade, and it approached things differently than the Haganah. The Haganah had become expert in preparing the crew and passengers of its Aliyah Bet ships for a violent confrontation with British boarding parties. The Haganah knew that if the British were to be resisted, it was necessary to drill the passengers, to create in them an appetite for battle. But many in the Irgun were scornful of the Haganah practice of involving the passengers in this manner. As one of the American representatives of the Irgun put it: "We fight, but we don't ask refugees to fight." Whatever the reason, ideology or inexperience, the passengers of the *Abril* were not trained to challenge the British soldiers who stormed the ship.

Ironically, the British were particularly fearful of the *Abril*. Because the ship belonged to the more radical Irgun, the British expected an even more violent confrontation than they had experienced with Haganah ships. They had no idea that no such confrontation would be forthcoming. Instead, the crew gambled on being able to maneuver the ship through the blockade, with some last-minute help from the Irgun in Palestine. In an operation timed to coincide with the ship's arrival, Irgun soldiers attempted to divert the British by attacking a coastal police station near Tel Aviv. The attack failed – a number of Irgunists were killed – and the British boarded the *Abril* without incident. Intent on not taking any chances, the British intercepted the *Abril* more than ten miles outside of Tel Aviv, well beyond Palestine's territorial waters.

As the ALFP had instructed them in New York, the crewmen made no effort to hide among the passengers or elsewhere on the ship. Instead, they identified themselves as American seamen, and were duly arrested. The British towed the *Abril* to Haifa harbor, where they transferred the passengers to a prison ship bound for Cyprus. There, the British had erected an enormous prison camp to house Jews caught trying to enter Palestine in defiance of British regulations. The crewmen were at first jailed in Haifa lock-up, together with other prisoners in a large, somewhat bare cell. Hoping to learn more about the Irgun's Aliyah Bet operations, the British infiltrated a number of informants into the cell. The informants tried to ingratiate themselves with the Americans, but Gutmann, Heavy and the others were suspicious and maintained their distance. One of the British police officers did approach Gutmann openly, and the two got to know each other in the few days that Gutmann spent in the lock-up. They talked politics, in particular the merit, or lack thereof, of Britain's immigration policy. Although neither persuaded the other of his position, Gutmann enjoyed the exchanges.

The *Abril* crew were not the only Americans in the Haifa jail. A little more than a week before the *Abril's* capture, the Haganah ship *Ulua/Chaim Arlosoroff* had succeeded in ramming its way through a gauntlet of British warships and beaching itself at Bat Galim, near Haifa. Despite the dramatic conclusion to that voyage – which would prove to be the only successful beaching of a post-World War II Aliyah Bet ship – nearly all of the passengers and crewmen were captured by British forces who waited on shore. Like the *Abril*, the *Arlosoroff* had a mostly American crew. The *Arlosoroff* crew, consistent with Haganah practice, had tried to avoid capture by disguising themselves as displaced persons. They dressed like the DP's and spoke only in Yiddish, the language most prevalent among the passengers. Some of the Americans had grown beards during the voyage, and pretended to be religious Jews. The *Arlosoroff* crewmen maintained their distance from their fellow Americans, fearful of blowing their cover and not willing to trust men who had sailed on an Irgun ship.

After a short stay in Haifa, the *Abril* crew was transferred to Acre prison. The main part of the prison was a former crusader fortress, built in the twelfth century by the Knights of St. John of Malta after Baudouin I captured the port of Acre. The fortress appeared to be impenetrable. Its rock walls were seventy feet high, and these were surrounded by a moat that was forty feet deep and fifteen feet across. The British considered Acre prison to be so secure that they chose to imprison there the captured members of the Irgun and the Stern Group, the two most militant underground forces. However, since the British didn't regard the *Abril* crew as a security threat, they placed them in barracks that were located outside of the main fortress.

As the men examined their new lodgings, it soon became clear they were not the first Aliyah Bet crewmen to be imprisoned there. Spanish slogans like "*Viva La Republica!*" ("Long Live the Republic!") and "*Franco Es Marecon*" ("Franco is a homosexual") covered the walls. These were clearly the work of Spanish Loyalists who had sailed with Aliyah Bet. The crew was housed in a large, barracks-style room, with an adjoining bathroom and kitchen. Britain's relatively tolerant attitude toward the Americans was reflected not only in the decision to keep them out of the main fortress. Incredibly, the British never searched the men's sea bags. In addition to their more innocuous possessions, they brought with them cameras and at least one gun – a Luger that belonged to crewman Bob Nicolai.

Although they were not housed in the main fortress, the crewmen were allowed to move between the fortress and their barracks. The British assigned a Christian Arab policeman named Ahmed to guard the Americans. Ahmed became more a guide than a prison guard. He took the men on tours of the fortress, leading them on walks along the parapets and explaining the history of the crusader-constructed building. The freedom of movement ran in the other direction as well. Representatives of the Irgun and Stern Group came to visit the new arrivals. They introduced themselves, and checked on the sailors' belongings that might be useful to the men in the main prison.

As disenchanted as Gutmann had become with the Irgun's American political operatives, the men that he met in prison had the opposite effect on him. They were tough, quiet men, who seemed incapable of the kind of posturing that he had seen in New York. Gutmann spent a lot of time with the Irgunists and Sternists in the main prison. He became particularly friendly with Yosef Dar, a member of the Stern Group who had been captured after an attack on the Haifa railroad workshops. Dar tried to recruit Gutmann, explaining that the Stern Group could use the services of a sailor like the young American, someone who could get in and out of ports without drawing any unwanted attention – the perfect saboteur. Gutmann agreed to consider Dar's proposal.

When they were not spending time with the other prisoners in the main fortress or touring with Ahmed, the *Abril* crew found more traditional prison pastimes to keep themselves occupied. They played a lot of chess. Gutmann, an amateur artist, made sketches using paints and a sketch block that he had brought into the prison in his sea bag. The men also read a great deal, sprawled out in their barracks or in a neighboring courtyard. One of the crewmen, Harry Herschkowitz, was an acquaintance of Henry Miller, and had brought with him *Tropic of Cancer* and other of Miller's banned writings, which the men read with considerable enthusiasm. The spring weather was warm and mild, and the Jewish Agency made sure that the men were properly supplied with clothes and food, including kosher salamis. Considering the circumstances, the men found that the days passed pleasantly enough.

One day, the Irgunists and Sternists asked Bob Levitan to bring his camera to the main prison. They directed Levitan to a particular cell and, when he arrived, he found a chair placed in front of a large white sheet. One by one, he photographed a procession of prisoners – full face and profile. When he finished, one of the Sternists, Matityahu Shmuelevitz, asked for the film. Shmuelevitz did not explain why the photographs were needed, and Levitan didn't ask. The reason would become obvious a short time later.

Although the Irgun had always expected, and perhaps hoped for, a trial of the American crewmen, the British decided after some reflection that no benefit would come from such a proceeding. It was an uncharacteristically wise decision by the British, who seemed never to fail to deal with Aliyah Bet in ways that appeared brutal and callous to world opinion. The British notified the crewmen that they would soon be released from Acre, and deported from Palestine. When the other prisoners learned of the impending release, they invited the crewmen to the fortress for a farewell party. There, the Irgun gave each man a medallion, hand-carved from olive wood and bearing the Irgun insignia – a fist clenching a rifle, superimposed over a map of Israel on both sides of the Jordan river. On each medallion was inscribed the words: "To a brave sailor from his comrades, members of the *Irgun Zvai Leumi*, Acre Prison."

A few days later, after spending five weeks at Acre, the men were deported. But before the British released them, each crewman had to sign a statement pledging, under threat of criminal prosecution, not to ever again assist in the illegal immigration of Jews into Palestine. In late April, the men were taken to Haifa and placed on the *Marine Carp*, a converted troop transport ship from World War II, for a twenty-day voyage back to New York.

While at sea, the men learned of dramatic events in Palestine. On May 4, 1947, the Irgun and the Stern Group engineered a mass prison escape from the main fortress at Acre. Some one hundred twenty Irgunists and Sternists escaped through the fortress walls, using smuggled explosives to blow a hole in the seemingly impregnable structure. The prison break was aided by Irgun and Stern Group soldiers from the outside, who linked up with the escaping prisoners on the other side of the breached wall. The escapees included Gutmann's friend Yosef Dar, as well as

Matityahu Shmuelevitz, the man who had arranged the photography session with Bob Levitan. Levitan's photographs, the *Abril* crewmen later learned, had been smuggled out of the prison and used to create forged identity cards for the men scheduled to participate in the escape. The daring escape from a crusader fortress captured the imagination of the world, though it was not without cost. The British killed five of the escaping prisoners, as well as four of those who attacked from outside of the prison. Many, including Dar and Shmuelevitz, were ultimately recaptured. The news of the escape electrified Gutmann and the others. Gutmann, for one, was sorry not to have been there when it happened. "Bloody hell, they released us too soon. That would have been the way to get out," he told the others.

After nearly a month at sea, the *Marine Carp* finally docked in New York in May 1947. The *Abril* crew disembarked. Most of them would never sail together again. Whether because of the pledge extracted by the British or for other reasons, it was the last Aliyah Bet voyage for most. However, they would come together as a group one final time. Within weeks of the crew's return to New York, the ALFP hosted a dinner honoring Ben Hecht, the prime benefactor of the *Abril*. The crew was invited, and their efforts were recognized as well. Afterward, they returned to their former lives, the adventure completed.

✡ ✡ ✡

Gutmann, though, had been hooked. He immediately contacted Haganah offices in New York, anxious to join another ship. He spoke with Akiva "Kieve" Skidell, a Haganah representative who had lived for many years in Canada and the U.S. before emigrating to Palestine. A short while later, Skidell telephoned Gutmann to instruct him that a ship was ready and that he was to depart immediately. Gutmann grabbed his sea bag, and raced to the docks at Brooklyn Heights. There, he caught his first glimpse of the S.S. *Paducah*, a former U.S. Navy gunboat that had seen action in both world wars. Like the *Abril*, the nine-hundred-ton *Paducah* was a relatively small ship – only one hundred ninety feet long and thirty-six feet across. But Gutmann, who had been through the drill already with the *Abril*, was not concerned about the ship's ability to make the voyage. He was delighted to learn that Heavy and Lou Brettschneider, two of his crewmates from the *Abril*, would be making this trip as well. A second Aliyah Bet adventure awaited the three sailors, this time under the command of a non-Jewish captain, a veteran merchant seaman named Rudolph Patzert.

The *Paducah* would not be making its run alone. It was paired with a second Aliyah Bet ship, the *Northland*, a twenty-year-old icebreaker that had recently been refitted in Baltimore. Like the *Paducah*, the *Northland* had an American crew. Both ships left the U.S. in May, headed to the Azores for supplies and refueling and then on to Bayonne, a French port near the Atlantic border with Spain. The ships arrived in Bayonne in June for additional refitting. As with the *Abril*, it was necessary to fill each ship, to the extent possible, with wooden bunks to accommodate all of the DP's. Between them, the two ships were to transport more than 4,000 passengers to Palestine.

At Bayonne, a Palestinian agent of the Haganah named Moka Limon came on board. Although Rudolph Patzert remained operationally the captain of the ship, Limon became the commander for what in essence was a military mission. Limon would communicate to Patzert the details of the ship's plans as the Haganah radioed them from Palestine, at a pace that Limon deemed appropriate. Once the ship reached Bayonne, it remained the responsibility of the American crew, but it came under the authority of the Haganah and for the first time truly became a Haganah ship.

Before the men were allowed to disembark at Bayonne, Limon briefed them on security. He instructed them not to reveal to anyone they met any information regarding the ship. Even when talking among themselves, Limon asked the men to be careful, and to use code words so that no one overhearing their conversation might learn anything about the voyage. They were to refer to Palestine as "Oklahoma," the Haganah men as "shu-shus," and the passengers as "bananas." Gutmann found the emphasis on security to be a refreshing change from the publicity that had so frustrated the *Abril* crew.

Limon's addition to the crew was not the only personnel change to take place in Bayonne. Typically in Aliyah Bet voyages originating in the U.S., the arrival in Europe after the voyage across the Atlantic represented a turning point for the crew. Those who were not prepared to risk internment or arrest in Palestine would leave the ship in Europe. In some instances, these same men would later serve as crewmen on the first leg of other Aliyah Bet voyages. Those who stayed knew that once the ship left Europe there would be no turning back. The loss of crewmen required some shuffling of assignments. Gutmann, an oiler for the first leg of the trip, became one of the ship's engineers. It was a good fit for Gutmann, who had worked in engine rooms during his stint with the U.S. Merchant Marine. Lou Brettschneider and Larry Kohlberg also received promotions to engineer positions. Technically, the three engineers were supposed to receive new titles. One was to be the second engineer, one the third engineer, and one the day engineer. Instead, they decided to share equally the responsibility of all three positions, as well as the titles. They named themselves "The Three Deuces."

Despite his new job, Gutmann again found the refitting period to be one of relatively little activity, at least as far as shipboard responsibilities were concerned. He, Heavy and the others looked for ways to amuse themselves. Frequently, the men would travel to the nearby resort town of Biarritz, to enjoy its cafes and bars. The men would take the "Bayonne Al Biarritz" trolley, or "B-a-B" as it read on the signboard. Heavy promptly renamed it the "Big-Assed Bird." The men also discovered that bullfighting was a big attraction in Bayonne, an obvious product of the influence of nearby Spain. Gutmann went to a number of bullfights during the refitting period, the first he had ever seen.

The *Paducah* and *Northland* were finally ready to leave Bayonne in August, having been fitted with bunks, a speaker system, and other structures necessary to accommodate the passengers. But events in Palestine during the layover in Bayonne would alter the rest of the *Paducah's* journey. It was then that the capture of the *Exodus 1947*, another Aliyah Bet ship, shocked the world.

✡ ✡ ✡

One of the *Exodus'* crewman was David Starec, a Polish-born Jew who left his rabbinical studies at the Yeshiva University in New York to make the voyage. Tall and slight of build, Starec had thick, black hair and an intense personality. He was nine years old when his parents left the small town of Rokitno Volinia in Poland, saving most of his immediate family from the Holocaust. But the rest of his family had remained in Poland, and while at Yeshiva University Starec learned that all but three had been murdered by the Nazis.

The discovery had a profound impact on Starec's life. The Holocaust shook him to the depth of his being. He began to question his faith, and slowly lost interest in becoming a rabbi. Instead, he found an outlet in the Zionist organization Betar, a youth group closely identified with the Irgun. Starec liked the Irgun because it believed in fighting for a Jewish home-land in Palestine – the only fitting response, in Starec's view, to the hor-rors of the Holocaust. Starec soon decided to venture beyond youth group activities. He spoke with Akiva Skiddel of the Haganah, the same man who had recruited Gutmann for the *Paducah*. Although Starec had no maritime training, he did have one valuable skill. A gifted linguist, Starec spoke nearly a dozen languages, including English, Yiddish, Polish, French, and Hebrew, an obvious asset given the varied group of passen-gers the typical Aliyah Bet ship carried. Skiddel told him to report to Baltimore, where an Aliyah Bet ship was being refitted.

Before boarding the train for Baltimore, Starec prepared a letter to the university, explaining his actions. The letter was timed for delivery after his departure, to avoid any attempt on the school's part to prevent him from going. Because Starec's mother lived in Brazil, he was techni-cally the responsibility of the university. In his letter, he explained his desire to personally take part in the building of a Jewish state. Starec closed with a flourish, writing in Hebrew: "*Im epol, epol b'chavod, veloh b'clhima*" ("If I fall, I shall fall with honor and not in shame").

The ship that Starec was to meet was the *President Warfield*, a three-hundred-and-thirty-foot luxury steamboat that had originally been de-signed to ferry up to four hundred passengers across the Chesapeake Bay. By the standards of Aliyah Bet, the *Warfield* was an enormous ship. The Haganah hoped to use it to transport more than 4,000 passengers to Pal-estine.

Paul Shulman, a young U.S. Naval Academy graduate, had helped the Haganah select the *Warfield* and most of its crew. Shulman was no stranger to the Zionist cause. Both of his parents were active Zionists who frequently hosted emissaries of Palestine's Jewish community in the Shulman's Connecticut home. In 1941, while still a cadet at the Naval Academy, Shulman had met Jewish Agency head David Ben Gurion. The man who would later become Israel's first prime minister was quite taken with the young Jewish naval officer. Ben Gurion told Shulman that he was glad to see Jewish boys studying to be naval officers, because they would be needed someday in the Jewish navy. "I hope you have a fine navy," Shulman responded politely, but added that he planned to spend his career as an officer in the American navy. At the time, Shulman's attention was occupied by the recent attack on Pearl Harbor and the war raging in Europe. He went on to serve as an officer on board the U.S.S. *Hunt* in the Pacific Theater. With World War II over and the struggle for Jewish independence intensifying, Shulman joined the Haganah's Aliyah Bet operation, taking his first step toward fulfilling Ben Gurion's wish.

Starec joined the ship's crew during the refitting, a process that would prove to be exceptionally difficult. It was not just the disastrous condition of the ship that was responsible. Of the forty or so Americans who made up the crew, most, like Starec, lacked the proper training for maritime work. One of the few experienced sailors assigned to the ship was Bill Bernstein, a twenty-three-year-old graduate of the U.S. Merchant Marine Academy. After taking stock of his shipmates, Bernstein wrote to his brother: "We have everything aboard except sailors."

The ship left the U.S. for France on February 25, 1947. That voyage, the first for the *President Warfield* as an Aliyah Bet ship, nearly ended in disaster. The *Warfield* wallowed in stormy seas, taking on water and very nearly sinking. With the help of the U.S. Coast Guard, the ship limped back to Norfolk, Virginia. After more repairs, the *Warfield* finally left the U.S. for good on March 29, 1947, bound for the Azores.

The ocean crossing was uneventful, and the ship arrived in Ponta Delgada in the Azores on April 5th. The British, who had known for months that the *Warfield* was an Aliyah Bet ship, had earlier alerted the Portuguese authorities that the *Warfield* would be arriving. News of a Jewish refugee ship entering Ponta Delgada to refuel spread to the townspeople, and hundreds of locals crowded onto the dock to watch. It was obvious to the *Warfield's* captain that the townspeople, who had likely never seen a Jew before, were anxious to catch a glimpse of the Jewish crewmen and passengers. He believed that most expected the classic hook-nosed Jew portrayed by anti-Semites. The captain decided to send a member of the crew down to greet them. For the occasion, he chose John Stanley Grauel, a Methodist minister who was making the voyage as a representative of the American Christian Palestine Committee. The blond haired, blue-eyed minister strode down the plank, sporting, as was his custom, a large crucifix around his neck. As the people stood and watched in shock, Grauel stepped forward and pronounced a blessing over them.

From Ponta Delgada, the ship eventually made its way to Port de Bouc, where French workers installed enough bunks to transport more than 4,500 passengers. On the evening of July 9, 1947, the *Warfield* headed to the small French port of Sete to load the refugees. Seventy trucks, all filled with displaced persons, awaited the steamboat. Under cover of darkness, 4,554 men, women and children crowded onto the Palestine-bound ship.

After the ship was fully loaded, Starec began to search for survivors from his hometown. Desperate to find out how his family members had met their end, he waded through the crammed holds, asking in Yiddish and Polish for anyone from Rokitno Volinia. He was surprised to find several people from the small Polish town, including members of a family who had lived across the street from his childhood home and another man in whose backyard Starec had once played. These passengers were able to tell Starec more about what had happened to his family. The Nazis had ordered most of the town's Jews to the central market across from the synagogue. There, Starec's aunts, uncles, and all but three of his cousins were machine-gunned. The story only deepened Starec's commitment to become involved in the struggle for a Jewish homeland.

By the time the passengers were loaded, the British were well aware of the true identity of the ship, and its purpose. As soon as the *Warfield* left France's territorial waters, a British man-of-war moved into position behind the refugee ship. As the *Warfield* sailed closer to Palestine, the British presence grew, with two minesweepers and a destroyer joining the *Warfield's* initial lone pursuer. Every few hours, one of the British ships would close to within megaphone distance, and Starec could hear the British broadcast in several languages: "Jews! You have no chance to break the blockade to Palestine. Follow us to Cyprus." It was, of course, a message the crew ignored.

The conditions on the *Warfield* were dreadful. It was the middle of July, and passengers on the severely overcrowded ship wilted in the humid afternoon heat. Meals consisted of a dried mixture of beef, suet, raisins, and sugar. Within days, seasickness and diarrhea swept through the ship, further worsening conditions on board. To make matters worse still, movement aboard the *Warfield* had to be carefully regulated. The slender design of the overcrowded ship meant that even the slightest shift in weight could prove disastrous.

The Haganah anticipated the grueling conditions of the voyage, stationing eight doctors on each deck and setting up a makeshift hospital on one of the decks. But because the ship would not have adequate facilities to deal with complicated medical emergencies, the Haganah forbade all women in their last month of pregnancy from making the crossing. Nevertheless, two women were able to conceal the advanced stages of their pregnancies during boarding, and made it onto the ship. Both gave birth during the voyage. The first woman delivered her baby without complication, but the second mother died during childbirth. With no other choice, the crew asked the first woman to also breastfeed the child of the woman who had died. Out of concern for the health of the rest of the passengers, the crew prepared the dead woman's body for a burial at sea. Two of the American crewmen placed the body in a sack, together with lead weights, and sewed it shut. They painted a Star of David on the outside of the bag, and the ship was stopped briefly as the body was dropped into the ocean.

The size of the Royal Navy's escort of the *Warfield* continued to grow. By the morning following the funeral, Starec awoke to find the refugee ship surrounded by four destroyers, two minesweepers, a cruiser, and a frigate. Despite Britain's show of force, the Haganah continued to hold out hope that the smaller, more maneuverable steamboat could make it to the shores of Palestine. The plan was for the *Warfield* to stay three miles offshore – just beyond Palestine's territorial waters – until the evening of Thursday, July 17. The *Warfield* would then sprint for the beach, relying on the steamboat's ability to sail in shallower water than the warships dared enter. The Haganah intended to send a force of 30,000 Palestinian Jews to rendezvous with the ship and secure the off-loading of its passengers. The Haganah believed that the resulting confrontation with Britain's forces had the potential for triggering a nationwide uprising against the British. The British were determined not to let the *Warfield* make it to shore.

On the last full day of the voyage, the crew announced the ship's Aliyah Bet name. The ship was to be named after the Jews' biblical exodus from Egypt, "*Yetziat Europah Tashach*" ("Exodus from Europe 1947"). On wooden boards where the name "*Warfield*" formerly appeared, the crew painted in large block letters: "HAGANAH Ship Exodus 1947."

On Thursday afternoon, hours before the planned beaching, the crew met to discuss how to defend the *Exodus* in the likely event that the British tried to board her. The Haganah wanted the crew to defend the ship by force until it reached the designated landing area near Bat Yam. No firearms were brought on board the ship, however, for fear that an armed confrontation would endanger the lives of refugees and crew. Instead, the crew stockpiled potatoes, bottles, and cans of food – all to be used as projectiles against British boarding parties. The crew also fastened barbed wire around the deck to further complicate the task of landing troops on board.

The consensus among the crew was that the British would try to intercept the refugee ship around five o'clock in the morning, as the *Exodus* reached the territorial waters of Palestine. It therefore came as a complete surprise when, more than two hours earlier and with the ship still in international waters, the British attacked. Starec was working in the engine room when two British destroyers illuminated the refugee ship with blinding searchlights. A megaphone blasted a prepared statement to the crew, claiming that the ship had crossed into the territorial waters of Palestine, and ordering the crew to stop the engines and prepare the ship to be towed into Haifa port.

As Starec raced to his battlestation, the destroyer *Childers* rammed *Exodus'* old steel hull across the port side. On his way to the wheelhouse, which he was to help defend, Starec first stopped off at his own cabin. There, he had previously set aside three objects to take into battle: an iron rod to fend off British attackers, a life-jacket in the event he jumped or was thrown overboard, and his father's phylacteries.

The destroyer *Chieftain* rammed *Exodus* from the starboard side, sandwiching the small vessel as it repeatedly changed speed and course in an effort to squirm free. As the ships bounced off of each other, the

British vessels lowered newly-constructed drawbridges, engineered to allow the rapid deployment of soldiers onto the deck of the *Exodus*. Starec stood ready, iron bar in hand, as the first wave of British marines began streaming onto the ship. The invaders were met with a hail of canned food and potatoes. The initial resistance and the *Exodus'* continued maneuvering made it difficult for the British to send over large numbers of marines. Needing to gain control of the *Exodus'* navigational controls, the boarding party's primary target was the ship's wheelhouse. Five British soldiers managed to make it past the barrage of food, clubbing their way to the wheelhouse with steel-tipped truncheons.

While the Palestinian captain and an American volunteer disconnected the steering controls in the wheelhouse, Starec and Bill Bernstein defended the entrance to the navigational room. Starec swung his iron bar furiously, while Bernstein held up a fire extinguisher to fend off the boarders. As the British broke through, Starec hammered one soldier after another with his iron pipe until one of the British landed a severe blow to Starec's skull. Semi-conscious, Starec could see that Bill Bernstein was being dragged off, also the victim of a blow to the head. Bernstein would never recover. He died the following morning from his injuries.

Two hours later, Starec woke in his own cabin, barely able to lift his bandaged head. He struggled to his feet, his mind consumed with fury at the British. Starec was reminded of a quote he had read in *Underground to Palestine*, a book by American journalist I.F. Stone about an earlier Aliyah Bet voyage. On the first page of the book, Stone had quoted a Jewish partisan: "The Germans killed us. The British don't let us live." Starec had brought the book with him, and he ripped out the page with the quote and pinned it up on the wall.

The battle continued to rage, even after the British seized control of the wheelhouse. The crew succeeded in transferring rudder control from the steering wheel to deep inside the hull of the ship. Meanwhile, the fusillade of canned goods and potatoes continued unabated, and several of the boarders were disarmed and thrown overboard. Two hours after the battle had been joined, the British had been able to put only forty men on the *Exodus*, and all four of the Royal Navy destroyers had suffered extensive hull damage.

But the confrontation was taking a terrible toll on the *Exodus* and her passengers. The ramming had splintered the ship's wooden sides above the water line, leaving holes the size of automobiles. The crew and passengers had suffered many casualties, including a number with gunshot wounds who required immediate medical attention. The captain feared that further resistance might result in the sinking of the ship, and a catastrophic loss of life. He radioed Haganah headquarters, and received authorization to surrender the ship.

Once the surrender order was given, the crewmen disguised themselves as refugees and mingled with the passengers. One of the Palestinian crewman approached Starec and told him that he would not be continuing with the rest of the crew and refugees to Cyprus. Because of Starec's head injury, he would likely be taken off the ship in Haifa and brought to a hospital. Later, Starec was told, the Haganah would arrange for him to slip out and join a fighting unit. But as the British carried him off the ship on a stretcher, his head in a bandage, Starec could not control his anger. "Down with the British! Down with Bevin!" he shouted. A British officer who heard Starec called out: "Take that bloody terrorist onto the prison ship."

All of those who were not in desperate need of medical attention were placed on one of three prison ships, presumably for the one-day journey to the internment camps in Cyprus. Each ship was capable of carrying 1,500 refugees in crowded, prison-like conditions. Giant wire cages enclosed the decks of each ship, to prevent passengers from trying to jump overboard and swim to freedom. The convoy departed Haifa the following evening.

Unbeknownst to the Haganah, the British were rethinking their policy of deporting illegal immigrants to Cyprus. There were those in the British government who believed the threat of internment in Cyprus was not sufficient to deter refugees from trying to run the blockade, and that more punitive measures were necessary. England's Foreign Minister Ernest Bevin, a man reviled in Palestine for his hostility to the Zionist cause and the person that Starec had referred to in his outburst at the Haifa pier, shared this view, and decided to make the *Exodus* a test case for a new policy.

For those on the prison ships, the first inkling that something was amiss came the next day, when they found themselves still in the open sea instead of within sight of Cyprus. When another day passed and the prison ships were still at sea, some on board took a rough plot of their position, and concluded that the ships were heading back to Europe. While conditions on the prison ships were tolerable for a single day's journey between Palestine and Cyprus, they were nearly unendurable for an extended voyage from the Mediterranean to Europe. The passengers received only two meals per day. The first meal, served at ten in the morning, consisted of five maggot-infested C-ration biscuits and a cup of tea. At five in the afternoon, they received potato soup and more contaminated biscuits. One of the survivors observed that conditions on the prison ships were worse than what he had lived through at Auschwitz.

After a voyage of more than a week, Starec saw lights on the horizon, and immediately recognized the French port of Port de Bouc. Britain's new Aliyah Bet policy, it was now clear, would be to forcibly return the immigrants to the country where the voyage originated. In Bevin's view, this would "teach the Jews a lesson." It would also, of course, express British displeasure with countries that allowed Aliyah Bet ships to sail for Palestine. But the British had failed to secure France's cooperation in the forcible return of illegal immigrants, or to properly judge the extent of the refugees' determination.

The French refused to allow the use of force to remove the refugees from the ships. Instead, the government offered to allow the Jews to temporarily settle in France, until they found a permanent place to live. But the passengers announced they would accept nothing less than legal entry into Palestine. For three weeks, the prison ships remained in Port de Bouc. The British hoped the summer heat and the desperate conditions on board would weaken the Jews' resolve. But they stood firm. During the stand-off, many of the refugees looked to the American crew, to see how they would act in the crisis. The refugees saw the Americans, who came from a wealthy country and who had not suffered during the war, as soft. They jokingly referred to the Americans as "*chocolatniks*." The resolve of the Americans to stand firm with the other passengers helped strengthen the spirit of the refugees.

Finally, on August 21, Britain announced that unless the refugees left the ships by six p.m. the following day, they would be taken to the British zone of occupation in Germany. The world community condemned

Britain for threatening to transport the Jews, most of whom were Holocaust survivors, to the blood-soaked soil of Germany. But by this point,
the British had passed the point of no return. Only twenty-one of the
refugees left the ships following Britain's announcement, joining another
sixty or so of the aged and sick who had left during the preceding three
weeks. That still left some 4,500 passengers and crew on board the prison
ships. Within twenty minutes of the passing of the deadline for disembar-
kation, the three ships weighed anchor and headed for Germany.

More than two weeks later, on September 8, the ships arrived in Ham-
burg. Again the refugees had to decide on a course of action – to leave the
ships voluntarily or to resist. Most of the refugees, weakened by the extended struggle, had reached the limit of their ability to fight back. They
left the prison ships voluntarily. On the *Ocean Vigour*, Starec's boat, a
few hundred decided they would not leave without a fight. British troops
armed with clubs stormed the ship, and a melee ensued – although on a
far smaller scale than that original battle at sea. Starec, who again found
himself in the middle of the action, received a second blow to the head.
But the refugees did not have a lot of fight left in them, and soon the
British took control of all three ships. Starec was so furious with the British by this point that every time he saw a British soldier that day he shouted
"Heil Bevin!" The British took Starec and the other passengers to two
displaced person's camps, Poppendorf and Amstau. The voyage of the
Exodus was finally at an end, an unmitigated public relations disaster for
the British. Starec's personal journey, though, was far from over.

✡ ✡ ✡

The Haganah had arranged for the *Paducah* and *Northland* to em-
bark their passengers in Bulgaria, behind the Iron Curtain, and the ships
sailed separately for the Black Sea. This was part of the Haganah's response to the fate of the *Exodus*. While the British might try to forcibly
return DP's to France, they would not risk a confrontation with the Soviets by trying the same thing in Bulgaria.

Despite the Haganah's elaborate security procedures, and to no one's
real surprise, the British discovered that the *Paducah* and *Northland* were
Aliyah Bet ships. British destroyers began to follow both ships through

the Mediterranean and Aegean seas to the Dardanelles. The British warships drew near to the *Paducah*, close enough to ask its destination by loudspeaker. By megaphone, Limon responded that the *Paducah* was headed for Italy. As the crew stood on deck looking over at the British sailors, Heavy noticed some men on one of the destroyers in plain clothes. "Don't let them get a good look at you," he warned the others. Those are CID men." The CID was Britain's Criminal Investigation Department, one of the agencies charged with stopping Aliyah Bet. "Later they'll try to identify the crew members," he advised. The British ships halted their pursuit at the Bosphoros, as the *Paducah* and *Northland* continued on into the Soviet-controlled Black Sea.

The *Paducah* was the first to arrive in the Bulgarian port town of Varna. Varna was not exactly a sailor's dream port. It was small, its clean streets lined with two and three-story buildings. There were a few nightspots in town, but these were tame by the crew's standards. Patzert overheard one crewman complain: "At ten o'clock it's so dead you could fire a cannon down the main street and not hit anybody." In Varna, the crew continued with their efforts to keep secret the true nature of their voyage. Some of the crew, including Gutmann, spoke a little Spanish, and they began to use it as a cover language. But they failed to realize there was a community of Sephardic Jews in Varna, who spoke Ladino among themselves. Ladino was something of a cross between Hebrew and Spanish – the Sephardic equivalent of Yiddish. When the locals heard the crewmen speaking in Spanish, they became convinced the ship had come to transport the local Jews to Palestine.

In September, after the ship spent a few weeks in Varna, the Haganah ordered the *Paducah* to proceed to the nearby port town of Burgas, still in Bulgaria. The *Northland*, which by then had arrived in Varna, was also ordered to Burgas. One evening shortly after the arrival of the two ships, the embarkation process began. All night, trains arrived at the port, bringing thousands of Jewish refugees willing to trade the displaced persons camps of Europe for the risks of an Aliyah Bet voyage and almost certain internment in a new camp in Cyprus. Gutmann saw a powerful symbolism in trains bringing the Jews to the ships. In the Holocaust, the trains had carried millions to the concentration camps, and the train had become synonymous with death. Now, as they brought the remnants of the

Holocaust to the ships that would take them to a new life in Palestine, those trains in the night meant life.

By this point, the Haganah had reduced the loading of Aliyah Bet ships to something of a science. Each passenger received a numbered card, which corresponded to a number on one of the bunks. It was the responsibility of the crew to direct the passengers to their assigned places on the ship. The first refugees to board were the orphans, some as young as five or six. Some of the children walked alone, while others – members of Zionist youth groups – together marched and sang as they came aboard. The sight of so many parentless children, bravely heading into the unknown, was intensely moving for the crew, many of whom wept. The adult passengers followed, until there was simply no further room on the deck or below. The *Paducah* took on 1,388 passengers, the *Northland* 2,664, mostly Rumanian and Hungarian Jews. The *Northland* filled first, and departed while it was still dark. The *Paducah* pushed off as the sun rose over the horizon. As the ship left the port for the open sea, everyone on deck joined in the singing of "*Hatikvah*" ("the Hope"), the Zionist anthem.

The ships headed out of the Black Sea, reversing their original course from several weeks before. As always with Aliyah Bet, life on board was difficult. The sheer number of passengers left the crew only able to serve two meals a day, each dispensed chow-line style. Even at that reduced level, preparation of one meal followed almost immediately the conclusion of the one before it. Washing had to be accomplished at one of the jerry-rigged water faucets located on deck – another product of the Bayonne refitting – which dispensed unheated sea water. Each morning and evening, groups of men and boys would gather on the starboard side of the deck to pray. Even the irrepressible Heavy couldn't help but be moved by the obvious emotion of their prayers. "They give it hell, don't they," he commented to Patzert.

The Aliyah Bet ships passed through the Bosporus and the Dardanelles. As they emerged from the Dardanelles into the Aegean Sea, the Royal Navy was waiting. With their British escorts in tow, the *Paducah* and *Northland* continued through the Aegean to the Mediterranean. Originally, the Haganah had planned for the two ships to converge upon entering the Mediterranean, with the *Paducah* transferring its passengers to the *Northland* and then returning to Europe for another run. The Haganah had done this once before, moving the passengers from the *Norsyd/ Haganah* to a Turkish vessel, saving the *Norsyd/Haganah* for an additional voyage. But with the *Northland* already dangerously overcrowded with 2,700 passengers, there was no way to make the transfer, and the idea was abandoned.

As they entered the final leg of the journey, the *Paducah* and *Northland* assumed new names. The *Paducah* became the *"Geulah"* (the "Redemption"). The *Northland* became the *"Medinat Hayehudim"* (the "Jewish State"). To the cheers of the passengers, the crews of each ship unfurled giant banners with the Hebrew names. While everyone else's spirits rose as the journey's climax drew near, Gutmann became more and more tense. As a former prisoner of the British, he knew the police and the CID would be looking for him. He began to have a recurring anxiety dream, in which the *Paducah* sailed into Haifa Bay with Gutmann standing alone and exposed on the ship's fore-deck, as the hooting destroyers closed in.

To make it more difficult for the British, the *Paducah/Geulah* and *Northland/Medinat Hayehudim* separated. The *Paducah* headed for Haifa and the *Northland* for Tel Aviv. Aboard the *Paducah*, preparations continued to resist a British boarding. Instructions from the Haganah brought that to an abrupt halt. The British had been publicly agitating against the ship, claiming that it carried arms and warning of a bloody confrontation. With the wounds of the *Exodus* still fresh, and with the British apparently itching for a fight, the Haganah decided the ships would not actively resist the British boarders.

When the ship crossed to within twenty miles outside of Palestine's territorial waters, the crew began their final preparations. They put on disguises, trading their American clothes for the peasant garb worn by the passengers. Gutmann had grown a beard, and he now wore wire-rimmed glasses and a collarless shirt buttoned to the neck – the very image of a Talmudic scholar. The crew soon observed that one of the British destroyers now had a boarding platform jutting over its side, level with the *Paducah's* bridge. The attack was about to begin.

It happened some five miles outside of Haifa. The destroyer with the platform rammed the *Paducah*, dropping a boarding party onto the deck.

The British were taking no chances. They sent their finest troops – airborne soldiers known as the Red Devils. The ramming put events rapidly into motion on board. Patzert signaled the men in the engine room, who sabotaged the engine. That left the ship dead in the water, compelling the British to tow her to Haifa. With the *Exodus* experience in mind, the Haganah wanted to ensure that the British could not sail the ship, with its passengers, back to Europe. The crew, now disguised, left their stations to hide among the refugees. Gutmann climbed into a crowded bunk below decks as he felt the impact of the ramming.

After the ship reached Haifa, the passengers, with crew mixed in, were herded down the gangway. The British stripped them of their possessions, separated the men and women, and sprayed everyone with DDT. Although the British intended to transfer the passengers to prison ships for deportation, presumably to Cyprus after the embarrassment of the *Exodus* affair, they still hoped to locate and arrest the crewmen. Everyone stood in long lines, guarded by British troops, waiting to be interrogated by a British officer who spoke Hebrew and Yiddish. During the voyage from Europe, the crew had prepared themselves for this type of confrontation. They chose new names and homelands and learned how to answer basic questions in their new native tongues. Not trusting his Yiddish, Gutmann had decided to try to pass as a Ladino speaker.

As Gutmann stood with the other passengers, waiting to be interrogated, a British officer suddenly pulled him out of line. The Brit, apparently suspecting that Gutmann was a Palestinian and hoping to trick him, barked a question in Hebrew. Gutmann, whose Hebrew was rudimentary in any event, didn't take the bait. He and the other crewmen made it through the interrogation. Some seven hundred of the passengers, Gutmann included, were immediately herded onto the prison ship *Empire Rival*, one of the same ships that had transported the *Exodus* passengers back to Europe, for the one-hundred-thirty mile trip to Cyprus.

Gutmann found a spot in the cramped lower deck of the prison ship, where he spent an uncomfortable night. In the morning, he made his way to the caged portion of the deck. It was a crisp, sunny Mediterranean day. As he looked around, Gutmann noticed a French Jew, speaking in animated tones to a group of DP's around him. On the other side of the cage, a young British soldier stood guard. Gutmann could tell that the Brit was embarrassed by this duty, and he passed a cigarette through the wire to Gutmann. Gutmann took it. The soldier also offered one to the French DP, who refused it. Softened by the gesture of kindness, Gutmann commented to the Frenchman that the Brits didn't seem to be such bad people. The DP, a French intellectual whose family had died in the camps, shrieked at Gutmann in fury: "They put us in cages like animals, and you forgive them because they hand you a fucking cigarette." The DP turned away, and broke into heaving sobs. Embarrassed, Gutmann threw away the cigarette.

As daylight began to fade, the *Empire Rival* arrived at the Cypriot port of Famagusta. The passengers were taken off, sprayed with DDT a second time, and loaded onto army trucks for the trip to the camp. By the time the vehicles were loaded and ready to move out, night had fallen. The trucks moved through the countryside, and began to climb a hill. In the distance, a camp began to come into view, its electric lights glistening. The barracks were solid, and the streets nicely laid out. The DP's had by now been in many camps: concentration camps, slave labor camps, and the DP camps of Europe. They knew how to evaluate a camp and they liked what they saw. *"Dus es a guter lager"* ("This is a good camp"), Gutmann heard several say in Yiddish. As the trucks entered the camp, some of its residents came into the street. Suddenly, Gutmann heard shouts of "Heil Hitler," and saw that many of the people were raising their arms toward the trucks in Nazi salutes. The camp was not for the DP's. Instead, it housed German prisoners-of-war, members of Rommel's Afrika Corps. Gutmann was furious. "Fucking limey bastards," he said to himself. He thought back to his days in Acre prison, to Yosef Dar's invitation to join the Stern Group. If a Stern Group recruiter had appeared right then, Gutmann thought, he would gladly sign, in blood. The trucks continued through the POW camp, and on into the darkness.

A short while later, the trucks reached their destination, a collection of prison camps known as Xylotymbou. The passengers climbed down, and the British again separated the men and women. The men were led to a large Nissen hut for a last search and interrogation before entering the camp. This was the final hurdle. Because the British stayed out of the camp itself, the crew members knew that if they could make it past this checkpoint, they faced no further risk of discovery. But the British were more thorough at Cyprus than they had been at Haifa. Leaving nothing to chance, the British made a practice of strip-searching the passengers, a measure that would prove to be Heavy's downfall.

Heavy undressed as ordered, only to be revealed in his full glory as a tattoo-covered American sailor. If there had been any doubt as to Heavy's nationality, the American flag on his chest removed that. "Sir, we seem to have a terrorist here," called out a British sergeant. A cluster of troopers, armed with Stens, appeared as if from nowhere and surrounded Heavy, guns pointed. It was Heavy's moment. He looked at the soldiers with scorn, fluffed his dungarees in the air like a housewife shaking out her laundry, and snorted: "Oh, blow it out your ass." The Brits took Heavy away.

Gutmann and the others made it through, and entered the camp. They soon discovered that Xylotymbou was far inferior to the German POW camp they had passed through. In place of the well-constructed wood barracks in the German camp, Xylotymbou had a mix of small tin huts and army tents organized along red clay roads, and divided into a series of smaller camps. The entire complex housed more than twenty thousand Jewish refugees.

Although the crewmen were able to remain together in smaller groups, life in the camp proved to be difficult. Food rations were meager, with the British providing each resident with only 1,800 calories per day. There was no hot water, and, to make matters worse, the showers were outdoors. The latrines were slit trenches filled with lime and covered with boards. They were open, and their smell wafted throughout the camps, filling the heavy night air. The open latrines were a serious health hazard. Flies were rampant, carrying disease from the latrines to the food. At one point or another, it seemed that every member of the crew suffered from dysentery. At Xylotymbou, the British had done the least required to comply with the Geneva convention regulations for the treatment of prisoners of war.

The residents of Xylotymbou had organized themselves according to religious and Zionist affiliations. There were groups of Orthodox Jews, Labor Zionists, Revisionist Zionists, and others. The Americans were placed in Camp 65, where the orphans lived. The young children, who had known worse conditions and who knew that they were closer to reaching Palestine, were happy. They filled their days in organized study, and playing. They were reverential to the Americans, whom they referred to as "Our Sailors." As he had done at Acre, Gutmann passed the time reading and playing chess.

The American crewmen had an advantage over the other residents of the camps. They knew they would not have to remain long at Cyprus. The British allowed Jews who were deported to Cyprus to emigrate to Palestine at the rate of 1,500 per month. Because Xylotymbou already housed more than 20,000 Jews, the DP's could expect to remain there for as long as two years. But the Haganah had a policy of getting the crews out early, so they could participate in future voyages. The crewmen would take the places of DP's who were scheduled for release, but who had volunteered to surrender their immigration certificates to the Haganah.

In November, after some two months at Xylotymbou, the Americans received word that they would be leaving with the next group heading for Palestine. Heavy, though, would not be joining them. Since his capture, he had been held in isolation in a separate part of the camp. While he could communicate with other detainees, he sent word to the crew not to approach him. Heavy was under constant surveillance, and he feared that anyone who spoke to him would come under suspicion as an Aliyah Bet crewman. Heavy's imprisonment would continue for more than six additional months, until after the State of Israel was declared.

Together with the other DP's whose turn had finally come to leave Cyprus, the Americans made the one-day trip back to Palestine. The ship docked at Haifa, and the refugees prepared to disembark. Gutmann walked to the top of the gangplank, and started to descend. Suddenly, he froze. A British soldier stood at the bottom of the gangplank, scanning the passengers as they disembarked to see if any Aliyah Bet crewmen were among them. Gutmann recognized the Brit. He was the same soldier Gutmann had gotten to know when he was jailed in Haifa lock-up with the *Abril* crew.

Other passengers began to crowd behind Gutmann, and they asked him to move forward. In Yiddish, Gutmann whispered, "*Se ist du polizei vus kennen mir zehr git*" ("There are policemen down there who know me very well"). The passengers standing around him quickly improvised. Gutmann was given a wife who took one arm, an aged mother-in-law who took the other, and a baby to hold. Together, the group proceeded down the gangway. The soldier looked right through Gutmann, never recognizing the young American he had met some months earlier.

Gutmann could not have known it then, but the *Paducah* and *Northland* would be the last Aliyah Bet ships to try to run the British blockade. Events thousands of miles away would make these dangerous confrontations unnecessary. On November 29, 1947, only a few days after Gutmann arrived in the country, the United Nations General Assembly voted to partition Palestine into Jewish and Arab states, with Jerusalem to remain an international city. That vote came nearly a year after the British, frustrated with their inability to govern Palestine, had submitted to the U.N. the question of the country's future. It was a vote the entire Jewish community of Palestine awaited, breathless with anticipation. When the local radio reported the U.N. resolution had passed, the Jews poured into the streets to celebrate the joyous moment. But the celebration was premature. The British were still in the country, where they would remain for five and a half more months. The British would no longer be the greatest barrier to Jewish independence, however. That mantle now passed to the Arabs of Palestine and beyond, who were furious over the U.N. vote and unwilling to accept a Jewish state in Palestine of any size. The battlelines would be redrawn, but the fighting would continue.

NOTES

[1] Josiah Wedgewood was a member of the British Parliament who was sympathetic to the Zionist cause.

4

SCHOOL LETS OUT

On November 30, 1947, the first full day after the U.N. vote, the celebrations continued. Throughout Palestine, the scenes were the same. Jews sang and danced in the streets, waiving Zionist flags. In some places, even British troops joined in, either out of sympathy with the Jews or because they knew that soon their occupation duty would end. Little noticed, a number of Americans were among the celebrants.

With the end of World War II, the U.S. Congress had passed the GI Bill of Rights. It gave educational benefits to returning veterans, and thousands entered universities under the legislation. Although American schools were the typical choice for those studying under the government program, a number of European schools were also authorized to accept GI's. Through the efforts of an American veteran named Bernie Popkin, two schools in Palestine also received permission to take GI's under the program – the Hebrew University in Jerusalem and the Technion in Haifa. For the 1947-48 academic year, more than one hundred Americans enrolled in these Jewish universities. Most of the Americans were GI's, though there were a number of non-GI's as well. Hebrew University, because it was in Jerusalem and also because of its liberal arts programs, was by far the more popular of the two institutions. The Technion, a school oriented toward the sciences, attracted less than ten American students.

At Hebrew University, the Americans received a gracious reception. Most lived relatively comfortably in the Pension Pax, a three-story rooming house in the Kiryat Moshe section of Jerusalem that the university had rented for the Americans. At the start of classes, Judah Magnes, the university president and a former American himself, invited them to a special tea. The university also arranged meetings for the Americans with prominent members of the Zionist establishment, including Golda Meir – then a member of the Jewish Agency Executive and later the Prime Minister of Israel. There was a powerful self-interest behind the Jewish community's warm welcome for their brethren from America. Palestine's Jewish leaders believed that American Jews could be persuaded to emigrate en masse to Palestine once the Mandate ended. They looked upon the small group of American students as an advance party, in effect, for a group of some five million potential new immigrants.

Despite the best efforts of their hosts, the Americans found Palestine a difficult place to study. Hostilities with the British and the Arabs frequently interrupted classes, particularly in Jerusalem where the students had to travel every day through Arab areas to Hebrew University's Mount Scopus campus. More and more, the American students came to view these interruptions less as observers and more as participants. As the 1947 school term began, many found themselves becoming drawn into the conflict raging around them – most often as recruits to the Haganah.

The U.N. resolution intensified everything. As it became clear that the Arabs would violently resist the formation of a Jewish state, studies essentially were abandoned and the schools closed down. Recruitment of university students, including the Americans, intensified. For the Palestinians, there was little question what they would do. Palestine was their homeland, and they would fight. The Americans had another option, though. They could leave the country, and many were pressured by their families to do so. For most, that pressure was too great and, however reluctantly, they left.

Irv Fellner and Leon "Lee" Reinharth were two of the American GI students who joined the Haganah. They were both New Yorkers and had become friendly during the first months of their studies in Palestine. On the evening of November 30, 1947, the day after the U.N. vote, they were sworn into the Haganah, together with hundreds of Palestinians, at a mass ceremony in a gymnasium in the Rechavia neighborhood of Jerusalem. The swearing-in was conducted in the finest tradition of the underground. For security purposes, the windows were shuttered and the room lit only by candlelight. Following a speech by a Haganah representative, Fellner, Reinharth and the others took the oath of allegiance, becoming members of the Jewish community's largest underground army.

Many of the Americans, including Reinharth and Fellner, made sacrifices to come to Palestine. For virtually all, the trip meant, at the very least, an extended separation from their families. Once the schools closed, remaining in the country also meant putting educational plans on hold. Reinharth's decision to come to Palestine involved an unusual sacrifice, though. It led him to being expelled from New York's Jewish Institute of Religion, where Reinharth was studying to be a rabbi.

The Jewish Institute was a non-denominational seminary founded by the noted American Rabbi Stephen Wise. In its classrooms on 68th Street in New York City, Orthodox, Conservative, and Reform Jews studied together, with the common goal of receiving ordination as rabbis. Reinharth and eight other Institute students, all of whom had already finished their first year of classes, decided to go to Palestine for the 1947-48 academic year, before returning to New York to complete their training for the rabbinate. They met with John Slonimsky, the dean of the school, to advise him of their plans and to propose that, in the future, a year in Palestine should become a regular part of the Institute's curriculum.

But Slonimsky, who had been arrested years earlier for demonstrating against America's entry into World War I, was hostile to their plans. "I know why you fellows want to go, you want to get involved in the violence in Palestine," he told the group. "I'm a pacifist, and I'm telling you now that if any of you dare to go, you will not be readmitted to the school." Slonimsky's warning had a powerful effect on the students and, in the end, only Reinharth made the trip. Much later, after Reinharth had returned to the U.S. from Palestine, he met with Dean Slonimsky to request readmission to the Jewish Institute. "Do you remember what I told you?" he asked Reinharth. "You're not going to be readmitted." Reinharth went to see Rabbi Stephen Wise, the school's founder and a preeminent American Zionist, to seek his intervention. "How can you with your Zionist approach allow your dean to expel me because I went to help the

Jewish community in Palestine?" Reinharth asked the seventy-five-year-old rabbi. Wise expressed sympathy with Reinharth's position, but declined to lend his support, saying that he was too old and feeble to argue with Dean Slonimsky over the matter. Thus ended Reinharth's rabbinic career.

There had been something else unusual about Reinharth's journey to Palestine. Danny Schind, a Haganah representative in New York, learned in advance of Reinharth's planned departure. Schind asked Reinharth to bring with him on the ship to Palestine a car for David Ben Gurion, then the head of the Jewish Agency and later Israel's first prime minister. Reinharth agreed. When he went to board the *Marine Carp* for the voyage to Palestine, a 1947 Dodge that the Haganah had purchased for Ben Gurion was there to board the ship with him. Reinharth later met the future prime minister when, as a member of the Haganah, he was assigned to night time guard duty outside of Ben Gurion's apartment.

After the swearing-in ceremony in the gymnasium, Fellner and Reinharth received some initial training with the motley collection of small arms and explosives used by the Haganah. The two were then assigned with some forty others to take part in a night raid on a large house in an Arab neighborhood of Jerusalem. The Arabs had been using the solidly-built, three-story structure as a base for sniping at the Jews, and the shooting had already killed one Jew and wounded three others. The Jewish leadership had first asked the British to put a stop to the Arab attacks, but they refused. With the end of the Mandate in sight, the British were determined to avoid any activity that might lead to British casualties. That attitude left the Jews to defend themselves, constrained by Britain's refusal to allow the Jews to carry arms, much less bring weapons into the country for the coming war. The British as well as the Arabs were on the minds of the Haganah attackers that night – the Arabs to be overcome, the British to be avoided.

The members of the assault force were divided according to their responsibilities and the weapons each would be carrying. Fellner and Reinharth were assigned to guard the operation's flank. They were to use grenades and primitive landmines to block any attempt the British might make to intervene. The fear was that the sound of the attack might draw in the unwilling British, interfering with the Haganah's plans to demolish the house.

The attackers moved toward the house in the darkness. As they drew nearer to the target, the men separated according to their assignments. In one position, Fellner and two Palestinians hid at the side of an approach road, which they had mined against the arrival of a British armored car. Reinharth was in another position guarding a different approach, a grenade at the ready. They waited in silence for the attack to begin. They heard an exchange of gunfire as the men in the assault group rushed the house. Then there was a sharp explosion – the Haganah had blown open the door of the house to place the larger charge that would bring it down. Finally the deep boom came, followed by silence. A billowing cloud of grey smoke replaced the three-story structure.

As the sounds of the short battle rang out, Reinharth kept watch down the road. Suddenly, out of the darkness, an armored car approached. He pulled the pin on his grenade, keeping his hand grasped on the handle, ready to throw it when the vehicle came within range. At the last possible moment, though, the armored car turned around, and left the scene. Had he still been in the U.S. Army, Reinharth would have simply thrown the grenade, to avoid the risk of attempting to replace the pin. But he was acutely aware of the arms shortage faced by the Haganah, and didn't want to waste a valuable grenade. On the other hand, he had little confidence in his ability to replace the pin. He decided to bring it with him to the building where the attackers were to rendezvous after the raid. There, still clutching the live grenade, Reinharth explained the problem to his commander. As he spoke, Reinharth noticed a seventeen-year-old Yemenite Jew, with a skullcap and earlocks, listening with a look of disgust on his face. The teenager walked over, grabbed the grenade, and unceremoniously inserted the pin. For Reinharth, it was a defining moment. He decided that with soldiers like these, the Jews of Palestine would certainly triumph over the Arabs.

Reinharth carried that belief with him for decades after he returned to the U.S. In May of 1967, the Arab states massed to attack Israel, and it appeared that Israel was on the verge of annihilation. On June 6, war broke out. That day, Reinharth received a call from a Jewish friend. The friend had scheduled his son's bar mitzvah for the second week of June. But with Israel in such jeopardy he wasn't sure he should go forward with what should be a happy ceremony. His faith in Israel's soldiers undiminished, Reinharth comforted his friend. "Don't worry about it. Go ahead with all of your preparations. By the time of the bar mitzvah, you will be celebrating not only a bar mitzvah but a great victory." As Reinharth prophesied, there was a victory to celebrate, as Israel overcame the combined armies of Egypt, Jordan and Syria in only six days of fighting. His friend, who went forward with the bar mitzvah at Reinharth's urging, forever after believed that Reinharth had possessed some inside knowledge of Israel's military plans.

The Hebrew University students answering the call of the Haganah included women as well as men. Zipporah Borowsky, the daughter of a prominent American Zionist leader, had been studying at the Hebrew University on a scholarship from the Zionist Organization of America. Like Fellner and Reinharth, Borowsky also joined the Haganah. The Haganah was an egalitarian fighting force. Borowsky often served as a courier, transporting small weapons that had been hidden under her blouse. Women were frequently used in this fashion by the Haganah. A Jew caught by the British carrying arms potentially faced the death sentence, but the British were loath to search women, making them the perfect candidates for this work.

Herbert Hordes and Max Alper were among the small group of Americans studying at the Technion. Both decided to join the Haganah. Unlike most of the American students, Hordes, who had just completed his freshman year at the University of Michigan, was not a GI. As a result, he had been forced to jump through more hoops than the others to get to Israel. Although the British granted some student visas to non-GI's, they did so sparingly. This was out of concern that student visas might be used as a conduit for illegal immigration. To prevent immigrants from falsely claiming to be students to get into the country, the authorities required those seeking to study in Palestine to post two years' tuition. Fortunately for Hordes, his parents agreed to put up the money.

Max Alper served as a B-29 mechanic in the Marianas Islands during the Second World War. He had interrupted his studies at UCLA to come to Palestine, enrolling at the Technion at the suggestion of the Haganah after first trying to sign on as a crewman for an Aliyah Bet ship. Alper came from a family of committed Zionists. At the same time that he was in Palestine training with the Haganah, his brother Phil was smuggling military equipment to Palestine. The equipment that Phil Alper and others were smuggling included machines for making grenades. Phil had shown Max a sample grenade casting from one of these machines before Max left for Palestine.

In December, Hordes and Alper were part of a group of nearly eighty Technion students that the Haganah sent to the mixed Jewish/Arab town of Safed for guard duty. The group travelled in a convoy of two busses and two trucks, passing through a series of British army checkpoints before reaching Safed late in the day. Hordes was riding in a truck at the end of the convoy as it entered the town. Safed was shrouded in a deep fog, making it difficult for the driver of the lead truck to find the way. Uncertain where he was going, the driver turned into the Arab section of town. The driver's error immediately became clear. An Arab threw a grenade into the back of the truck. One of the other students traveling with Hordes quickly picked up the grenade and threw it back out, where it exploded harmlessly. The shaken driver quickly turned the truck around and got back to the convoy going to Jewish Safed.

Hordes and Alper were in Safed for a month. Their job was to guard Jewish Safed, using as a base a school on the edge of the Jewish half of the city, some fifty yards from the nearest homes in the Arab part of town. The Technion group's responsibility was to ensure the Arabs made no attempt to advance any further toward Jewish Safed. The group was lightly armed, with rifles and some primitive grenades.

A few days before New Year's, Hordes was sitting at the school in Safed, reading an American newspaper that had somehow found its way into the city. He read with great interest a story about a search for a number of men who were wanted for attempting to smuggle TNT out of the Jersey City, New Jersey port. According to the story, the ringleader of the operation was Phil Alper. Hordes called Alper over: "Look, somebody with your name was arrested in New York." Alper scanned the article. "That's my brother," he told Hordes proudly. A few days later, a shipment of grenades arrived in Safed. Alper examined the grenades, which came in a crate marked *"Totzeret Ha'aretz"* ("Made in Israel") with special satisfaction. He recognized them as having come from the machine his brother had smuggled from New York.

Although the Jews and Arabs in Safed traded potshots each day, the Arabs made no attempt to attack while Hordes and Alper were there.

Their month of guard duty completed, they returned to Haifa.

The scale of the conflict with the Arabs continued to increase, as the Arabs grew increasingly bold. The Jews of Palestine had to concern themselves with more than their Arab neighbors, as the first Arab forces from outside of the country began to make their presence felt. In December of 1947, several units of the Arab Liberation Army (ALA) entered Palestine with the knowledge of the British. The ALA was an irregular Arab force made up of volunteers from Syria, Iraq, Lebanon and Palestine. In January of 1948, it attacked Kfar Etzion, one of four Jewish settlements in the Etzion Bloc. The Etzion Bloc was in the Judean mountains, some nine miles southwest of Jerusalem. The Liberation Army soon expanded its attacks to the other Etzion Bloc settlements. The remote location of these settlements made them depend for their survival on regular supply convoys from Jerusalem. Arab attacks on those convoys had reduced the stream of supplies to a trickle, making the situation of the settlements critical. The Haganah believed that unless reinforcements could be sent in, the Etzion Bloc would fall to the Arabs.

In an act of desperation, the Haganah decided to send a platoon at night through the mountains to relieve Kfar Etzion. Fellner and Reinharth learned they would be part of the relief platoon. Both men knew they were about to take part in what could be a suicide mission. Reinharth quickly penned a farewell letter to his parents, to be sent if he failed to return. But the hand of fate intervened. Only five minutes before the platoon was scheduled to depart, the Haganah decided to make some personnel changes. Fellner and Reinharth's unit was out, and another took its place.

The replacement unit also had an American soldier. Like Fellner and Reinharth, Moshe Pearlstein was a GI from New York, who had also been studying at Hebrew University. This was not Pearlstein's first mission for the Haganah. In a prior operation, Pearlstein and a group of other Haganah soldiers, including Fellner, had stood guard over a Jerusalem house. Pearlstein had guarded the front of the house, while Fellner stood watch in the back. The other soldiers slept inside, to be awakened by Fellner if anything happened. After a time, Fellner saw eight Arabs appear out of a nearby wadi, heading toward the front of the house. Fellner pulled on a rope that was connected to a bell inside, a crude alarm system that was supposed to wake the sleeping soldiers. But nothing happened. Just then, Fellner saw the Arabs running back toward the wadi, with Pearlstein at their heels. When Pearlstein felt as though he had a clean shot, he pulled the trigger, but nothing happened. His gun had failed. Pearlstein hoped the Etzion mission would be more successful.

The mission to the Etzion Bloc did not begin smoothly. The men left Jerusalem late in the evening of January 15, 1948. They needed to reach Kfar Etzion under cover of darkness, in order to evade attack by Arabs in the area. But they had left Jerusalem too late. Day broke before the platoon reached its destination, and the men were exposed. A group of Arab villagers opened fire on the group. The platoon returned fire, and sought cover on a small, tree-covered hilltop. But soon Arabs from other villages joined the attack, surrounding the Jewish fighters. The exchange of fire continued throughout the day, with the pace of return fire from the hilltop slowing as the intensity of the Arab attack increased. By sunset it was over. The entire platoon was wiped out. Moshe Pearlstein was, of course, among the dead. Later, Reinharth would take Pearlstein's effects to his family in New York.

At Kfar Etzion, the residents anxiously awaited the platoon's arrival, having been informed by radio of the soldiers' departure from Jerusalem. Among Kfar Etzion's defenders was an American named Jack Yeriel. Yeriel had been a crewman on the Aliyah Bet ship the *Northland*, and had joined the Haganah after arriving in Palestine. Unlike David Gutmann and the others who had served on the *Paducah*, Yeriel had been able to avoid internment on Cyprus following the capture of his ship. Just before the British boarded the *Northland*, the ship's radio operator pulled Yeriel aside. "How would you like to walk the streets of Haifa tonight a free man?" he had asked. He explained that the Haganah intended to hide some of the crew in the ship's watertanks. The Haganah would then smuggle the men off the ship after the passengers were taken away. Yeriel wanted to join in, and the radio operator took Yeriel to the ship's Haganah commander, Yosef Almog. Almog cautioned Yeriel: "We can't take responsibility for you if anything happens. The British could open up the tanks, and panic and start shooting. It is your responsibility." But Yeriel had already made up his mind. He would go into the tank.

Yeriel and about ten others slid through the hatch into the small compartment. They laid down side by side in the tank, a space that had a height of only about three feet. The area was so confined that it was impossible to stand, much less sit up. It was also completely dark. As they lay silent, not moving, they could hear the British trampling directly above them. Finally, they heard someone shout, "Come on, let's go." The British were evacuating the ship. But still the men had to wait; the hatch could only be opened from the outside.

Fortunately for Yeriel and the other men hiding in the water tank, when it came to cleaning the captured Aliyah Bet ships, there was something of a prissy quality about the British. They regarded the Aliyah Bet passengers and their ships as filthy. Once they captured the ships, the British wanted them cleaned, but were unwilling to do it themselves. They insisted that the Jewish Agency clean them, and the Jewish Agency was all too happy to comply. It sent in Haganah crews, who would free any hidden sailors and smuggle them off the ship disguised as cleaners. And so it was with Yeriel's group. After about twenty-four hours of lying like sardines in the tank, with nothing to drink and only a few chocolate bars to eat, the men heard someone fumbling with the latch. The door opened, and the crew saw the beam of a flashlight. It was the Haganah cleaning crew. They pulled the men out of the tank, gave them clothes to disguise them as workers, and the entire group walked off the ship to freedom.

Yeriel had learned from his commander that the Haganah was sending reinforcements to Kfar Etzion. But the platoon was now several days late, and the commander was growing nervous. On the night of January 18, Yeriel was on guard duty with a Palestinian when they saw the headlights of an approaching jeep. Instantly, they knew it was a British jeep – the Arabs wouldn't drive with their lights on. But they were only partially comforted; no one was sure of the intentions of the British in the period following the U.N. vote. Yeriel and the Palestinian decided that Yeriel, an English speaker, would go out to meet the vehicle. The Palestinian would stand behind a nearby tree. If anything went wrong, Yeriel would dive to the ground and the Palestinian would start firing.

Yeriel strode up to the jeep, and a British soldier stepped out. "I'm sorry, we have some very bad news. We have the bodies of thirty-five of your men who were killed last night. But they put up a good fight. The

Arab losses were five to one," he said solemnly. The residents of Kfar Etzion took the bodies and buried them. The loss of the platoon was devastating, and ultimately sealed the fate of the Etzion Bloc.

Pearlstein's death, the first of an American in the conflict, threw a spotlight on the presence of Americans in the ranks of the Haganah. The American consulate had previously suspected such involvement. The consulate had also been concerned by the apparent cessation of university studies – a state of affairs inconsistent with the continued receipt by Americans of GI assistance to study in Palestine. At one point, the consulate raised the subject directly with Hebrew University, demanding to know whether the American students were still engaged in university studies. "They are studying just as much as the other students are," the university representative had assured the consulate, a technically accurate statement.

But now there could be no denying that Americans were taking up arms in another nation's conflict. On January 30, 1948, only two weeks after Pearlstein's death, the consulate announced that the U.S. would recall the passports of any Americans found taking part in the fighting, to be returned only for a trip back to the United States. Under the circumstances, it was a mild reaction. The threat was intended to express the U.S. government's disapproval of activities such as Pearlstein's, without putting too much real pressure on Americans to avoid the fighting. The increase in hostilities was doing the consulate's work in any event. By the time of Pearlstein's death, most of the American students had already left.

As Britain's departure from Palestine and war with the Arabs became more imminent, the Haganah realized it needed help from abroad. Its makeshift arsenal of small arms would be no match for the advanced weapons of Palestine's Arab neighbors. The Haganah needed the modern weapons of war, and the men who were expert in their use. They sought both in the U.S. and Canada.

5

THE TIGER

In Canada, the Jewish community began early to recruit volunteers to fight in Palestine. On November 30, 1947, one day after the U.N. passed the partition resolution, Lionel Druker and Art Goldberg each had the same thought – now was the time to begin recruiting Canadians to fight for a Jewish state. Goldberg and Druker had served in the Canadian army together at the end of World War II, and had stayed in touch after their service. Both were enrolled in university. Druker was studying law at Halifax, while, on the other side of the country, Goldberg was a student at the University of British Columbia. The passage of the partition resolution profoundly moved both men, and they could think only of the implications of the U.N. vote for Palestine's future – and their own. On November 30, Goldberg and Druker each took out a sheet of paper, and wrote to the other, suggesting they join together to recruit Canadians to fight in Palestine. Several days later, on the same day, each received the other's letter. Thus began Goldberg's and Druker's role in Canadian recruitment.

Other Canadians would become involved as well. In Montreal, a committee of five formed to facilitate the recruitment of Canadian veterans and the purchase of Canadian weapons. One of the committee members was Syd Shulemson, a highly decorated veteran of the Canadian air force. Shulemson served as a bomber pilot during World War II, earning the

Distinguished Service Order for leading a massive bomber attack on a German convoy sailing off the Norwegian coast. After he finished his active World War II tour, Shulemson helped outfit the RAF's Mosquito bombers to fire rockets. Ultimately, Shulemson became the RAF's top rocket expert.

Each day, the five-man committee would meet for lunch to make decisions regarding recruitment and arms purchases. The group tried to maintain a low profile; each day's lunch was held at a different restaurant. What they were doing was not illegal – Canadian law did not prohibit its citizens from fighting under a foreign flag. Still, Shulemson and the others feared that too public an operation might invite pressure on the government to enact proscriptive legislation. Illegal or not, the Royal Canadian Mounted Police closely monitored the recruitment of Canadian Jews to fight for Palestine.

After a time, the Montreal committee decided that a second recruitment base was needed, this one in Toronto. A prominent Canadian named Ben Dunkelman headed the Toronto operation. Dunkelman was a huge man, six foot three and some two hundred sixty pounds, and a former major in the Queens Own Rifles of Canada. He was also a highly decorated veteran of the Second World War. Like Shulemson, Dunkelman had earned the coveted Distinguished Service Order.

Both the Montreal and Toronto groups primarily sought volunteers among Canadian Jews who had served in World War II. They would invite veterans to large gatherings and encourage them to go to Palestine to fight. Ben Dunkelman and another Canadian named Ben Adelman typically spoke at these events. Adelman was originally from Saskatoon, but he had emigrated to Palestine with his family in the 1930's. He had a particularly bold style of speaking, concluding his remarks with a challenge: "Eighty generations of Jews are looking over your shoulder, waiting to see what you will do." Sid Halperin of Toronto, a six-year veteran of the Canadian army, attended one of these gatherings, to hear a speech by Ben Dunkelman. After Dunkelman outlined the need for trained volunteers, he asked for those who were truly interested in joining to stay for further discussion. The others were asked to leave. Halperin thought over what Dunkelman had said. Having spent six years as a Canadian Jew in the Canadian army, Halperin decided he could spend one year as a Jewish Canadian in the Palestinian army. He stayed.

The goal of the Canadian recruiters was not simply to find individual Canadian Jews willing to fight in Palestine. Dunkelman in particular was more ambitious. As he told the gathering that Halperin attended, he hoped to create an all-Canadian infantry brigade that would fight as a unit. By March 1948, the recruiters had put together the first group of Canadians ready to leave for Palestine. Lionel Druker headed the group of twenty-seven volunteers. On March 5, 1948, the Druker group sailed from New York on the *Marine Falcon*, a former liberty ship. The route these first volunteers took would become familiar to nearly all of the Americans and Canadians who joined Israel's ground forces. The ship sailed first to Le Havre, France. From Le Havre, the Canadians travelled to Marseilles, passing briefly though Paris. At Marseilles, they stayed at Grand Arenas, a local DP camp. There they received some rudimentary military training – training the experienced soldiers regarded as a waste of time. From Marseilles, they sailed on to Palestine, arriving some six weeks after leaving New York. On May 3, 1948, the Haganah assigned the group, together with Sid Halperin and a handful of other Canadians who had travelled separately, to the 52nd Battalion of the newly-formed Givati Brigade. Soon, this group of Canadians would come to be known as the Canadian Platoon.

As the Druker group was making its way to Palestine, recruitment continued in Canada. An early question faced by the Montreal committee was whether or not to accept non-Jewish recruits. Shulemson did not want mercenaries, and for that reason opposed any recruitment of non-Jews. But that position ran headlong into the determination of George "Buzz" Beurling to fly for Israel.

A non-Jew, Beurling was Canada's leading World War II ace. He shot down thirty-one and one-third enemy planes, twenty-seven of these in just fourteen days of air combat in Malta.[1] His success on Malta earned him the nickname "the Falcon of Malta." Many, Shulemson included, regarded Beurling as the greatest living fighter pilot. Beurling's success was the product of his fanatical devotion to the craft of air-to-air combat and, in particular, to his refinement of the deflection shot. In the 1940s, a fighter pilot downed another plane by firing his machine guns and sometimes his cannons at the enemy. But unless the aggressor could position himself directly behind his foe, the kill had to be accomplished with a deflection shot. A deflection shot was not fired directly at the target, but at the place where the target would be at the critical moment when the bullet or cannon shell arrived. In a matter of seconds, the pilot had to factor in his own rate of speed and that of his enemy, together with the angle of flight of both planes, before taking aim. The calculation was too complex for many fighter pilots, who were incapable of making difficult deflection shots under the pressure of combat.

Beurling's mastery of the deflection shot did not come without effort. During breaks between flights, he would spend hours calculating different deflection angles and carefully recording them in notebooks. Beurling practiced his craft as well, using training techniques he designed himself. Beurling had been a model plane builder in his youth, and he carved wooden models representing the British Spitfire and the German Messerschmitt. He inserted wooden dowels into the bottoms of these planes. Holding one dowel in each hand, Beurling practiced different angles to simulate air-to-air combat.

While stationed at Malta, Beurling honed his shooting skills with another novel training method, lizard hunting. On the days he wasn't flying, Beurling would find a place on the island where lizards roamed freely. Then, standing motionless in the sun, he would wait for his prey. But Beurling would only shoot lizards a certain distance away, that at which the lizard approximated the size of a Messerschmitt or an Italian Macchi at three-hundred yards – the Spitfire's maximum effective range.

Beurling also worked to improve his vision, a pilot's greatest ally in 1940's-style air combat. He would train his eyes on an object a few feet away, equivalent to the distance between his eyes and the control panel in a Spitfire. Then, quickly, Beurling would lift his eyes to the horizon, trying to reduce as much as possible the amount of time needed to adjust his focus.

Beurling's hard work and single-mindedness may have made him one of World War II's greatest fighter pilots, but those qualities were not enough to make him popular with his commanding officers. Despite Beurling's incredible successes in the air, both the British Royal Air Force, with whom he began his flying career, and the Royal Canadian Air Force, with whom he finished it, regarded him as a serious discipline problem. Beurling didn't have the typical fighter pilot's vices; he didn't drink or chase women. He did, however, march to the tune of his own drummer, a trait not highly regarded in military circles. Beurling's superiors believed he was too much of a loner in the air. When flying as another pilot's wingman, he would freely leave the flight leader if he saw enemy planes nearby. To Beurling, nothing came before the hunt. His individuality showed in other ways. To the consternation of his commanders, for months he refused a promotion to flying officer, fearing the higher rank would mean increased administrative duties and less flying time.

Oddly for a man of Beurling's flying skill, he was involved in a large number of crashes – nine to be exact. Although injured a number of times, he always managed to come through in one piece. In one instance, his survival was nothing short of miraculous. On November 1, 1942, after completing his tour of duty on Malta, Beurling boarded a Liberator bomber for the flight back to Canada, where a hero's welcome awaited him. Also on the plane were eighteen other passengers, including two babies, and a crew of six. The Liberator attempted to land in Gibraltar for refueling. But a raging thunderstorm made it difficult for the pilot to find the landing strip. As the plane descended out of the clouds, the pilot quickly realized he had overshot the runway and needed to come around again. He opened up all of his engines and the plane climbed to forty feet. Then, suddenly, it nosed down and plummeted into the sea. Beurling had sensed that the Liberator was in trouble, and leaped from his seat and yanked open the emergency exit just as the plane hit the water. Beurling crawled out, his leg still in a cast from a recent crash landing, and managed to swim to shore. Two other passengers also escaped. Everyone else on board was killed.

As events heated up in Palestine, the local Canadian press began to speculate about the possibility that Beurling might participate in the fighting for the Jews or for the Arabs. Beurling, who had befriended a number of reporters during his glory days, openly encouraged the speculation. More quietly, though, he sought out the right person to put him in touch with the Jews. Finally, through the efforts of a mutual friend, Beurling and Shulemson arranged to meet privately. Concerned about the publicity surrounding Beurling and suspecting his motives, Shulemson painted a dark picture of life as a pilot in the Jewish air force. He explained to Beurling that the Haganah did not yet have any fighter planes, and there was no guarantee that Beurling would ever get to fly a fighter, much less one of his beloved Spitfires. Beurling would also not profit monetarily from his actions. There would be no pay beyond expenses. But Beurling was undaunted; he still wanted to go.

Over time, Shulemson's resistance to the recruitment of non-Jews wilted in the face of Beurling's determination and undeniable value. That determination was the stuff of legend in Canada. After the Canadian air force turned him down at the beginning of World War II, Beurling hastily boarded a ship to England to volunteer for the RAF. Those were the days when the German wolf packs hounded Atlantic shipping, and the convoy that Beurling's ship sailed in was attacked. The Germans torpedoed several of the ships, though not Beurling's. Unfazed by the ordeal, he raced to the RAF recruiting office immediately upon arriving in England. The RAF told him they would be delighted to have him, but first needed to see a birth certificate. Beurling had forgotten to bring it with him. No matter. He got right back on another ship and returned to Canada, surviving another torpedo attack on his convoy. He retrieved the birth certificate and made a third voyage across the Atlantic, finally joining the RAF.

The decision to recruit Beurling was too big for Shulemson to handle alone. Ben Dunkelman met with Beurling as well. During that meeting, Beurling explained that he was sympathetic to the Jewish cause, in part because he was troubled by the DP camps in Cyprus. Beurling again insisted he was not interested in money. Like Shulemson, Dunkelman became convinced that the fighter pilot wanted to join for the right reasons and should be recruited. Finally, Shulemson communicated with Haganah agents, in New York, seeking their approval to bring Beurling on board. In their conversations, they used a rudimentary code, fearful of wire-tapping. Shulemson referred to Beurling as the "Tiger," a name Shulemson chose because he believed that, if you had Beurling on your side, you had a tiger by the tail. Ultimately, the Haganah became persuaded of Beurling's value, and Shulemson told Beurling to travel to New York. Others would meet him there, and arrange his transportation to Europe. The Haganah had its tiger.

✡ ✡ ✡

Like their Canadian counterparts, the Jews of the United States quickly got into the recruitment act following the partition resolution. The situation in the United States was more complicated than in Canada, however. U.S. citizens wanting to fight in Palestine had to struggle with a number of legal barriers. American law did not then permit dual citizenship; an American who became a citizen of another country lost his or her U.S. passport. Worse, acts short of formally accepting foreign citizenship could be deemed a violation of the law. Swearing allegiance to another country, or voting in another country's election, were also considered inconsistent with continued American citizenship. The fear of losing their American citizenship would deter many from going to Palestine to fight. That fear would continue to plague those who went anyway, despite the risks.

It was also clear that the U.S. government had no intention of providing any special dispensation for those wishing to fight in Palestine. Although the U.S. had voted for partition, the State Department lobbied the White House throughout the period between the U.N. vote and Israel's proclamation of independence not to support the creation of a Jewish state. As a concrete expression of American ambivalence toward Israel's establishment, the U.S. steadfastly refused to sell arms to the Haganah – or later to Israel after it proclaimed its independence in May of 1948. Indeed, the U.S. would later join in an embargo of arms to the region, an embargo that for all practical purposes affected only the Jews.

For a time, before it became clear that such activity would not be tolerated, it appeared there might be large-scale, public recruitment of American Jews to fight in Palestine. On March 30, 1948, 2,500 people attended a rally at Madison Square Park in New York. The purpose of the rally was to announce the formation of a George Washington Legion – a name choice obviously influenced by the Abraham Lincoln Brigade that fought in the Spanish Civil War – made up of American soldiers who would fight for the creation of a Jewish state. The George Washington Legion was the brainchild of the American League for a Free Palestine, the same group that had organized the *Abril's* voyage. Barney Ross, the former world welterweight boxing champion and a decorated marine, spoke to the crowd. "All I've got left is my heart and two good hands to talk for me," he announced. There would be other publicity for the George Washington Brigade and an office was even established in New York to accept recruits. Ultimately, though, in the face of government opposition, nothing would come of it. On the very day of the rally, the State Department announced that passports would be refused to U.S. citizens seeking to join the fighting forces of either side in Palestine.

Recruiting in the U.S. would have to be done secretly. In the end, a handful of Haganah emissaries from Palestine headed the American recruiting effort. Some of these men, like Ehud Avriel, had been part of the Haganah's Aliyah Bet operation. Aware of the legal barriers to this activity, the Haganah created a front organization, Land and Labor for Palestine. Land and Labor ostensibly recruited men and women for non-military jobs in Palestine. In fact, its mission was to find former American servicemen willing to fight for Jewish independence. The man in charge of Land and Labor, which had offices in New York, Chicago, Los Angeles, and Cleveland, was Major Wesley Aron, a Jewish veteran of the British army.

Land and Labor sought volunteers in different ways. Aron and other representatives sometimes gave speeches to Jewish groups, saying enough about the organization's purpose to attract the truly interested to more private, closed meetings. Land and Labor also sought out Jewish war veterans, who had sometimes been identified with the help of other Jewish groups, directly soliciting these men to fight in Palestine. Over time, as the existence and true purpose of Land and Labor became better known within the Jewish community, many who were interested in volunteering, like former marine Tiny Balkin, contacted the organization directly. Ultimately, the vast majority of American volunteers would come to Israel through Land and Labor.

The best known of the American volunteers, however, came by a different route. In December of 1947, Moshe Shertok, the head of the Jewish Agency's Political Department, approached American General John Hilldring, an Assistant Secretary of State. Hilldring had earned a reputation during the post-war years as a friend of the Jews, because of his efforts to help Jewish refugees in the American zones of occupation. As part of its campaign to find experienced soldiers from abroad, the Haganah was particularly interested in finding high-ranking officers who could act as advisers to the Haganah in its transformation from an underground force into a modern army. While many in the Haganah had fighting experience, few had been commanders in regular armies. The expertise the Haganah needed would have to be found abroad. Hilldring recommended a Jewish officer to Shertok, a man who had formerly been under Hilldring's command. That officer was Colonel David "Mickey" Marcus.

A West Point graduate, Marcus had a distinguished military background. For some six months during the early part of World War II, he had run the army's Ranger training school, teaching soldiers the skills they would need for jungle warfare. The army then rotated him back to the Pentagon, where he held a series of high-level staff positions. Marcus served on the American staff for some of the major inter-Allied conferences of the World War II period, including Yalta, Cairo, Teheran, and Dumbarton Oaks. Marcus, who had obtained a law degree after graduating from West Point, also drafted the surrender terms for Italy and Germany.

But Marcus, the 1923 intercollegiate welterweight boxing champion, was a fighter at heart. Throughout the war, he lobbied for a field command of some kind, but he was always turned down. Marcus was considered too valuable as a staff officer. Still, for a short time during the war, he got his wish. In May 1944, Marcus was assigned to the Supreme Headquarters of the Allied Expeditionary Force in London, "to act as an observer in the implementation of military government policies for France." Marcus had asked for the assignment, knowing it would bring him closer to the action. As D-Day approached, Marcus grabbed his opportunity. He sought out the commanding general of the 101st Airborne Division, one of the divisions scheduled to parachute into France during the first part of the invasion. Without telling his superiors at the Pentagon, Marcus obtained permission to go into battle with the 101st. On D-Day, June 6, 1944, Marcus parachuted into Normandy with the rest of the airborne assault force. Of the 10,000 soldiers who jumped that day, Marcus was one of only two men who had never before jumped from a plane. In the next few days, Marcus was involved in more than a dozen engagements with the Germans, on one occasion leading a squad on a successful raid against a German machine gun nest. Soon, though, the Pentagon tracked Marcus down and had him shipped back to Washington – bringing an abrupt end to Marcus' brief combat tour.

Shortly after the end of the war, Marcus, by then a full colonel, was offered a promotion to general. The promotion carried a price, however. He would have to accept an assignment to the American embassy in the Soviet Union. But Marcus had just spent much of the prior seven years overseas and away from his wife. He reluctantly turned the army down, and returned to civilian life.

The Haganah dispatched Shlomo Shamir, a senior Haganah commander, to approach Marcus. At the time, Marcus was working to establish a private law practice. Initially, the Haganah was not interested in Marcus himself. It had hoped to find a general, and Shamir asked Marcus to recommend possible candidates. The West Point graduate agreed to help Shamir, and went to work trying to find someone suitable. After several weeks of searching, it became apparent there were no other candidates – it had to be Marcus. He agreed to leave behind his fledgling law practice and travel to Palestine to serve as an adviser to the Haganah. In January of 1948, Marcus and Shamir flew from New York to Paris. For security reasons, Marcus travelled under the alias Michael Stone. Delicately, Shamir asked Marcus where he should be buried if he were killed in Palestine. "West Point," Marcus answered proudly.

In Paris, Marcus and Shamir were greeted by Paul Shulman, the Annapolis graduate who was working for the Haganah in Europe. Marcus and Shulman kidded each other, each claiming to have attended the finer military academy. From Paris, Marcus and Shamir continued on to Palestine.

Marcus' mission was to evaluate the Haganah, and to report the results directly to Ben Gurion. Marcus immediately dove into his assignment. In the course of three months, he travelled the length and breadth of Jewish Palestine. Marcus toured Haganah units, met soldiers and commanders, and inspected the organization's arms and equipment. He had a way about him that appealed to Haganah soldiers at all levels. He believed in the importance of close relations between a commander and the men he commanded, and he made a special effort to get to know some of the Haganah's young recruits. When Marcus wanted to speak with a soldier, he would invariably call out, without any trace of sarcasm: "Come here, young hero." On a visit to one base, Marcus saw a number of soldiers doing chin-ups. A firm believer in the benefits of strength training and sports, he walked over to talk with the soldiers. With characteristic directness, one of the young Palestinians asked Marcus why he had come to Palestine. Marcus rolled up a sleeve, exposing a muscular arm. "You see this," he said, pointing to a bulging vein, "the blood of Abraham flows through these veins."

Marcus was respectful toward the Haganah's officers, as well. Although the Haganah prided itself on its informality, Marcus was careful to address its chief of staff Yaakov Dori as "Sir." He was also adept at finding a common language with members of the two competing factions within the Haganah's command – those like Shlomo Shamir who were veterans of the British army and who wanted to pattern the Jewish army along the same structured lines, and the Palmach commanders who favored a less formal, more democratic army.

In the first week of March 1948, Marcus reported the results of his evaluation to Ben Gurion. Marcus was blunt. He decried the poor level of physical fitness, the inferior training, and the lack of routine. He was particularly caustic in his assessment of the Haganah's commanders, advising Ben Gurion that there was no one who could lead a battalion – or even a platoon – into battle. Marcus observed that the Palmach had its share of courageous leaders, but these men were capable only of leading small units into combat. He recommended the establishment of a school for battalion commanders, where officers could be put through a four-week training course, and offered to run the school himself. Marcus also suggested bringing some two dozen brigade commanders from the U.S. to help with instruction. Despite the criticisms, or perhaps because of them, Ben Gurion was delighted with Marcus' efforts.

Haganah Chief of Staff Yaakov Dori was concerned, however, about the vacuum that would be left if he pulled senior Haganah commanders from their units for a one-month course. In Dori's view, given the delicate nature of the Jewish community's security situation, it was a luxury the Haganah could not afford. He decided that Marcus should prepare written training materials, and then visit each brigade for a two- or three-day period to personally instruct the battalion commanders, using the materials as a guide. Marcus immediately went to work preparing the manuals, writing in longhand hundreds of pages of material, which were promptly transcribed and translated into Hebrew. The school for battalion commanders that Marcus recommended would not be established until February of 1949, when Israel's War of Independence was virtually over. The school used Marcus' manuals, unedited.

In April 1948, Marcus returned to the States. There were several purposes for the trip. He felt he needed to spend some time with his wife, who had become ill in his absence. After spending so much time away from her during World War II, he hated inflicting a further separation. He also felt he could best help the Haganah by personally recruiting qualified officers to return with him. Marcus identified eleven Jewish graduates of West Point he believed would come to Palestine. Marcus contacted each, requesting their assistance. To his shock and disappointment, all eleven turned him down. Marcus would return to Palestine alone.

After less than a month in the States, Marcus was back in Palestine. With his wife's health restored, he was ready to get back to work.

NOTES

[1] A pilot is credited with one kill for each enemy plane he destroys in air-to-air combat. Fractions are awarded where more than one pilot shoots at the same plane, making it impossible to apportion credit among them for the kill. Beurling's one-third of a kill represented an incident in which Beurling and two other pilots combined to destroy one enemy plane.

6

ATC

At the same time the Haganah was trying to create a viable army, it was also attempting to build an air force. If Marcus was concerned over the absence of trained infantry officers in the Haganah, he would have been even more dismayed by the situation in the air force. At the time of the partition resolution, the Haganah's primitive "Air Service" consisted of less than two dozen light civilian aircraft, primarily single-engine Austers. The Haganah had no transport planes, no bombers, and no fighter planes in its arsenal. In short, it had none of the aircraft needed to fight a modern war.

In late 1947, Shlomo Shamir of the Haganah, the same man who recruited Marcus, contacted Al Schwimmer, then a flight engineer with TWA. Shamir sought Schwimmer's help in locating American transport planes, to be used at least initially to bring illegal immigrants to Palestine. Schwimmer was thirty years old and a veteran transport pilot who had served in the Air Transport Command of the U.S. Air Force. He was a tall though not imposing man, with thinning hair and a quiet manner. But Schwimmer's placid demeanor masked a tremendous inner strength. He would prove to be one of the most important recruits to the cause of building a Jewish air force.

Shamir's recruitment of Schwimmer did not represent the first time the Haganah looked to the United States for help in establishing an air force. In the late 1930's, the Haganah established a small flight training school based in Cream Ridge, New Jersey. The Zionist youth group Hashomer Hatzair owned two farms in New Jersey, one in Cream Ridge and one in Heightstown. There, idealistic young American Jews who dreamed of starting a new life on a kibbutz in Palestine learned basic farming skills. The Cream Ridge farm became the base for the school, while the actual flight training took place at a small airfield a few miles away. The initial class of ten students included a Palestinian named Aharon Remez, who later became the first commander of Israel's air force. Hyman Schechtman, later Remez's deputy, and American Percy Tolchinsky, another future member of the Israeli Air Force, also learned to fly at Cream Ridge. To celebrate the opening of the school and to raise money, the Haganah hosted a gala opening at the Heightstown farm. One of the speakers that day was Nobel Prize-winning physicist Albert Einstein, a committed Zionist and then a professor at nearby Princeton University.

But as the Haganah looked to the U.S. after World War II, it was more interested in purchasing planes than in training pilots. One of the odd, and, to the Haganah, frustrating aspects of U.S. arms policy was the fact that in 1947, the U.S. had an almost unlimited supply of every kind of surplus military hardware. Left over from the war were hundreds, if not thousands, of planes of every type. Many were being sold for a mere fraction of their original cost, often to former military pilots who were trying to start their own airlines or transport services. Schwimmer was well aware of this market, and sought to tap it. Between December of 1947 and February of 1948, Schwimmer arranged the purchase of three Lockheed Constellations and ten Curtis Commando C-46's. The Constellation, the larger of the two planes, could carry sixty passengers, and was the same aircraft TWA used for its trans-Atlantic flights. The C-46 was also a big plane by the standards of the day, and in fact was one of the largest twin-engine planes ever built. Most important to Schwimmer, as the focus shifted from ferrying illegal immigrants to transporting weapons, the C-46 was able to carry up to 18,000 pounds of freight, making it an ideal transport craft.

The planes were not in good condition. They had taken a beating during the war, and needed to be substantially overhauled before they could reliably be used for transport. The overhaul also became

Schwimmer's responsibility. He hired experienced mechanics, explaining to them that he was forming a new airline that would eventually operate out of Italy, but concealing the connection between these planes and the fighting in Palestine. Schwimmer's story was not false, as far as it went. At that time, the Haganah did plan on setting up a base in Italy, and from there to ferry arms purchased in Europe to Palestine. The men that Schwimmer hired to service the planes would, Schwimmer expected, work out of the Italian base. Most of the mechanics, men like Mike Ondra, Glen King, T Taylor, Shorty Barker, and Freddie Dahms, were non-Jews. The "cobbers," as they liked to call themselves – borrowing the Australian slang for "buddy" – were all veteran air force mechanics who had hoped to become part of an airline after the war, but had encountered a frustrating lack of opportunity. Before meeting Schwimmer, they had given up on that dream, finding employment outside of the airline industry. Seeing a chance to hook up with an airline, the cobbers were only too eager to respond to Schwimmer's offer.

For security purposes, the Haganah decided it would be useful to form a front American airline with these planes. Nahum Bernstein, an American lawyer working for the Haganah and a veteran OSS agent, figured out an easy way to accomplish it.[1] An air force veteran named Irwin "Steve" Schwartz had contacted Bernstein, trying to sign on as a radio operator for an Aliyah Bet ship. Schwartz's desire to help the Haganah dated back to 1946. That year, while based in Cairo for TWA, he visited Palestine and saw the arrival of an Aliyah Bet ship. Stirred by the experience, he decided to get involved himself.

Talking with Schwartz, Bernstein had learned about Service Airways, a former charter airline that had ceased operations, but that still existed on paper. Service Airways was headed by a friend of Schwartz's named Irvin "Swifty" Schindler, a Jewish veteran of the U.S. Air Force's Air Transport Command. It was a perfect match. The revived Service Airways leased Schwimmer's planes, and opened a four-room suite of offices on West 57th Street in New York. With its fleet of ten C-46's and three Constellations, Service Airways became overnight the largest non-scheduled airline in the world.

Two bases of operations were established to put the planes back in flying condition and to train the crews to fly them. Initially, all of the planes were hangared in Burbank, California, at the Lockheed air terminal. Over time, one Constellation and five C-46's were flown to Millville, New Jersey, where the refurbishing work continued at Millville Municipal Airport. The ultimate goal was to get all of the planes to New Jersey, a convenient jumping-off point for the flight across the Atlantic to Italy.

The Millville airport was a former U.S. Air Force training base. It had a 5,000 foot runway, long enough to accommodate the C-46's and Constellations. The airport was far enough from a major town so that the Service Airways operation would not attract attention, yet close enough to the New York headquarters to still be convenient.

While the planes were being refitted in New Jersey and California, the recruiting of pilots and navigators to fly them was also underway. Steve Schwartz was responsible for this, with one notable exception. Schwimmer personally recruited Sam Lewis, TWA's first Jewish captain, and the man credited with breaking the airline industry's "Jewish Barrier." Lewis had literally fought his way to his lofty position at TWA, once breaking the jaw of an airline executive who told him that no Jew would ever sit in the left seat – the captain's seat – of a TWA plane. But in response to a plea from Schwimmer, with whom Lewis had flown in the U.S. Air Force's Air Transport Command, Lewis resigned his hard-won captaincy.

One of Steve Schwartz's early recruits was Bill Gerson. Gerson was a former major in the U.S. Air Force and a father of two, who dreamed of a new life in Palestine with his young family. Older than most of the other volunteers and a skilled flight instructor, Gerson was placed in command of Millville. Schwartz also signed up several former B-17 pilots, including Norm Moonitz and Ray Kurtz, two oversized, wise-cracking Brooklyn firemen, who brought light moments and natural leadership to the operation. Marty Ribakoff was one of the most experienced pilots to join Service Airways, having already seen action in two wars. He had flown for the Loyalists in the Spanish Civil War, and flew C-46's over the Hump with the U.S. Air Force in World War II. Hal Auerbach, a thirty-one-year-old former navy pilot, was another hire. The softspoken Auerbach had been powerfully influenced in his decision to volunteer by newsreels of the British capture of the *Exodus*. Another early arrival was Trygve "Tryg" Maseng, a tall, quiet, former B-26 captain, who had been studying creative writing at Columbia University. The blond-haired and blue-eyed Maseng, of Norwegian descent, was one of the more unexpected additions to the Haganah's ranks. A skilled flyer, Maseng became the check pilot, checking out new recruits on the C-46 to see if they had the skills they claimed.

Service Airways did not accept everyone who volunteered. Some would-be pilots overstated their qualifications, a fact that Maseng would typically discover during their first flight. One obviously qualified pilot was turned away for a different reason. Al Raisin, a former B-17 captain who flew twenty-five missions for the Eighth Air Force during World War II, tried to sign up at the suggestion of his friend Harold Livingston. Livingston had already joined Service Airways as a radio operator, and thought Raisin could contribute as well. Raisin met with Sam Lewis. Lewis reviewed Raisin's flight background, and determined that Service Airways could use the B-17 pilot. Lewis told Raisin he would need to get a passport. Raisin explained he already had one.

A few months earlier, Raisin told Lewis, Raisin had agreed to help a New York rabbi and Zionist activist named Baruch Korff. One of Korff's schemes was to parachute illegal immigrants into Palestine, and Raisin was recruited to pilot that plane. Because the flight was to leave from Europe, Raisin had already secured a passport. The operation had fallen apart when Korff was arrested in Paris and the plane confiscated. With Korff's activities going nowhere, Raisin was available to fly for Service Airways.

But Rabbi Korff was not affiliated with the Haganah, and he was considered to be something of an extremist. (Korff never would become part of the mainstream of the American Jewish community. Years later, he became known as "Nixon's Rabbi" because of his strong support for the Republican president.) Another Korff scheme had been to drop anti-British leaflets from a Piper Cub onto the deck of the *Queen Elizabeth* as it sailed into New York harbor with British Foreign Minister Bevin on board. Raisin was to pilot this flight as well, which had to be canceled because of bad weather.

Service Airways was not interested in associates of Rabbi Korff, Lewis told Raisin, and turned the B-17 pilot away. Raisin tried to explain that he had no interest in politics, and that he had only agreed to help Rabbi

Korff as a way of helping the Jews of Europe get to Palestine. But Lewis was adamant.

Although the planes were now part of an official airline, they still could not leave the country without certification from the Civil Aviation Administration. That certification was not forthcoming; the CAA wanted more modifications to the planes than Schwimmer thought necessary, or for which he had the time or funds to make. But without CAA certification, Service Airways could not get its planes out of the country. Through Swifty Schindler, a solution was found. Schindler had run into an old friend named Martin Bellefond, a former major in the U.S. Air Force who had secured a franchise to start an airline in Panama before losing his financial backers. Bellefond knew the nephew of the Panamanian president, who was enthusiastic about the plan. Panama, as it turned out, had the perfect facility for the new airline, a large, modern air terminal at Tocuman. Panama's leaders had political reasons for wanting to see an airline based at Tocuman. The airport was virtually unused, and had as a result become a liability for the ruling government, which faced elections in April of 1948. Schwimmer's planes, which had first been leased to Service Airways, were now leased to the new Panamanian airline – Lineas Aereas de Panama, Sociedad Anonima, or LAPSA. Because the planes were now foreign registered, they no longer needed CAA certification.

Panama was attractive to the Haganah not only because it solved the certification problem. The U.S. government was closely monitoring Service Airway's operation, suspecting the planes were connected to the Haganah. The threat of exposure, and thus the possible loss of the planes, was a serious one. By moving the planes to Panama, the Haganah could escape the prying eyes of U.S. government agents, while preparation of the Italian base continued. On March 13, Sam Lewis flew a Constellation from Millville down to Panama, the first LAPSA plane to make the trip.

A short while later, the Haganah decided to fly one of the C-46's to Italy, to look over the airfield the Haganah had located near the town of Perugia. Leo Gardner who, like Al Schwimmer and Sam Lewis had been an ATC ferry pilot during the war, captained the flight. Steve Schwartz was the navigator. After hopscotching their way across the North Atlantic, they landed the transport plane on a dirt strip at the Perugia airfield. Immediately, it became clear that the field was in no condition to be used by the huge LAPSA transport planes. Another field would have to be found. Still, Schwartz's arrival in Italy would prove to be fortuitous for the Haganah.

Back in the States, the need to get the planes out of California and New Jersey became critical. On March 26, 1948, President Truman issued a proclamation that, after April 15, 1948, no further exports of aircraft weighing more than 35,000 pounds – a weight that all of Service Airway's planes exceeded – would be permitted without clearance from the State Department. The Haganah knew clearance would never come. The proclamation made it essential to accelerate the pace of work on the planes, so they could be spirited out of the country by April 15.

The Millville planes were the first to leave. On April 10, the four C-46's were ready to depart, official clearance having been received for the flight to Panama. Or so it seemed. The Treasury Department had been monitoring the Millville operation from its inception. Every day two agents, each wearing the T-man's classic overcoat and fedora, observed the activity at the airfield from a black sedan. Each night, a second team of agents replaced the first. With the planes ready to taxi to the runway, the agents finally made their move. They strode up to Schindler, and told him they suspected the planes were carrying contraband. They informed him they would not permit the planes to leave. Schindler argued with the agents, reminding them that the planes were foreign registered. The agents were unpersuaded. One pointed to the planes, telling Schindler: "Those planes have U.S. numbers." "I'll be back in a second," Schindler told them, and headed for one of the hangars.

Less than two minutes later, he returned, this time with two of the mechanics. The men carried with them a bucket of paint, a brush and a ladder. Hurriedly, they painted the LAPSA registration numbers on each of the four C-46's: RX-135, RX-136, RX-137, and RX-138. The T-men were unmoved. They got into their black sedan and drove it in front of the first C-46, now bearing the number RX-135, refusing to let the plane leave. The stand-off continued for several hours, until Schindler decided it was time to act. "I am ordering my airplanes to take off immediately," he informed one of the agents. Then, to Hal Auerbach, the pilot of RX-135, he called out: "Okay, Hal, get going!" The agent shouted at Schindler: "By government order, you are prohibited from leaving the United States!"

But Schindler would have the last word that night. "If you want to stop them," he said as he walked to his own C-46, "you'll have to shoot them down." Auerbach then pulled around the sedan, taxied onto the runway, and roared into the night. The other three C-46's followed, in rapid succession.

Schindler's mad dash around the agents exemplified Al Schwimmer's strategy for the whole operation. Schwimmer knew that he and the others were breaking U.S. law by buying the planes and exporting them out of the country under false pretenses. But Schwimmer also knew that the U.S. government worked slowly. He believed that if his men moved quickly enough, they could get the planes out of the country before the government would have time to act.

On April 13 and 14, just before the April 15 deadline, the last five C-46's flew out of Burbank, also headed for South America. Bill Gerson, Hal Auerbach, Sam Lewis and Marty Ribakoff were part of the operation. For Gerson, Auerbach and Lewis, it was their second flights to Panama. Each had previously flown a New Jersey plane down to South America. Because of the shortage of pilots, the three had travelled to California on commercial airliners to help bring the rest of the C-46's. In fact, the crew shortages were so acute that some of the cobbers had to be pressed into service as co-pilots for this last ferry flight. One of the ground crewmen, a non-Jewish recruit named Glen King, was assigned to fly as Gerson's co-pilot for the trip from Los Angeles to Panama.

The California C-46's did not fly empty. The entire ground operation had been quickly loaded onto the planes, to be reestablished in Panama. Spare parts, tools, and communication equipment filled to capacity each plane's cargo area.

The heavily-laden C-46's flew without incident through the first four legs of the trip, arriving in Mexico City for the final stretch to Panama. In the thin air of Mexico City, some 7,300 feet above sea level, they lined up for take off. Sam Lewis went first. The altitude and the C-46's heavy load made takeoff difficult. Lewis' plane needed the entire length of runway and an unpaved area beyond it to get airborne. Ribakoff went second, and he too needed the whole runway. Next it was Gerson's turn, and Ribakoff looked back to watch his friend take off. Gerson also needed most of the runway before he could get his plane into the air, lowering his flaps at the last instant to provide extra lift. The trick worked, and the plane slowly climbed to one hundred feet. Suddenly, Gerson lost an engine, and his left wing dropped. The plane tumbled into a dry river bed at the end of the runway. The force of the impact tore the left engine loose, driving it backwards into the cockpit. The engine flattened the pilot's chair and badly burned Gerson. Glen King, Gerson's co-pilot, was killed instantly.

Ribakoff watched, horrified, as Gerson's plane crashed. Momentarily too shaken to continue the flight, the veteran pilot relinquished the controls to his co-pilot until he regained his composure. Back on the runway, Auerbach was waiting in his C-46, engines idling, when he saw Gerson's plane drop from view. Auerbach raced his plane to the end of the runway at near take-off speed, and taxied as close as possible to the airport fence. Auerbach jumped out of his plane, climbed over the fence, and ran a mile to reach the crash site. He found Gerson, who had been thrown clear of the wreckage, moaning in pain. An airport rescue crew placed Gerson onto a stretcher and loaded him into an ambulance. Auerbach clambered on board, and the ambulance careened through the crowded streets of Mexico City toward the hospital. It seemed to Auerbach that the Mexico City drivers were oblivious to the ambulance's wailing siren. At nearly every intersection, the rescue vehicle barely avoided an accident. They finally reached the hospital, with Gerson still clinging to life. Gerson was taken to a room, with Auerbach at his side. Auerbach, ever the optimist, tried to encourage the nearly-unconscious Gerson: "Bill, if you live, the miracle will not be that you survived an airplane crash, but that you survived the ambulance ride through Mexico City." But his injuries were too severe, and Gerson died a short while later. His dream of a new life in Palestine with his family would not be realized.

Before the planes arrived in Panama, Marty Bellefond had worked hard to put things in order. He arranged to house the men in two large apartments in a fashionable section of Panama City. Maintaining the LAPSA facade, Bellefond also opened a LAPSA ticket office, featuring a plastic model of the LAPSA Constellation – the airline's flagship.

The group in Panama included the early recruits like Moonitz, Kurtz, Auerbach and Lewis, who had been part of the Millville and Burbank operations. In the weeks after the last of the C-46's arrived in Panama, more men would join them, filling out the crews necessary to fly the fleet of planes to Italy. Jules Cuburnek was one of the new additions. A navigator/bombardier, Cuburnek had flown twenty-five combat missions in a B-17 during World War II. Moe Rosenbaum, another veteran navigator, left his studies at Cornell University to come to Panama. Ed Styrak, a radio operator, was another one of the newcomers. Styrak, of Polish extraction, was an Aliyah Bet veteran who had sailed with David Gutmann and Heavy Greaves on the *Abril*.

Sam Lewis was working at the airfield one day when he looked up to see yet another new recruit arrive. To his surprise, it was none other than Al Raisin, Rabbi Baruch Korff's pilot. A short time after being dismissed by Lewis, Raisin received a phone call from Land and Labor. When he learned the purpose of the call, Raisin cut off the caller, explaining that he had already tried to volunteer. Raisin related the episode with Lewis, and said that he had no interest in being turned down again. But the caller assured Raisin that Land and Labor was not interested in his earlier work for Korff. Raisin signed on, and Land and Labor sent him to Panama. The first person Raisin ran into when he arrived was Sam Lewis. "What are you doing here?" Lewis gasped. "I'm part of the group," Raisin answered. This time, Raisin had the last word.

The flight crews trained at Tocuman according to a schedule set by Hal Auerbach. The training was essential. Many of the flyers were rusty; they hadn't flown since the war. Navigator Jules Cuburnek fell into this category. He was working as a druggist when he decided to volunteer, and had not flown since his tour of duty with the U.S. Air Force ended in 1944. He was concerned about the state of his navigational skills, and he needed the training to restore his confidence. Moe Rosenbaum, whose navigational skills were fresher than Cuburnek's, gave a refresher course for Cuburnek and the other navigators.

When the men were not training, they spent their time enjoying Panama City's night life. Panama City boasted a wide selection of bars and restaurants, and even a government-operated casino. The men made the rounds of the different establishments, while Moonitz became particularly fond of the Hotel Internationale casino. Moonitz was soon rolling in money. Each night he dined at the best restaurants. Together with radio operator Harold Livingston, Moonitz purchased a 1936 Buick Phaeton for trips around town. Livingston wondered about the source of

Moonitz's new-found wealth. He learned the secret one night at the casino, when he saw Moonitz and one of the blackjack dealers disappear into the restroom. Livingston followed, and listened as the two men spoke in one of the stalls. He soon realized that the dealer, in return for a percentage of the profits, had been letting Moonitz win.

During this period, the men learned more about their travel plans. They had known from the beginning of the operation that May 14 would mark the end of the British Mandate. That date became their deadline; they would have to be ready to go when the Jewish state was declared. They also had known already that the plan was to fly the planes to Italy, or more specifically to Catania, Sicily, where the Haganah had found an alternative field to the one at Perugia to use as a base for ferrying supplies to Palestine. Now, they were told how they would be going. The new American ban on the export of aircraft made a refueling stop in the U.S. impossible. Instead, the planes would first fly overland to Natal, Brazil. From Natal, the planes would fly over the Atlantic to Dakar, French Senegal. The next stop after Dakar would be Casablanca. Finally, after Casablanca, the planes would reach their destination in Catania.

As May 14 drew nearer, the men increased the pace of their preparations. In addition to the pressure they faced from events in Palestine was the pressure the Panamanians were exerting. The Panamanians believed that LAPSA was a real airline, and were becoming impatient at its failure to commence operations. Finally, on May 6, the first group of five C-46's was ready to leave. LAPSA told the Panamanians that the five planes would be departing on a survey flight, to determine the best routes to Europe for the airline's passenger and cargo services. The departure was a gala event, with a number of representatives of the Panamanian government on hand to celebrate the airline's inaugural flight. One after another, with Auerbach in the lead, the five C-46's took off for Natal. When the final C-46 had cleared the runway, Auerbach circled one final time over Tocuman, and waggled his wings to the cheers of the dignitaries gathered below.

The five C-46's arrived without incident in Natal, though two required repairs before they would be ready for the ten-hour flight across the ocean to Dakar. Moonitz's plane was one of the two that were stranded. Always adept at finding a way to entertain himself, Moonitz bought a marmoset in town. With the monkey on his shoulder, the pilot walked the streets, bedecked in a bush jacket, khakis, and leather boots, and carrying a swagger stick in one hand and an ivory cigarette holder in the other. As he strode through town, a cluster of adoring shoe shine boys chased after him, calling: *"El Capitano Mooney! El Capitano Mooney!"*

The first wave of C-46's left Natal for the next stop on the journey, Dakar. From there, as planned, they flew on to Casablanca. A major surprise awaited them. They would not be flying on to Catania, Sicily, as originally planned. American and British pressure on the Italian government had made Catania off-limits. The new supply base, the men were shocked to discover, was in Czechoslovakia, behind the Iron Curtain.

NOTES

[1] The OSS was the predecessor of the CIA.

7

THE UNOFFICIAL WAR CONTINUES

During the months the Haganah was attempting to develop an air transport arm with Service Airways and LAPSA, events in Palestine did not stand still. The decimation of the Haganah relief platoon bound for the Etzion Bloc was receding in memory as the pace of Arab attacks and Jewish counter-attacks quickened. Increasingly, as the Mandate's end drew nearer, the British were becoming less willing to keep the peace in Palestine. In the waning days of the Mandate, the British seemed only interested in protecting British lives.

One particularly violent battleground was the Jerusalem-Tel Aviv highway. That road, which wound its way between wooded hilltops as it climbed from Tel Aviv to Jerusalem, was the only artery connecting Jerusalem to the rest of Jewish Palestine. Each day, convoys of vehicles from Tel Aviv travelled to Jerusalem, transporting food, water, gasoline, and other vital supplies. Those convoys were the holy city's lifeline; without them, it did not seem possible the Jews of Jerusalem could survive.

Unfortunately for the Haganah, Arab villages dotted the hills surrounding the Jerusalem-Tel Aviv road. Armed Arabs used those villages to snipe at the convoys as they passed below, making it increasingly difficult, and deadly, to resupply Jerusalem. The British refused to ensure free passage, forcing the Haganah to improvise its own solution. The Haganah built makeshift armored buses to carry the supplies. These buses, which were only minimally effective in stopping the bullets, became known as "sandwiches." The name referred to the primitive plating the Haganah surrounded each bus with – two thin metal sheets sandwiched around a layer of wood. Slits were cut into the sides of the sandwiches to permit armed Haganah guards travelling on the buses to shoot back at the Arab snipers. One of the Haganah's armed guards was David Starec, the former *Exodus* crewman.

Starec's journey to Palestine had been a long one. For most of the *Exodus* crew, their service ended with the capture of the ship and internment in Germany. One by one, with the help of the Haganah, the crewmen made their way out of the British zone of occupation and back to the U.S. Not all ended up back home, however. Ben Foreman, Bernie Marks, Myron Goldstein and a few others continued on to Palestine to join the fighting. Starec too was determined to continue his part in the struggle for Jewish independence.

But Starec first needed to get out of Poppendorf, the DP camp where the British had imprisoned him. Initially, the British maintained a tight watch at the camp. After several months, though, the British abandoned Poppendorf, leaving the occupants unguarded but still stranded within the British zone of occupation. With this opening, the Haganah decided to take the crew members out of the British zone and into the American area, a necessary first step toward escaping from Europe. The Haganah dressed Starec and a group of others as soccer players and transported them in a lorry through British and American checkpoints to the American zone. The group explained to the soldiers that they were soccer players, travelling to another refugee camp for a match.

While waiting in Poppendorf, Starec had learned that one of his cousins from Poland was in a DP camp in the American zone. After Starec and the others made it to the American zone, he visited his cousin in the DP camp there. Starec told his cousin of his plan to continue on to Palestine. But his cousin could not understand why Starec had entered the American zone, instead of leaving Europe as most of the other crewmen had. "You should know what I am doing here," Starec replied. "Where is my family, where are my cousins, where are my uncles?"

In November of 1947, Starec finally left Germany, bound for France. At a DP camp near Marseilles, the Haganah gave Starec his first formal military training. But he was getting impatient; he wanted desperately to finish the journey to Palestine. Finally, in January, the time came. The Haganah gave Starec a ticket on a Greek ship leaving Marseilles, bound for Palestine. A few days later, nearly ten months after leaving the U.S. on the *Exodus*, he finally reached Palestine, this time to stay.

During the months since he left New York, people had often asked Starec which of the underground groups he supported: the Haganah, the Irgun, or the Stern Group. His answer was always the same: "I support the one that throws more bombs." Ultimately, Starec decided the Palmach, the elite "striking force" of the Haganah, was the toughest group. He joined its ranks, and was assigned to the Harel Brigade. His brigade commander was a young Palestinian named Yitzhak Rabin.

Starec underwent several weeks of training at a kibbutz near the seaside town of Caesaria, before his unit received orders to go to Jerusalem. On March 3, 1948, Starec's platoon commander told the men that their orders were to defend a convoy of supplies bound that evening for Jerusalem. Another member of the platoon who was to guard the convoy was a DP Starec knew from the *Exodus*, a Jew from a North African country who spoke only French. Starec, who counted French among his many languages, had befriended the North African during the voyage. Now they would be together again for another battle.

That night, Starec and the others climbed into the sandwiches, positioning themselves for the dangerous journey ahead. Before they could challenge the Arabs, however, they first needed to deal with the British. Although they refused to guarantee safe passage to Jerusalem, the British also refused to allow the Haganah to openly arm the convoys. To enforce this policy, the British searched each vehicle in the convoy before the trip to Jerusalem. The Haganah was therefore forced to hide its weapons. Once the British soldiers completed the search, they waved Starec's convoy through. Only then did the Haganah guards remove their weapons from their hiding places, ready to run the gauntlet of fire from the Arab gunmen.

As the convoy passed the Arab town of Latrun, the bullets began to rain down. They pinged against the sides of the sandwiches, with increasing frequency as the Arabs found their range. Starec heard shouts from the Arabs above – "*Alihu Itbach al yahud*" ("Slaughter the Jews"). Then he heard shouts from the other convoy vehicles, calling out that people had been hit.

Starec and the other Haganah guards fired back through the slits. Suddenly, the commander shouted at Starec: "When you shoot, shoot straight ahead at the enemy, not up at the sky!" With only a few weeks of military training, Starec was still learning the rudiments of soldiering. The convoy made it through, with the guards returning fire the whole way. The Arab gunmen had wounded two people, one fatally. The dead man was Starec's friend from the *Exodus*. The Haganah buried him at Kibbutz Ha'anavim, just outside of Jerusalem. But in the hectic pace of events, neither Starec nor any of the other members of the unit had ever learned the soldier's name. He was buried under a headstone that read only: "A Passenger on The *Exodus*."

Starec's convoy was one of the last to get through to Jerusalem. By the middle of March, Arab attacks made the Jerusalem-Tel Aviv road impassable. The residents of the holy city, now cut off from the rest of the country, were besieged. Jewish Jerusalem had been utterly dependent on the supplies of food, water, and fuel brought by the convoys. Although the Haganah had started to stockpile in preparation for a possible cutting-off of the city, no one believed Jerusalem could hold out for long without a renewal of the supply line. Unless the Haganah found a solution quickly, the city would be lost to the Arabs.

Jerusalem was but one of the Haganah's many concerns. Like Jerusalem, the port city of Haifa had a mixed Arab and Jewish population. Also like Jerusalem, Haifa had seen an increasing wave of hostilities since the U.N. vote. The Haganah wanted to take control of the Arab section, to protect the city's Jewish residents. It waited for the right moment to move in.

On April 21, the Haganah got the break it was looking for. That day, the British announced they would immediately evacuate their forces from positions throughout the country, redeploying them in military camps in southern Palestine and in Haifa's port. The purpose of the British action was to remove their troops from harm's way, positioning them instead in the areas they would be needed to secure Britain's safe departure from Palestine on May 14. The Haganah moved decisively in response to the British announcement. On April 22, it launched Operation Misparayim

("Scissors"), the goal of which was to capture the Arab section of Haifa.

The Haganah's Carmeli Brigade spearheaded Operation Misparayim. Many in the brigade had been students at Haifa's Technion, including Herbert Hordes, the American from the University of Michigan. Hordes, who at nineteen had never before served in an army, was proud to be a soldier. When he received his first rifle, he carved the name of his girlfriend Nesia into the stock.

Operation Misparayim was not Hordes' first action in Haifa. In the spring of 1948, before that battle, Hordes was assigned, with other members of his unit, to guard Haifa's flour mills. The Grand Mills, as they were known, had been established with the help of the Rothschild family at the end of the nineteenth century. The mills were in the eastern part of Haifa, near the Arab section of the city. While food was in short supply generally in the country, the Grand Mills were home to a seemingly limitless supply of matzah. Hordes and the other members of his unit ate their fill. One day, during his stint guarding the mills, Hordes received a message that his brother-in-law in America had sent him a package. To get to the post office, Hordes had to travel in a lightly armored bus through the Arab section of Haifa at a cost of half a pound – a handsome sum in those days. When he arrived at the post office, he learned he would have to pay an additional pound as duty on the package. Hordes paid that sum as well, and left the post office. On the return trip to Jewish Haifa, Arabs fired on the bus, and several shots pierced the thin metal sheets that were supposed to protect the passengers. Although unhurt, Hordes was shaken up. He returned to his barracks and opened the package, only to discover that his thoughtful brother-in-law, concerned about whether Hordes would be able to properly celebrate the approaching holiday of Passover given the country's food shortage, had sent a box of Manishewitz matzah.

For the capture of Haifa, Hordes' platoon went to battle with four Davidka mortars. The Davidka was one of the classic Israeli weapons of the War of Independence. Its design was crude and its heavy shells caused little physical damage. But a shell fired from a Davidka exploded thunderously, and it was a potent psychological weapon. The Davidka shells that Hordes fired had two charges. There was a small cache of explosives at the bottom of the shell, and a much larger charge of dynamite – weighing more than twenty pounds – at the top. The smaller charge was what

The *Abril* anchored at Port de Bouc. *(Photograph by Shepard Rifkin, Courtesy of American Veterans of Israel)*

Refugees make their way to Port de Bouc, to board the *Abril*. *(Photograph by Shepard Rifkin, Courtesy of American Veterans of Israel)*

Abril crewmen David Gutmann *(standing)* and Lou Brettschneider in the Haifa lock-up, before being transferred to Acre prison. *(Courtesy of David Gutmann)*

David Gutmann made this sketch while in the Acre prison barracks. *Abril* captain Bob Levitan is seated. The figure standing on the right is Walter "Heavy" Greaves. *(Courtesy of David Gutmann)*

The *Abril* crew tour the fortress walls of Acre prison, accompanied by their prison guard Ahmed. David Gutmann *(top row, first from left)* and Captain Bob Levitan *(bottom row, fourth from left)* admire the view with binoculars. *(Courtesy of David Gutmann)*

Refugees prepare to board the *Exodus*, which is docked in Sete, France. *(Courtesy of David Gen)*

The *Exodus*, splintered and smashed from her encounter with British warships. *(Courtesy of David Gen)*

After taking control of the *Exodus*, white-helmeted British soldiers stand guard on the deck, amidst hundreds of refugees. Note the Zionist flag, still waving defiantly in the background. *(Courtesy of Abraham Segal)*

The Aliyah Bet ships *Northland* (*The Jewish State*) *(left)* and *Paducah* (*Geulah*) docked in Haifa harbor after British "Red Devils" stormed the ships, seized control of them, and towed the vessels to port. *(Courtesy of David Gutmann)*

Haganah agents bribe French police to allow an immigrant ship to dock in Port du Bouc. *(Courtesy of Aaron Levin)*

Jewish refugees see Haifa for the first time as their ship enters the harbor. *(Courtesy of Aaron Levin)*

The Cyprus prison camps. These housed as many as 20,000 Jews at one time; all forcibly interned by the British for trying to emigrate to Palestine in defiance of a British naval blockade. *(Courtesy of David Gutmann)*

Life on board an immigrant ship. *(Courtesy of Aaron Levin)*

Major Ben Dunkelman in the uniform of the Queens Own Rifles. Dunkelman commanded the Seventh Brigade. *(Courtesy of National Archives of Canada)*

A national hero, Beurling is greeted by Canadian Prime Minister King upon returning from Malta on November 19, 1942. Less than three weeks earlier, Beurling narrowly escaped death when the plane that was returning him to Canada crashed into the sea off Gibraltar. *(Courtesy of National Archives of Canada)*

George "Buzz" Beurling, the "Falcon of Malta," records another kill. Canada's leading World War II ace, Beurling shot down twenty-seven planes in just fourteendays of air combat over Malta. *(Courtesy of National Archives of Canada)*

George Beurling's *(left)* distaste for administrative responsibilities led him to refuse a promotion to flying officer. *(Courtesy of National Archives of Canada)*

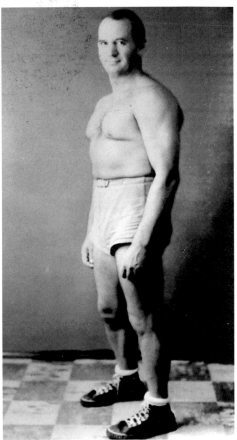

Right: Lieutenant Colonel David "Mickey" Marcus, Commander of the Rangers Training School in Hawaii. *(David Marcus Collection)*

Left: Marcus conducting a briefing at the Pentagon. *(David Marcus Collection)*

Major General Hildring (*left*) congratulates Marcus after awarding him the Distinguished Service Medal on May 18, 1945. It was Hildring who recommended Marcus to the Haganah. (*David Marcus Collection*)

Albert Einstein visited a Zionist training farm in Heights Town, New Jersey in 1939 for the opening of a Haganah pilot training course. Aharon Remez, Israel's first air force commander, received his first flight training at Heights Town. (*Courtesy of Yechiel Sasson*)

Bill Gerson, a major in the U.S. Air Force, stands in front of his B-26. Gerson was killed when the C-46 he was piloting crashed on take-off at Mexico City, Mexico, April 14, 1948. (*Courtesy of Eddy Kaplansky*)

Glen King, one of the "cobbers." King was pressed into service as Bill Gerson's co-pilot for that fateful fight from Mexico City. *(Courtesy of Eddy Kaplansky, Evie Dahms)*

Above and two below: The many faces of Limey Miller, a soldier in the British, American and Israeli Armies. *(Courtesy of Milton "Limey" Miller)*

Annapolis graduate Paul Shulman, the first commander-in-chief of the Israeli Navy, shows Prime Minister David Ben Gurion how to use a sextant. *(Courtesy of American Veterans of Israel)*

George "Buzz" Beurling's gravesite in Haifa. At his patents' request, Beurling's body was moved from Italy to Israel for reburial. *(Courtesy of American Veterans of Israel)*

A C-46 flies over Tel Aviv. *(Courtesy of Arieh Jacoby)*

Norm Moonitz *(second from left)* piloted the C-46 that crashed on approach to Ekron air field, May 24, 1948. *(Photograph by Howard Binder, Courtesy of American Veterans of Israel)*

Ed Styrak, the radio operator for the May 24, 1948 flight. Moonitz and co-pilot Sheldon Eichel saved Styrak's life by pulling him through a cockpit window and dragging him away from the burning plane. *(Photograph by Shepard Rifkin, Courtesy of American Veterans of Israel)*

Canadian Ralph Moster *(center)*, the commander of the Negev Squadron. *(Courtesy of Eddy Kaplansky, Sonny Wosk)*

A Piper Cub from the Negev Squadron. *(Courtesy of Arieh Jacoby)*

American fighter pilots Lou Lenart *(left)* and Giddy Lichtman *(center)*. Lenart led the raid that stopped the Egyptian advance on Tel Aviv. Lichtman recorded the first kill of an enemy fighter. *(Courtesy of Red Finkel)*

Draped in the flag of the nation he helped to create, the body of Mickey Marcus, the first general of the Jewish people in nearly 2000 years, is readied for transport back to the U.S. *(David Marcus Collection)*

Marcus' funeral procession in New York. *(David Marcus Collection)*

propelled the shell out of the mortar and toward the target, where the larger charge was supposed to detonate on or near impact. The Davidkas in Hordes' platoon were particularly primitive. To fire the mortar, Hordes had to manually light two fuses – a quick-burning one for the propelling charge and a slower burning one for the exploding charge.

As other units fought below, Hordes' platoon positioned themselves on Hadar Hacarmel, the hillside area where most of the city's Jews lived. From that vantage point, they could fire their mortars at the Arab forces in the lower part of the city. As the battle progressed, Hordes and the other mortarmen received the order to fire. They lit the four mortars and, within seconds, Hordes heard three loud booms as the shells were hurtled toward lower Haifa. But there was no sound from Hordes' mortar. During training, he had learned to count to fifteen after lighting the propelling charge. If that charge did not fire by then, its fuse was defective. But unless the fuse on the larger charge was also defective, the shell would explode in the tube. More than fifteen seconds had passed. Hordes was terrified. He wanted to shout a warning to the others to take cover, but he couldn't think of the right words in Hebrew. In a frenzy, he shouted the closest thing he could think of: "*Mapa, Mapa!*" ("Table cover, table cover!"). Somehow, the other soldiers realized what had happened and ran for cover. The main charge was not a dud; with a deafening sound, it exploded, spraying pieces of the Davidka in all directions. The force of the blast threw Hordes to the ground. He was uninjured, but the thunderous roar of the explosion caused his ears to ring for two days afterward. The blast lightly wounded another soldier, and he and Hordes were taken to the hospital. In the confusion, Hordes lost his prized rifle.

The destruction of Hordes' mortar did not affect the outcome of the battle. The operation was a stunning success. Within twenty-four hours, and with relatively few casualties, the Haganah realized its objective – all of Haifa was in Jewish hands.

The British redeployment of forces provided the Haganah with other opportunities. The Haganah decided that it was now safe to bring in the C-46 that Leo Gardner and Steve Schwartz had flown into Perugia in March. On May 5, 1948, the C-46 took off from the dirt strip at Perugia, bound for the Aquir airfield, just south of Tel Aviv. Arnold Ilowite, another Service Airways pilot, was at the controls. Ilowite's co-pilot was

Canadian Jack "Jock" Goldstein, a Syd Shulemson recruit. Goldstein had served as a radio operator with the Royal Canadian Air Force's bomber command during the war. He was "promoted" to co-pilot for the C-46 flight, with no one else available to sit in the right-hand seat.

Ilowite and Goldstein negotiated the route from Italy to Palestine safely, and landed at Aquir late in the evening of May 5, 1948. The very next day, the Haganah put Ilowite and Goldstein to work. Kibbutz Yechiam, located on a small hilltop in the extreme north of the country, had been without supplies for weeks. As they had done with Jerusalem, the Arabs had been able to stop the passage of supply convoys to the kibbutz. The Haganah decided to use the C-46 to airdrop supplies to Yechiam's starving residents.

The morning of May 6, Ilowite and Goldstein headed the C-46 north from Aquir, its cargo area filled with huge steel tins of food. Riding in the back of the plane were several Palestinians, who were to push the tins out over the kibbutz once Ilowite maneuvered the plane into position. Ilowite approached the hilltop kibbutz, which he noticed was surrounded on all sides by larger hills. Arab gunners had taken positions on that high ground. Those gunners, who over the past weeks had sniped at the kibbutz, now turned their attention to the C-46, letting loose with a barrage of machine gun fire.

Maintaining a safe altitude for the drop, Ilowite approached the kibbutz. He yelled for the Palestinians to push out the first group of tins, and then watched, disappointed, as they sailed past the kibbutz. He and Goldstein realized they would have to find a more accurate method. They made a second pass. This time, Ilowite slowed the C-46 to near stalling speed and came in low. Goldstein dropped the landing gear, further slowing the plane, while lowering the flaps to provide enough lift to keep the lumbering C-46 airborne. The intensity of the ground fire increased, with the transport plane now flying at the height of the hills surrounding the kibbutz. Ilowite yelled to the Palestinians to push the food out, and the tins found their mark. Immediately, Goldstein retracted the wheels and raised the flaps as Ilowite applied full power and banked the lightened plane to the left.

Over the next week, Ilowite and Goldstein returned again and again to Yechiam, to drop more of the desperately needed supplies. Each time, they used the same low-altitude, low-speed approach, despite the withering ground fire. On May 13, Ilowite and Goldstein took off for their last run to Yechiam. As they approached the kibbutz, they cut the plane's speed and lowered the landing gear, dropping the food with pinpoint accuracy within the safe confines of the kibbutz. Goldstein raised the wheels and Ilowite applied full throttle, for the first time turning the plane to the right as they pulled out of their run. Suddenly, there was a sound of shattering glass followed by a rush of outside air, as bullets penetrated the windshield. Goldstein fell on to Ilowite as the force of the blast knocked both men from their seats. When Goldstein lifted himself up, he saw that Ilowite's shirt was drenched with blood. "Arnie, you're bleeding!" he shouted. "I'm not bleeding, you bastard, you are," responded Ilowite. The blood had come from Goldstein's face, lacerated by the flying glass. Ilowite quickly climbed back into the captain's chair and headed the plane south, landing it safely in Tel Aviv. Goldstein's wounds, it turned out, were superficial, and he was soon back in the air.

In addition to the northern settlements, the Haganah was also concerned with the country's less populous southern region. With the British departure only days away, and the surrounding Arab countries preparing for an invasion, the Haganah needed to strengthen its defenses in the areas along the projected Arab line of attack. It assigned its Givati and Negev Brigades the task of clearing out armed Arab fighters from the small towns which dotted the area south of Tel Aviv. Givati's 2nd Battalion, which included the Canadian Platoon, was ordered to attack the town of Bash-shit. The twenty-seven-member unit, commanded by Lionel Druker, was about to see its first action.

Immediately after arriving in Palestine in mid-April, the Canadians had begun to ready themselves for the fighting. Although nearly all of the men were Canadian army veterans, only two soldiers, including Sidney Halperin of Toronto, had significant infantry experience. With a full-scale war only days away, there was little time to get the unit into shape. After only ten days of training, in which the shortage of arms and ammunition limited the men to five practice shots each, the Canadian Platoon headed out for the attack on Bash-shit.

The Arab village was a collection of primitive two-story houses, loosely organized around a dusty town square. Most of the villagers kept a small collection of animals in the first floor of their homes, and lived on the second floor. Among the 1,600 Arab peasants living in Bash-shit, a Haganah reconnaissance patrol determined there were at least one hundred armed fighters.

In the early hours of May 11, the Canadian Platoon, together with three other platoons from the Givati Brigade, approached the village. The soldiers surrounded Bash-shit, laying mines and setting up machine gun positions. But the assault on the town, which was supposed to begin in darkness, was slow to develop. As day broke, Arab soldiers positioned on top of the homes found easy targets among the first Haganah soldiers to enter the town. While the Canadians anxiously waited to move in, two soldiers were killed and eight wounded in one of the adjoining platoons. The Canadians finally received the order to attack. They cautiously entered the village from the south, lobbing grenades at enemy positions and firing as they advanced.

Several of the Canadians, including air force veteran Syd Cadloff, pressed deep into the village. In the face of intense enemy fire, Cadloff and the unit's radio operator searched for cover. They spotted a shallow trench running through the town's courtyard, and started to make a run for it. Before he reached the trench, Cadloff noticed a small group of Arab men some fifty feet away. He swung his rifle across his body and fired, killing several of the Arabs. Cadloff and the radio operator then quickly dove into the trench.

The village had by then erupted in a mix of rifle shots, exploding grenades, and machine gun fire. Lying in the trench, Cadloff shouted over the din to the rest of the unit: "There's a machine gun very close by. I can hear him firing." Immediately, there was a shout from the radio operator, who had just taken a bullet in the leg. While Cadloff tried to help his wounded countryman, an Arab with a Bren gun opened fire on their position, and Cadloff too was hit in the leg. Both men yelled out that they had been hit, and a medic crawled over to render aid. When the medic took a look at Cadloff's leg, he froze – the lower leg was completely shattered, and Cadloff's foot was lying at an odd angle. As Cadloff and the platoon's radio operator lay wounded in the trench, another member of the unit also found himself in dire straits. Enemy fire had pinned Syd Beube behind a small house. He decided to make a break for it, and ran from the house, looking for cover. But before he could reach a position of safety, Beube was hit in the head and fell. His wound, though, proved to be superficial, and he was safely evacuated from the village.

Slowly, the wounded Canadians were pulled out of Bash-shit and taken to a field hospital. As he helped remove the wounded, Lionel Druker, the leader of the Canadian unit, was grazed in the neck by enemy fire. The Canadians still left in the town faced enemy fire from three sides after the Arabs had driven back a northern assault by another platoon. Isolated in the center of the village and without adequate support, the Canadian Platoon finally received orders to withdraw.

On the hills overlooking Bash-shit, the Canadians joined other troops in preventing Arab reinforcements from entering the village. Early the next morning, a fresh Haganah battalion arrived and launched a second assault on Bash-shit. In less than an hour, the village was captured.

Of the Canadians wounded in the fighting at Bash-shit, Syd Cadloff fared the worst. The damage to his lower leg was simply too great. Within days after the raid, the doctors amputated his leg above the knee. It had not escaped the notice of the Canadians that of the four "Sids" in the platoon, two had been wounded in the fighting at Bash-shit. Some had begun to say openly that it was bad luck to be named Sid.

After Bash-shit, the Canadian Platoon would never again see action as a unit. For reasons that were never entirely clear, the Haganah disbanded it within days after the Bash-shit raid. Most thought the unit was broken up because the Haganah worried that its relations with Canada would be harmed if the unit were to sustain heavy casualties. Others suspected that the government feared excessive balkanization of the country's fighting force from units comprised entirely of another country's nationals. Whatever the reason, the Canadians were promptly scattered throughout the army.

Between Bash-shit and the break-up of the Canadian Platoon, the Canadians saw limited action, mostly escorting convoys in the Latrun area. During one of these escort missions, the unit received word that two soldiers were missing. Sid Halperin, another of the Canadian "Sids," left the convoy with several others, to take part in a search for the two. Soon after starting the search, Halperin spotted the missing soldiers on a nearby hilltop. They were running toward Halperin and the others. Giving chase was a group of Arab fighters. The Arabs opened fire, and Halperin's right knee buckled as he was hit. The curse of the "Sids" had struck again.[1]

No vehicle was available to evacuate Halperin for medical treatment, and he was told to lie in a nearby ditch until transport was arranged. He remained in the ditch for thirty agonizing minutes, until finally an army truck arrived. Halperin was loaded on board, and taken to what he had been told would be a field hospital. But the tents of the field hospital were still being erected when Halperin arrived, and again he had to wait, this time for the hospital to be built. Finally, after what seemed like an eternity, Halperin was brought into one of the tents to be examined by a doctor. The doctor explained that the bullet had lodged in Halperin's knee. Because the newly-erected field hospital did not have an X-ray machine, removing the bullet would be too dangerous. "The best I can do right now is sew it up," the doctor told Halperin. The real bad news was yet to come. "It's also going to hurt because we have no anesthetics."

Halperin braced himself as the doctor began to stitch. It was, not unexpectedly, extremely painful. "Jesus Christ!" Halperin cried out. Startled, the doctor stopped stitching and looked at Halperin. "Aren't you Jewish?" he asked.

NOTES

[1] The curse would strike the fourth "Sid" – Sydney Rubinoff – the hardest. On July 17, 1948, months after the Canadian Platoon had been disbanded, Rubinoff died in battle.

8

THE WAR BEGINS

The five-month unofficial war was about to become official. On May 14, 1948, authority in Palestine formally passed from British hands. That day, at four-thirty in the afternoon, Jewish Agency chairman David Ben Gurion presided over a gathering of dignitaries at the Tel Aviv Museum. Standing in front of a portrait of Theodor Herzl, the father of modern Zionism, and flanked by two banner-size Zionist flags, Ben Gurion proclaimed the independence of the Jewish state. His proclamation put an end to speculation that the Jews might refrain from unilaterally declaring independence, hoping instead to negotiate a solution to the problem of Arab opposition to Jewish statehood. There was another, smaller bit of drama to Ben Gurion's speech. In it he revealed to the nation for the first time the name of the Jewish homeland – Israel.

The task of communicating Ben Gurion's speech to besieged Jerusalem fell to Milton "Limey" Miller, a member of the Haganah's communications section. Limey had arrived in Israel as a crewman on the Aliyah Bet ship the *Josiah Wedgewood*. The Haganah was Limey's third army. He had dual U.S. and British citizenship, and had served in communications units of both armies during the Second World War. Miller began his military service in the British army but, frustrated at the anti-Semitism he encountered, asked to transfer to the American army. He later regretted that decision: "The English were gentleman anti-Semites, but the Americans were anti-Semites – period." Miller's decision to leave his post-war life in New York and come to Palestine had been motivated by the Holocaust. Toward the end of the war, his American army unit had stumbled on a mass Jewish grave in Holland, and Miller was forever changed by the experience. Using Morse code, Miller tapped out Ben Gurion's historic words to Jerusalem.

The Arab response to Ben Gurion's speech was not long in coming. Within twenty-four hours, the armies of Lebanon, Syria, Iraq, Jordan and Egypt had invaded, opening five battlefronts for the new state to deal with.

Max Alper, the UCLA student who had joined the Haganah with Herbert Hordes, sat in the Tel Aviv apartment of some relatives as they all listened, riveted, to Ben Gurion's speech. Unlike Hordes, Alper had not entered the Carmeli Brigade. When he learned that efforts were underway to establish a Jewish air force, he volunteered his services, and for the last few months had been working as an airplane mechanic at Sde Dov. Sde Dov was a small airport on the outskirts of Tel Aviv, where much of the Haganah's primitive air service was based. It was work that suited Alper, a former B-29 mechanic in the Pacific during the Second World War. He helped maintain the Haganah's small planes, and also instructed Palestinians in the rudiments of his craft.

Alper had barely made it to Tel Aviv in time to hear Ben Gurion proclaim independence. A few days earlier, he had been sent north to the Ramat David airport to repair one of the planes located there. For the trip back to Tel Aviv, Alper had hitched a ride with a friend. On the road south they had passed columns of British vehicles heading to Haifa for the evacuation. Alper noticed that periodically, one of the British vehicles would break down. Rather than abandon the vehicles to the Jews, the ever-thorough British towed them to the side of the road and set them on fire.

Alper couldn't stay in his relatives' apartment to hear Ben Gurion finish his speech. He had orders to report back to Sde Dov that afternoon. Hurrying to his base, Alper climbed on his bicycle and pedaled through the empty streets of Tel Aviv. Everywhere, apartment windows were open and everyone was inside listening to Ben Gurion's speech. Ben Gurion's words echoed through the quiet streets, and Alper felt as though he was being born aloft through the city's streets. As he rode, he was reminded of the Biblical pronouncement: "I bare you on eagles' wings, and brought you unto myself."

Within hours of his arriving at Sde Dov, Alper and the other ground crewmen received orders to disburse the aircraft. "The state isn't even a day old, and already they think they're an army," Alper grumbled as he and the others began the hard work of towing the planes around the field. But their labor did not go for naught. The very next morning, May 15, the Royal Egyptian Air Force attacked. Several Egyptian Spits bombed the base, hitting the main hangar and the guard shack. After their bombing run, the Spits strafed the field. As the planes began their run, Alper shouted to the others, who were running away from the attack, to dive at ninety degree angles to the attacking planes, as he had been taught in the U.S. Air Force. Although the raid damaged three of the parked planes, most escaped unscathed. The prior day's disbursal had prevented a calamity.

As the crews attempted to clean up after the Egyptian raid, an army truck drove up. "*Heveinu neshek!*" ("We have brought arms!"), the driver called out. Inside the truck were several weapons, mostly pistols and rifles. There was also one thirty-caliber machine gun, with a tripod. Because only Alper had any training on the gun, he took it for himself. He and a trainee cleaned off the shipping grease, and set the gun up on its tripod. Alper showed the trainee how to feed the belt of ammunition, and then waited. Within hours, the Egyptians returned for a second attack on Sde Dov. As they approached, Alper began to fire, trying to remember his air force training. The phrases "lead the target" and "fire bursts!" danced through his head, as Alper fired at a Spitfire that was coming right at the base. The Spit roared overhead, and Alper swiveled to follow it, still firing. Within moments, the plane began to trail smoke. The Spitfire crashed near Herzliya, and Israeli forces captured the pilot. Alper's gun had brought down the first enemy fighter plane in Israel's history.

The Jordanian Legion directed its substantial power to the goal of capturing the besieged city of Jerusalem. The Legion was the most-feared Arab force. Its commander, John Glubb, was an Englishman, as were two-thirds of the Legion's senior offices. The Legion was well-trained and well-equipped – the most professional fighting force in the Middle East. Its four mechanized regiments boasted six-pound antitank guns, twenty-five-pounder artillery pieces, and some fifty armored cars. While even the best-equipped Israeli troops could not match the firepower of the Jordanians, the Legion was not facing the strongest forces that Israel had to offer. The prolonged siege, combined with Britain's refusal to allow the Jews to openly arm themselves, had prevented the Haganah from delivering the heavy guns and artillery pieces Jerusalem needed to hold off the Jordanians. On May 14, the day David Ben Gurion declared independence, the Etzion Bloc surrendered to the Legion. The fate of those lightly armed settlements had been sealed months before, when Moshe Pearlstein and the other members of the Haganah relief platoon had died trying to reinforce the area.

While the British officer corps of the Legion provided that force with one of its greatest strengths, it was also an unexpected source of weakness for the Jordanians. In the spring of 1948, before independence and the Jordanian invasion, the Haganah had learned of the presence in Jerusalem of Marlin Levin. Levin, a Pennsylvanian who had entered Palestine as a Hebrew University student, had been a code specialist in the U.S. Army. A graduate of the army's cryptography school, Levin served during the war in the cipher room at the Supreme Headquarters Allied Expeditionary Force in Paris. The Haganah persuaded Levin to help the Haganah establish a security system, using the experience he had accumulated at SHAEF.

Before Ben Gurion's May 14 speech, the Haganah began to intercept coded communications between the Legion's senior officers. Because most of these officers were British, the communications were in English rather than Arabic. The Haganah showed the communications to Levin, who quickly concluded that the Jordanian code was basic. Using a number of the intercepted messages, Levin worked out the key to the Jordanian code. With that key, the Haganah ultimately translated more than seventy Legion communications, including one that revealed a planned attack on the Jewish settlements of Neve Yaakov and Atarot, located just to the north of Jerusalem.

Those settlements were dangerously weak and exposed. While Ben Gurion vehemently opposed abandoning any Jewish settlement in the face of Arab invaders, the Haganah did not want to risk a massacre. On May 15 and 16, the Haganah successfully evacuated the exposed residents of Atarot and Neve Yaakov in advance of the approaching Jordanians. The early warning Levin made possible helped Israel avert a catastrophe in the first few days of the new state's existence.

At the same time the Haganah was trying to secure the new country's borders against the mass invasion, it was also attempting to establish Jewish control over the interior portions of the country. While the Haganah had captured Haifa in late April, armed Arabs still occupied several towns to the north of Haifa. The largest was the port city of Acre, the site more than a year earlier of the dramatic escape from the fortress prison. Acre consisted of a walled old city and a new city located outside the walls. Acre was a fearsome target for the Israelis. In 1799, the walled old city had successfully repelled an attack by Napoleon. But less than a month before independence, thousands of Arabs fleeing the fighting in Haifa had travelled by boat to Acre. The refugee's presence in the port city, living testimony to a recent Arab defeat, would prove harmful to the morale of Acre's defenders.

The soldiers of the Carmeli Brigade, Herbert Hordes among them, were given responsibility for taking Acre. Setting out from Haifa, the site of the brigade's earlier victory, Carmeli's first objective on the way to Acre was Tel Napoleon, a hill just outside of the city. Hiking through the night, Hordes' unit reached the area before dawn. Hordes was no longer a mortarman. The brigade did not have a replacement for his exploded Davidka. With a year of ROTC training under his belt and some skill as a marksman, Hordes became a sniper.

At the top of Tel Napoleon, the Arabs had turned a small stone building into a fortified gun position. From there, using a primitive World War I machine gun, they fired on the approaching Jewish forces. The Jews returned fire, and the gun fell silent. But Hordes' sergeant wanted to make sure they had eliminated the position. He told Hordes to move ahead and throw a hand grenade into the building. Hordes did as he was ordered. He crawled forward to within range of the stone structure, pulled the pin from his grenade, and hurled it toward the gun. The grenade exploded, and Hordes heard a tremendous shout from behind. A piece of shrapnel from the grenade had flown straight back over Hordes' head, striking his sergeant in the hand. In two actions, Hordes had now injured two of his fellow soldiers. He was starting to feel jinxed.

After taking Tel Napoleon, Hordes' unit carved slit trenches into the side of the hill to take cover from Arab fire from Acre. The next evening, they were to be relieved. Hordes waited in his slit trench as his replacement crawled to his position. When Hordes greeted the soldier, Hordes noticed the rifle the man was carrying. The name "Nesia" had been carved into the stock. It was the rifle that Hordes had carried before the mortar accident.

With the capture of Tel Napoleon, Israeli forces were in position to attack the new city. They proceeded block by block, wresting control of the city in fierce hand-to-hand fighting. That victory left the dreaded old city in Arab hands. But the history of Acre and its walled fortress would not repeat itself. To Israel's surprise, on May 17, the Arabs of Acre surrendered the old city without a fight. The Carmeli Brigade now could turn its attention to the Lebanese and Syrians who were invading from the north.

The capture of Acre was not the only significant event to occur on May 17. That day, Ben Gurion made Paul Shulman, the Annapolis graduate and Aliyah Bet activist, the commander of naval operations and training. In the final months of the Mandate, the Haganah had begun the arduous task of refurbishing the former Aliyah Bet ships, which the British had tied up and docked at Haifa harbor. The Haganah hoped to make these ships the nucleus of the country's navy, a force that the Haganah assumed would be commanded by the Palyam, the Palmach's naval arm. It was from the ranks of the Palyam that the men who had captained the Aliyah Bet ships had come.

Ben Gurion had other ideas. In truth, most of the Palyam members had only limited naval training, and Ben Gurion wanted the navy to be headed by an experienced officer who had served in a professional navy, someone who could lay the proper foundation for the new force. Shulman met Ben Gurion's criteria. It was a choice that the Palmach bitterly opposed. Undaunted, Ben Gurion summoned Shulman from Paris, where the young American was still working on the problem of transporting Jewish refugees to Palestine.

Although Shulman was young – he had just turned twenty-six – he was already a seasoned sailor. Beginning in the summer of 1944, he served on board the U.S.S. *Hunt*, part of the navy's Fast Carrier Task Force. The

Hunt saw a lot of action in the Pacific, taking part in the battles of Okinawa, Iwo Jima and the Philippines. On one occasion, when the *Hunt* was supporting air raids against Japan, the ship was hit by a kamikaze suicide plane. Shulman survived the attack and stayed in the navy until March of 1947, resigning with the rank of lieutenant, junior grade. In nearly three years of naval service, Shulman acquired a wealth of experience, serving at various times as a watch officer, an assistant engineering officer, a gunnery officer, and an executive officer.

When Shulman arrived in Palestine, he immediately reported to Ben Gurion. Israel's first prime minister reminded the young sailor of their conversation years earlier in Connecticut, when Ben Gurion had spoken of the need for Jewish naval officers to form the country's new navy, and Shulman had insisted that he would remain in the American navy. After naming him commander of the navy's training and operations, Ben Gurion asked Shulman to serve under the name Shaul Ben Zvi. Because Shulman still held a commission in the U.S. Navy Reserves, Ben Gurion thought the Hebrew name might avoid any embarrassing problems with the American government. That name change would not, in the end, keep Shulman out of trouble.

9

ZATEC

Despite the best efforts of the Haganah's representatives in the U.S. and Canada, the Israeli forces were still woefully underequipped during the early days of the fighting with the local and invading Arab forces. While Al Schwimmer had succeeded in purchasing a fleet of heavy transport aircraft and ferrying them out of the U.S., the army still needed machine guns, artillery pieces, half-tracks – in short, military equipment of almost every kind. For its part, the air force was desperate for fighter planes that could challenge the Arab forces, particularly the Egyptian Spits and Dakotas that had been bombing Tel Aviv continuously since the war began. The answer to both the army's and the air force's needs came from Czechoslovakia.

In late April, the Czechs agreed to sell Israel ten Messerschmitt Me 109 fighters, and to train Israel's pilots on the planes. The Messerschmitts were built in a Czechoslovakian factory the Germans had used during World War II. The factory was now used to turn out the same planes for the Czech air force. In virtually all respects, the Czech Messerschmitt was the same plane flown by the Germans during the war, a fighter that had held its own against the British Spits and the American Mustangs in the air war over Europe. But there was one critical difference between the German and Czech versions. A fire in September of 1945 had destroyed the factory housing the Czechs' reserve of powerful Daimler Benz engines, the engine the Germans used in their manufacture of the Me 109's. The Czechs could not replace the Daimler Benz engines; instead, they had to substitute less powerful and heavier Junkers Jumo engines, the engines the Germans used in their Heinkel bombers. The substitution was not successful.

The bomber engine made the Czech Messerschmitt slower than its German counterpart. As Chris Magee, one of the Americans who flew the Messerschmitt would later say: "It sure didn't climb like any homesick angel." But the plane's sluggishness was far from its most serious problem. The combination of the heavy bomber engine and the plane's narrow undercarriage caused the Me 109 to ground loop or to flip up onto its nose so often that every take-off and landing was a nail-biting affair. The Messerschmitt would prove to have other, equally dangerous, drawbacks, which Israel's flyers would learn over time. The Israelis, though, were not in a position to concern themselves with any of this. The Czech plane was the only fighter available, and Israel was desperate. A serious problem still remained, however. The Me 109's did not have nearly the range to fly directly from Czechoslovakia to Israel. The Israelis would have to find another way to get them to the fighting.

The Messerschmitt transaction was not the first arms deal between the Jews and the Czechs. Beginning in January 1948, the Czechs began to sell the Haganah rifles, heavy machine guns, mortars, artillery pieces, and ammunition. The early shipments of arms were smuggled into the country by sea or on chartered aircraft. With the arrival of the C-46's and the Constellation, Israel would now be able to conduct an organized, large-scale airlift of these desperately needed arms from Czechoslovakia to Israel. The Schwimmer planes also solved the problem of transporting the Messerschmitts to the fighting. With the help of Czech technicians, the ground crews determined that it was possible to transport the Messerschmitts in the bellies of the transport planes. Although an Me 109 was too big to be wedged inside in one piece, the fit could be accomplished by dismantling the fighter and loading the fuselage in one transport plane and the wings in another.

Perhaps as important as the Czech government's agreement to sell Israel weapons and fighters was its agreement to allow Israel to use part of a military airfield as a base for the airlift and for fighter pilot training on the Messerschmitts. The Czech airfield was outside the town of Zatec, in the Sudetenland portion of Czechoslovakia. (In the 1980's, that cobblestone town was the location for the Barbara Streisand film *Yentl*.) In 1938, Czechoslovakia had ceded the Sudetenland to Germany in a failed effort to appease Adolf Hitler. During the war, the town had been renamed Saaz, the main square the Adolf Hitlerplatz, and the best hotel the Kaiserhof. With the war over, Zatec regained its name and became reunited with Czechoslovakia. The Kaiserhof was now the Hotel Stalingrad – although the Germans were gone, Czechoslovakia was now behind the Iron Curtain and had the Soviet Union to contend with. The Hotel Stalingrad would become home to the air and ground crews for the C-46's and the Constellation, and for those who came to train on the Messerschmitts.

The Zatec airfield had been used by the Luftwaffe during the war, a fact to which the scattered wreckages of German Junkers 88 bombers gave vivid testimony. Zatec was a modest base. It boasted only one runway, and no control tower or hangars. The ground crews were forced to use small wooden sheds to house their equipment. By the third week of May, the first of the transport planes began to arrive, completing the odyssey that had begun in Burbank and Millville. Soon, Zatec would become a fully-functioning, secret Israeli base behind the Iron Curtain.

For flyers and ground crews alike, their first encounter with life in a communist country was memorable. They liked the simple beauty of the town and the lush countryside, and appreciated the friendliness of the people of Zatec. But they were also struck by the emptiness of the shops. There was simply nothing to buy. One of the mechanics, Mike Ondra, who was of Czech descent, learned firsthand about the poverty with which the Czechs lived. He took advantage of his unexpected posting in Czechoslovakia to reestablish contact with lost relatives. He found his family, but was dismayed to learn that everyone lived in one room, where they cooked, ate, and slept. While Ondra stayed with them, he slept on a straw mattress placed atop the oven.

Unlike Ondra, most of the men stayed close to the Hotel Stalingrad or to one of the other two hotels in town that housed Israeli personnel, the Zlaty Lev ("Golden Lion") and the Zlaty Andel ("Golden Angel"). The men spent most of their time in the hotel lobbies. Around the clock, crews could be found eating, drinking, playing poker or gin rummy, telling stories, and laughing. For most, it was like a return to the bars and officers' clubs of World War II.

The transport operation underwent some changes in Czechoslovakia. Although the LAPSA cover was still loosely maintained, the fleet now formally became known as the Air Transport Command, or ATC. Sam Lewis became head of the ATC's Zatec operation. By May 22, plans were firmly in place for the ATC's airlift of Czech arms to Israel. The planes would leave Zatec, now code-named "Zebra," in the middle of the night for a three-and-one-half-hour flight to Ajaccio, on the French-controlled island of Corsica. (The Italians had withdrawn permission to use the base at Catania as a refueling site, forcing the switch to Ajaccio.) At Ajaccio, which the ATC pilots renamed "Jockstrap" for its similar-sounding name, the crew would have a leisurely lunch at an airport restaurant overlooking the sea, while the plane was refueled and serviced. After lunch, the flight would continue on to the Israeli airfield of Ekron (formerly Aquir) – "Oklahoma" in the vernacular of the ATC – landing at about midnight.

The arrivals in darkness were critical. With the Arabs controlling the airspace over Israel, it was dangerous to expose the large transport aircraft during daylight hours. The solution was to bring the ATC planes in during the night, offload the weapons and refuel the planes, and then send them off with a fresh crew before dawn for the return trip to Zatec. Nighttime landings were dangerous, though, for a number of reasons. For virtually all of the ATC pilots and navigators, the first flights to Ekron would be their first flights to Israel – ever. But the airstrip could not be lit until the last possible moment, for fear of an Arab attack. This meant the crews would have to make their approaches in total darkness over unfamiliar terrain. That wartime necessity would prove costly.

On May 9, the first group of fighter pilots, five in all, arrived at Zatec for training on the Messerschmitts. The group included two Americans, a former marine pilot named Lou Lenart and Milton Rubenfeld, a veteran U.S. Air Force pilot. The flight training was extremely brief. After a short check-out flight on the Arado, a two-seat trainer, the men moved on to the Me 109. Lenart's first flight was a Keystone Cops affair. His nose-heavy plane hopped over a chain link fence at the end of the runway and then dropped back to the ground, before gathering enough speed to stay in the air. But with Israel desperate to get its first fighter planes into the fighting, there simply wasn't time for more. On May 20, the pilots climbed into the ATC's Constellation for the trip back to Israel. Fittingly, they travelled with part of one of the Messerschmitts. Less than a week after independence, Israel's fighter squadron was ready, quite literally, to get off the ground.

Four days later, two of the C-46's left Zatec, bound for the airfield at Ekron. The lead plane was piloted by Hal Auerbach. Auerbach's navigator was Norman Dobrowitz, another of the GI's who had been a Hebrew University student when the war began. Norm Moonitz flew the second plane, with a crew of three: radio operator Ed Styrak, the former Aliyah Bet crewman; navigator Moe Rosenbaum, the navigation instructor in Panama; and co-pilot Sheldon Eichel. Both planes were loaded to capacity with crates of weapons; each also carried half of a Messerschmitt fighter. Neither Moonitz nor Auerbach had flown into Israel before, and they approached the darkened airfield cautiously. But they had to contend with an unexpected problem. A thick fog filled the night sky, reducing visibility almost to zero. After several passes over the area where they thought the airfield should be, the pilots still couldn't find the runway.

Their choices were limited. They did not have enough fuel to return to Corsica, and there was no alternative Israeli field. The pilots would have to try to find Ekron or land their planes in the sea. Finally, Auerbach managed to find an opening through the fog, and got his plane down safely. He ran over to the control tower, where he waited anxiously with a cluster of pilots and air force officials for Moonitz's plane. As the minutes passed without any sign that Moonitz would be able to land, Auerbach grew increasingly tense. He knew that Moonitz's fuel situation was critical. Auerbach asked for permission to take his plane back into the air. With his lights on, he thought he could act as a beacon, and lead Moonitz back to the field. It was a risky strategy; there was no guarantee that Auerbach could find the airfield a second time. Since, there had not been enough time to unload his C-46, letting Auerbach take off meant putting two planes, both filled with precious cargo, at risk. Heyman Shamir, the deputy commander of the air force, rejected the idea.

Above the field, Moonitz continued to struggle. He swung back out to sea, and tried coming in just a few hundred feet above the water, hoping to slip below the fog. The gambit didn't work, and Moonitz climbed again. Suddenly, co-pilot Sheldon Eichel spotted a break in the clouds. Moonitz headed the plane for the dim row of runway lights. But the opening disappeared and Moonitz had to abort his approach. The minutes passed, and Moonitz became more desperate. Finally, he decided to try approaching blind, hoping that he would break through the clouds before reaching the field. At seven hundred feet, the runway lights reappeared briefly, only to be swallowed up again. But at least they knew they were on the right line.

Less than two hundred feet above the runway, the crew was jolted by an enormous impact. Slightly to the left of the runway jutted a small hill – an obstruction the fog obscured. The plane slammed into the hill. The force of the impact dislodged the Messerschmitt, which shifted forward into the navigator's station, killing Moe Rosenbaum instantly. The C-46 slid to a stop, as flames enveloped the cockpit. Burned but alive, Moonitz and Eichel struggled to get out. Styrak had a broken leg, and the six-foot, two-hundred-pound radio operator could not climb free from the wreckage. Moonitz and Eichel squeezed Styrak through the cockpit window, and dragged him from the burning plane. After a few weeks in the hospital, the three survivors returned to action.

10

ROME

Zatec was not the only Israeli air base operating outside Israel's borders on May 14. Although the Italians changed their minds about allowing Israel to use the Catania airfield as a refueling stop, they did agree to make Urbe, a small airfield just north of Rome, available for pilot training on C-64 Norsemans. The Norseman was a small, rugged, single-engine transport plane. It was relatively easy to fly and reliable. Nearly 1,000 of the model had seen action in World War II. Haganah agents in Spain had purchased the Norsemans from the U.S. government, using a front to mask the true destination of the planes.

It was to Urbe that the Haganah decided to send Buzz Beurling. On his way from Canada, Beurling passed through New York City, where he spent several days at the Henry Hudson Hotel on West 57th Street. The Hudson was popular with the civilian airlines, and the Haganah believed that Beurling would not attract undue attention in that setting. After several days in New York, the time came for Beurling to continue on to Rome. He spent his last evening in the city with Vivi Stokes, a nineteen-year-old socialite with whom Beurling was romantically involved. That night, Stokes gave Beurling a St. Christopher medal, with the words, "Please do nothing dangerous," engraved on the back. It was, of course, not the kind of advice Beurling was inclined to follow.

Two men from Land and Labor picked Beurling up at the Hudson, and drove him to the airport. Beurling brought only a small bag for the trip to Rome, but in it he carried his prized model planes. To again be the best, Beurling knew he would have to work on deflection shots using his old training techniques.

On the way to the airport, Beurling was clearly excited about his return to action. He regaled his companions with stories of his exploits in the air. One story in particular had a dramatic effect on Beurling's listeners. On July 12, 1942, flying off of Malta, Beurling came upon an Italian Macchi 202. The Macchi had barely escaped an earlier skirmish that same day. Its cockpit hood, including the pilot's rear view mirror, had been shot away. Beurling came up underneath the Macchi's tail. At about fifty yards away, Beurling began to weave back and forth behind the Macchi. Because of the missing rearview mirror, the Italian pilot didn't notice Beurling's Spit. Beurling closed the distance to thirty yards, and attacked from the left. Just before Beurling fired his guns, the Italian turned and looked at the Canadian. The two men were so close to each other that Beurling could see the details of the other pilot's face. Deadly accurate as always, Beurling fired a single burst directly at the cockpit. The bullets decapitated the pilot. Blood poured out of the headless body – so thick it eventually obliterated the white Italian cross on the Macchi's tail. "It gives you a feeling of satisfaction when you actually blow their brains out," he told the two men from Land and Labor.

One of the men in the car that day was horrified both by Beurling's story and by the apparent delight that Beurling had taken in what was obviously a gruesome event. But in truth, it was nothing more than an attempt by Beurling to play the role of the swashbuckling fighter pilot. The incident with the Macchi had forever scarred the Canadian, so much so that Beurling frequently cried out in his sleep, plagued by nightmares involving the Italian pilot.

From New York, Beurling flew to Rome, arriving on May 4, 1948. There, he found a bustling Israeli operation, centered around training on the Norsemans. Air and ground crewmen were billeted at local hotels. Rome was not the quiet, simple town that Zatec was, a fact reflected in the lively nightlife the men enjoyed in Italy. Although Beurling still abstained from drinking, he had become more outgoing in the years since

World War II. On one of his first evenings in Rome, he visited La Biblioteca, one of the city's more fashionable bistros. There, Beurling ran into Jack Nyhuus, a Norwegian who had flown Spitfires during the war. Nyhuus had earned a reputation as a train-buster for his punishing attacks on German freight and troop trains, attacks that required a mastery of deflection shooting. Nyhuus and Beurling spent hours trading war stories and talking about different deflection shooting techniques. But late in the evening a disturbance broke out, and the police were called. Beurling and some of the other patrons spent the night in jail, and soon all the reporters in Rome knew that Beurling was in town.

Beurling's reputation as an outstanding fighter pilot preceded his arrival at Urbe. Curious about the great Canadian ace, the other pilots studied him carefully. Like Beurling's mates in the RAF and the RCAF, they found him to be quiet and something of a loner. But, as always, he was generous with the secrets of his success as an air gunner. He entertained a number of the pilots in his room at the Mediterranee, explaining his system of deflection shooting. When Beurling wasn't with the other pilots, he was at work recalculating his deflection angles – which he originally calculated based on the Spitfire he flew in the RAF and the RCAF – to take into account the different design of the Czech plane he would fly for Israel.

One of the pilots who got to know Beurling in Rome was Gideon "Giddy" Lichtman, a veteran of the U.S. Air Force's 3rd Air Commando Group in the Pacific. The tough-talking, skirt-chasing Lichtman was a more typical fighter pilot than Beurling, but that didn't stop the two men from becoming friendly. Early one evening, Beurling offered to demonstrate for Lichtman his novel technique for using model planes to determine deflection angles. Beurling pulled down the window shade in his room, and moved the planes at different attack angles to each other, with their shadows reflecting on the shade. Lichtman was intrigued by Beurling's technique, but he soon tired of watching. More interested in Rome's bustling nightlife, Lichtman excused himself.

That nightlife was thick with intrigue. Rumors abounded of British and Arab agents who were spying on the Israeli pilots, and the men were urged to be cautious. One day Lichtman was standing in the hotel bar when an attractive woman approached him. He had seen the woman before and had been warned about her. Supposedly, she was a Jew working as an agent for the Arabs. The woman admired Lichtman's ring. "It's an air force ring," he explained. After more small talk, she invited him to her room. Lichtman thought about the warning, but decided to go anyway, more interested in sex than concerned about espionage. When they arrived at her room, she reached for the door. As she opened it, Lichtman suddenly had a sense there was someone standing inside the room, behind the opened door. He quickly turned and left.

On the afternoon of May 19, Beurling and five other pilots were called to a meeting at the Massimo De Seglio Hotel. The other pilots included Americans Julian Swing, Bill Malpine, and Al Trop, as well as a British volunteer named Len Cohen. The meeting turned out to be a briefing – the six pilots would crew three Norsemans on a ferry flight to Israel. The men were shown navigational charts and Cohen, who had the most knowledge of Israel's terrain, was put in charge of the mission. Malpine and Beurling had wanted to fly together as a team, but Cohen assigned Beurling to fly with him in the lead plane.

This mission would not be the first such ferry flight of Norsemans. On May 2, 1948, two of the planes had been successfully flown 1,400 miles from Italy directly to Palestine. Lou Lenart and Milton Rubenfeld, the two Americans who had just completed their training on the Messerschmitt, had flown as pilot and co-pilot on one of the Norsemans. Those planes had been immediately pressed into service as light transport craft, delivering small shipments of weapons throughout the country.

At eight-thirty the morning after the briefing, the three crews arrived at Urbe to check out on their planes. After completing his initial flights, Bill Malpine watched as Beurling and Cohen practiced touch and go landings. Beurling's plane had already made three successful landings when it came around a fourth time. When the plane was fifteen feet above the ground, Malpine saw flames shooting out from the exhaust. Suddenly, the plane wingtipped onto the runway, and was engulfed in flames. Malpine ran to the plane and tried to pull out Beurling, who was sitting in the left seat – the pilot's seat.[1] But the flames and heat were too great, and Malpine had to give up the effort. Beurling and Cohen were both killed. Beurling, who had survived nine previous air crashes, must have thought until the last moment that he would survive this one as well. The Tiger, as it turned out, only had nine lives.

The cause of the Beurling crash remains an unsolved mystery. Officially, the Italians ruled the deaths accidental, the result of a mechanical failure. But the Italians did not undertake a detailed investigation, and seemed interested only in quickly closing the matter. With the new state only five days old and fighting for its life, Israel was in no position to carefully investigate the crash itself. There are a number of facts that point to sabotage. The planes were left unguarded on the airfield, and a saboteur could have obtained access to Beurling's plane. Rumors were circulating before Beurling's death that enemy agents were in Rome, and were targeting the pilots. Lichtman thought he may have avoided an attempted assault – or worse – in the days before the fateful flight. Beurling was certainly a visible target; his presence in Rome had become well-known following his arrest at La Biblioteca. And Bill Malpine, who had been appalled at the lack of security surrounding the Urbe operation, recalled that news reporters appeared on the field immediately following the crash – "as if they were on the field beforehand and awaited the accident." If enemy agents were attempting to assassinate an Israeli pilot, they could have chosen no better target than Beurling. The man who had shot down twenty-seven planes in fourteen days of flying over Malta could have, singlehandedly, decimated the fighter squadrons of Israel's Arab enemies.

Rome's small Jewish community mourned the deaths of Beurling and Cohen. Rome's chief rabbi spoke at Beurling's funeral, and the Jews of the city closed their shops in tribute to the young Canadian. In Montreal, Syd Shulemson, the man who had recruited Beurling, received a call from Beurling's father. With a heavy heart, Shulemson drove out to meet the Beurling family, to console them in person on the death of their son. Shulemson was moved by his encounter with the intensely religious, plain-spoken Beurling family. The experience strengthened Shulemson's conviction that Beurling's decision to fly for Israel was a moral one.

To his surprise, Shulemson learned that Beurling had told his family not to believe any public reports of his death – unless Shulemson confirmed them. Before departing for Rome, Beurling had proposed a number of cloak-and-dagger schemes to help give the Israelis the upper hand against the Arabs. According to one, Israel would fake Beurling's death, causing the Arab fighter pilots to lower their guard – giving the Canadian ace an additional advantage in the sky. Shulemson confirmed the news reports were accurate. Beurling really was dead. In 1950, the Beurling family asked Shulemson to arrange for Beurling's remains to be transferred from Rome for reburial in Israel. He lies there still, at a military cemetery in Haifa.

Beurling's death made public the presence in Rome of foreign flyers bound for Israel. A few days after the crash, the U.S. government sent a message to the Americans at Urbe, summoning them to the U.S. Embassy in Rome. Not sure what to expect, the group sent one of their number, Jack Schwarz, to find out what was going on. The embassy told Schwarz that he and all of the other Americans were to be sent back to the U.S. Although Schwarz himself was trapped, he was able to warn the others. Arrangements were hastily made to move the American members of the group out of the country.

For Giddy Lichtman, the departure meant a hurried train trip to Geneva. From there he was to fly to Prague. The Israelis told Lichtman he would not need a visa to enter Czechoslovakia. Instead, he was only to ask for a Dr. Felix, who would whisk Lichtman past airport controls and arrange his transport to the airfield. Although Lichtman didn't know it, Dr. Felix had negotiated on Israel's behalf the purchase of the Czech Messerschmitts and weapons.

In Geneva, Lichtman was told to buy several cans of Nescafe – a present for Dr. Felix. Lichtman bought the Nescafe and flew to Prague. The Czech officials at the airport asked for Lichtman's visa; Lichtman asked for Dr. Felix. Unimpressed, the Czechs threw Lichtman in jail. From there, he called an emergency number he had been given in Rome: "You better come get me out of here, or I'm leaving." Within a few hours, Dr. Felix arrived and secured Lichtman's release. The two men finally met face to face, with Lichtman still fuming over his ordeal. "Where's my Nescafe?" Dr. Felix demanded of Lichtman. Lichtman's first impulse was to hit Dr. Felix in the head with the Nescafe. Instead, barely able to control himself, he handed the cans over. The two men left the airport.

At Zatec, Lichtman received the same hurried training on the Messerschmitt as the first group of pilots. By late May, less than ten days after Beurling's death, Lichtman and another pilot were crammed into the back of a C-46, together with the fuselage of a Messerschmitt, for the long trip to Israel.

Not all of the American flyers at Urbe followed the route that Giddy Lichtman took. Some were still needed to ferry the Norsemans to Israel. In the days following Beurling's death, the Israelis quickly made preparations to send over the remaining two Norsemans from the group of three that had already been prepared for the long-distance flight. American pilots Bill Malpine, who had logged more than 2,000 hours ferrying planes during the Second World War, and Bob Fine, another of the Service Airways pilots, would crew the lead plane on the harrowing flight over the Mediterranean. A third crewman, navigator Hugh Curtis from Britain, would fly with them. Al Trop, who like Malpine had been slated to take part in the originally-scheduled flight of three planes, would co-pilot the second plane. Beurling's death caused no small amount of consternation among the remaining flyers at Urbe. Bill Malpine, for one, strongly suspected sabotage. He was concerned that whoever tampered with Beurling's plane may have gotten to the others as well. One of the pilots at Urbe refused to continue with the operation to ferry the Norsemans after the Beurling crash, and Malpine thought seriously of doing the same. But Bob Fine, who was called in as a replacement, prevailed upon Malpine to continue.

It would be Fine's second ferry flight for Israel. In April, he had been a crewman on one of four Ansons the Haganah had purchased in Britain. The planes, which had only limited range, were to fly to Palestine by a circuitous route, hopscotching their way across the Mediterranean using small airports that were off the beaten path. The cover story for the flight was that the planes were going to Singapore, and the pilots had official-looking papers to reflect this. But when the Ansons landed at the Greek island of Rhodes in mid-April, the authorities became suspicious and arrested Fine and the others. Because most of the crewmen were Americans, the Greeks contacted the American embassy to help investigate the incident. The Americans called in the British, who quickly got to the bottom of the affair. The Greek authorities seized the planes, but allowed the crews to depart Rhodes.

The Norsemans would have to fly stripped down, if they were to be able to make the non-stop flight from Urbe to Israel. They would not carry tool kits, life rafts, parachutes, flares, or weapons. Further complicating matters, the condition of the planes was poor. There were no navigation or cockpit lights, and the compasses were not serviceable. The pre-flight briefing was also less than adequate. Little was known about the rapidly-changing military situation in Israel, and the pilots were given to believe that the Gaza Strip was in Israel's hands. In fact, Egypt held that area.

The Norsemans took off for the nonstop flight to Israel at ten o'clock on the morning of May 24. Three hours later, both pilots flipped a switch that was supposed to allow fuel to be fed from long-range tanks installed specially for the flight. But the mechanism failed in both planes, requiring an emergency landing on the Greek island of Heraklion. Al Trop's plane sustained minor damage as it touched down.

The Greek officials at Heraklion were extremely hospitable, and provided repair assistance for the damaged plane. The nervous crews were relieved there would be no fallout from Fine's earlier episode at Rhodes with the four Ansons. Still, taking no chances, they decided to leave at two o'clock the next day for the second leg of the flight for Israel. But two hours before the scheduled departure, a Greek C-47 landed at Heraklion. One of the passengers was a government official from Rhodes who had arrested Fine only a month earlier. Their eyes met, and the two men recognized each other. To avoid a repetition of the Rhodes debacle, the planes needed to leave immediately. Fine filed a flight plan for Cyprus, and the two planes roared off.

The flight to Israel was difficult. Fine's engine threw huge quantities of oil, which splattered onto the windscreen. To see, Fine had to open his window and wipe off the screen every two minutes of the eight-hour flight. When he opened the window, the rush of wind blew the maps all over the cockpit, making navigation all but impossible. By the time the two planes reached what the navigator thought should be Israel, the sky was completely dark. Searching for some sign of an airfield, Fine briefly noticed a flashing light, but it quickly vanished from view. The navigator thought they were over Haifa, in the north of the country, and instructed Fine to head south toward the Ekron airfield. After several minutes of flying, the planes reached a lighted area, which the men agreed must be the border with Egypt.

The two planes turned north again, and continued the search for the Israeli field, all the while sending out coded messages to the Ekron tower. But the planes were getting no response from the ground, and Fine's plane was running out of fuel. He instructed the navigator to send out an S.O.S. With only eight minutes of fuel left, Fine spotted a flare off in the distance. He told the navigator to radio for more flares, and suddenly a wave of flares lit up the sky, leading the planes to a landing strip that was illuminated with the headlights of more than fifty trucks.

Fine made a first pass at the field, attempting a landing at full power so he could check out the terrain. He found it too rough for a safe landing and took off again. Fine made a circuit around the field, trying to decide what to do next. At an altitude of five hundred feet, the engine cut out. With no other choice, Fine attempted a landing. He had been right about the field. After the plane rolled for a while, it hit a ditch and tilted up on its nose. The second Norseman followed Fine's plane down, landing safely.

Fine, Malpine, and Curtiss jumped out of the plane, fearing it would catch on fire. As they did, they noticed well-cultivated citrus groves in the area, confirmation they were near a Jewish settlement. They ran toward the headlights, calling out *"Shalom Aleichem"* so the Israelis would not mistake them for the enemy. But their greeting was met with a burst of gunfire, the first sign that something might have gone horribly wrong. "They're fucking Arabs," shouted Malpine, "head for the trees." The three men raced for the grove, with Fine and Curtiss staying together and Malpine running off separately. The men climbed into trees, and waited.

Within an hour, the three flyers heard a voice on a loudspeaker call out in perfect English: "We know that there are Americans in this field. Surrender! This is the Egyptian army calling. We will give you ten minutes to surrender. You will be treated according to the Geneva Convention as prisoners of war." Fine and Curtiss decided to give up, and walked toward the loudspeaker. They were met by an Egyptian lieutenant colonel, who asked where the missing crewman was. The Egyptians had already captured Al Trop and the pilot from the other plane, leaving Malpine as the only crewman who continued to elude the Egyptians. Concerned about his co-pilot's safety, Fine offered to call for him over the loudspeaker. He did this for some fifteen minutes, to no avail. Malpine was determined not to surrender.

Ignoring Fine's request, Malpine ran through the grove, until he reached a barbed wire fence. He jumped over the fence, tearing his clothes and cutting himself in the process. On the other side, Malpine quickly pulled out some papers that Buzz Beurling had left in his care, and hid them. He also discarded his shirt, passport and other identification, trying to get rid of anything that would identify him as being affiliated with Israel. Running across a dirt road, Malpine disappeared into a second grove. He could hear gunshots as he ran. He jumped over or crawled under three more barbed wire fences as he moved from grove to grove, hoping to get away from the Egyptians. Finally, he climbed into a small tree, camouflaged himself with leaves, and waited. For three days, he remained there without any food or water. Sleep was nearly impossible, and Malpine only managed an hour or two of rest each night.

On the fourth night, Malpine heard heavy artillery fire. Looking off into the nearby desert, he could see that a battle was taking place. He climbed out of the tree and headed toward the fighting, hoping to cross over to the Israeli side of the line. As Malpine walked through the desert, the firing stopped, and he had no idea where to head in the darkness. As he reached a small hill, machine guns suddenly opened up on him from all directions. He had stumbled onto an Egyptian gun position. Malpine hit the ground, and waited for the firing to subside, all the while shouting: "I am an American! I am an American!" Finally, after what seemed like half an hour, the shooting stopped. Within minutes, a group of Arab soldiers reached Malpine, and started to beat him with their rifle butts all over his body. As they struck him, they shouted: "*Yehoudi*" ("Jew"). One of the soldiers pulled out a pistol and was about to shoot the American when an officer came up and grabbed the soldier's arm. Malpine was blindfolded and carried away.

After being posed with a number of different Egyptian officers for propaganda photos, Malpine was taken by train to Cairo. The papers had announced that a Jewish pilot had been shot down over Gaza, and a frenzied crowd of more than 5,000 waited as Malpine and his guards got off the train. The people spat at Malpine and kicked him as he walked past, and his guards had to use whips to keep the mob at bay. He was then taken to the Abbassiye military prison, where he was held in solitary confinement for two weeks. Finally, Malpine was reunited with the other crewmen from the mission, and the five men were placed together in a large cell for the rest of the war.

NOTES

[1] For nearly fifty years, the question of who piloted the Norseman during that fateful flight has remained unanswered. Malpine's account, placing Beurling in the pilot's seat at the time of the crash, is given in an Israeli Air Force Intelligence debriefing of Malpine in early 1949. That debriefing remained secret until 1996, when it was declassified at our request.

11

THE ROAD TO JERUSALEM

Meanwhile, in Israel, the situation was grim. In the east, the Jordanian Legion had already captured the Etzion settlements and the Jerusalem suburbs of Neve Yaakov and Atarot. Both the Old and New Cities of Jerusalem were about to fall under the Legion's devastating pressure. From the south, the Egyptians were advancing steadily through the Negev desert, and were less than twenty miles from Tel Aviv. In the north, where the Lebanese, Syrians, and Iraqis had invaded, there were less dramatic Arab gains. Still, the engagements there prevented Israel from reinforcing the troops deployed against the Jordanians and the Egyptians.

On May 16, one week after arriving back in Israel, Mickey Marcus joined the Israeli forces arrayed against the Egyptians in the Negev. That first week was hectic. Marcus had been in the north to observe the fighting between the Haganah and local Arab forces. He had then returned to Tel Aviv to hear Ben Gurion declare Israel's independence. If Marcus had any doubt about the wisdom of returning to Israel, the events of that first week erased it. Before heading south, he wrote to his wife: "Sweetheart, my dear, it was the correct and proper thing that I came. Perhaps we will lose much in matters such as money, etc., but I know that I shall come home safe to you, with both of us knowing that the sacrifices made were justified."

The decision to send Marcus south may have been based, in part, on non-military considerations. The general staff of the army, distrustful of Marcus' close relationship with Ben Gurion, gave that order. Ben Gurion later complained that the army did so to keep Marcus away from the corridors of power in Tel Aviv. Marcus was aware of the general staff's feelings about him. "Those big shots treat me like a stray dog who landed in their lot. They can't make up their minds whether to befriend me or to defend themselves," he told an acquaintance.

There was at the beginning of the war a leadership vacuum in the Israeli Army. The chief of staff, Yaakov Dori, had been ill for months and couldn't devote himself fully to his duties. On Marcus' earlier tour, he advised Ben Gurion to replace Dori. Ben Gurion agreed, but finding someone acceptable to the Haganah's competing factions was a different matter. There were the veterans of the British army, like Marcus' recruiter Shlomo Shamir, who wanted the army fashioned in the image of Britain's. They saw a military force that was structured and disciplined, with strict separation between the officers and the enlisted men. Opposite them were the fiercely egalitarian leaders of the Palmach, who wanted the army to reflect the looseness and informality of the Haganah's elite striking force. The Palmach fighters detested many of the trappings of a modern army, including even salutes, ranks, and military insignias.

Ben Gurion thought Marcus, an outsider with no ties to either faction, might be the ideal replacement. He considered appointing Marcus as Dori's deputy or as inspector general of the army, either of which would make Marcus the de facto chief of staff. But before Ben Gurion could act, the general staff sent Marcus south, putting Ben Gurion's plans on hold.

The "Wild Beasts of the Negev," as the Palmach forces there were known, were trying to hold their own against the Egyptian invaders. But the Egyptians had better equipment, more soldiers, and, most importantly, air cover. Egyptian Spitfires patrolled ahead of the ground troops, strafing and bombing Jewish settlements and Palmach troops in the path of the Egyptian advance. With the Me 109's yet to arrive from Czechoslovakia, the lack of Israeli fighter planes to challenge the Egyptians had a demoralizing effect on Israel's Negev forces.

Although the fighter planes hadn't arrived, the air force still had a presence in the Negev. The Negev Squadron, commanded by Canadian

Ralph Moster, threw its single-engine, two-seat Piper Cubs and Austers into the battle against the Egyptians. Mostly, the small planes flew critical supplies between the scattered Jewish settlements, and sometimes evacuated individual wounded soldiers. These small planes were in the air constantly. One night, Moster alone completed thirty-five sorties.

The Negev Squadron also flew combat missions, perfecting a primitive form of stealth flying. For these, the pilot would fly his plane at night toward Egyptian lines, carrying a few small bombs on his lap. As the aircraft approached the target area, the pilot would idle the engine, so the plane would not be heard from the ground. Then, as the single-engine plane passed over the enemy troops, the pilot would toss out his bombs, apply full throttle, and dart back toward Israeli lines. Occasionally, there were dogfights with the Egyptian Spits. The only defense for the small Israeli planes in those situations was to head straight down and maneuver close to the ground around trees and other landmarks, trying to prevent the Spits from ever getting a clean shot. Often, these measures were not enough.

The pilots who flew these missions, men like Moster and his second-in-command, American Hyman Goldstein, dealt with the stresses of such dangerous flying in unusual ways. They often smoked cigars during their flights, and sometimes drank while flying. On one mission, Goldstein was given a primitive bomb, one with a fuse that had to be lit before it could be thrown at the Egyptians. Over the target, Goldstein used the end of the cigar he was smoking to light the fuse, before tossing the bomb out.

Despite the nonstop action, or perhaps because of it, Ralph Moster was delighted to be in Israel making a contribution. In a letter to his parents, he thanked them "for having brought me into this world at such a time that I have a chance to fight for a free land for the Jews."[1]

When Mickey Marcus reached the Negev, the Palmach commanders didn't know what to make of him. He was still not technically part of the army. Known only by his code name Colonel Stone, he lacked a formal Israeli rank or title. The Palmach could take or leave Marcus' advice on how best to fight the Egyptians. He gave it nonetheless. Marcus counseled the Negev fighters to use their superior night-fighting ability to attack and harass the Egyptians. He believed that a purely defensive response to the Egyptian invasion was doomed to failure. Above all, he urged the Israeli commanders to be decisive. "This is my opinion. Maybe it's not right. It's not drastic if you do it differently. But at least choose one way and don't attempt to do it both ways," he would urge them.

On at least one occasion, the Palmach followed Marcus' advice to be aggressive. The American colonel favored assaulting a hilltop Egyptian artillery position that was shelling the nearby Jewish settlement of Niram. Initially, the Israelis rejected the idea as impractical. But Marcus planned the attack, and persuaded the Palmach it could work. On the night of May 25, a small Israeli force made its way to the target. Marcus positioned mortars at three points around the base of the hill. On Marcus' order, all three mortars opened fire on the Egyptians. As Egyptian gunners fired at the mortar positions, an Israeli squad raced up the hill from a fourth point. The assault squad penetrated to within fifty yards of the Egyptians without detection. From there, it attacked swiftly and effectively, wiping out the Egyptian gun crews, and capturing an assortment of artillery pieces and light weapons.

Although the Negev forces continued to harass the Egyptians, they could only slow what seemed to be an inexorable Arab advance northward. By May 29, the Egyptians reached the town of Ishdud, only seventeen miles from Tel Aviv. From that point, only two of the Palmach's underequipped infantry companies stood in the way of an Egyptian assault on Israel's largest city. That same day, the air force completed the assembly of the first four Messerschmitts, and the planes were ready for their first flight. Because Israel had wanted to conceal the existence of the fighter planes from the Egyptians, the Messerschmitts had been reassembled inside a hangar at the Ekron air base. There they had stayed. There had been no flight testing, no firing of the guns, not even a starting of the engines. The first raid would come as a complete surprise to the Arabs.

Air force commander Aharon Remez wanted the Messerschmitts' first mission to be against the Egyptian airfield at El Arish, hoping to destroy Egypt's Spitfire squadron on the ground. But before Remez could launch the El Arish attack, he received a new target: the Egyptian troops at Ishdud. Shlomo Avidan, the commander of the Palmach troops that stood between the Egyptians and Tel Aviv, had pleaded for the use of the Me 109's against the Egyptian forces, fearful that the ground troops alone could not stop the advance.

Lou Lenart, the former marine pilot, would lead the flight of four. Just before 8:00 p.m., the pilots climbed into their planes. They started their engines and then, one by one, the planes pulled out of the hangars, onto the runway, and took off for the rendezvous with the Egyptians. Although Lenart was the flight leader, he was unfamiliar with the country and soon realized he was not even sure where Ishdud was. Because the planes had no radios, he had to use hand signals to communicate his confusion to Modi Alon, an Israeli piloting one of the other planes. Alon pointed Lenart in the right direction. Within minutes, the planes were over Ishdud. The town was filled with hundreds of Egyptian vehicles. Undeterred by the heavy anti-aircraft fire now coming at him from every direction, Lenart led several passes over the Egyptians, firing his cannon and machine guns. Almost immediately, Lenart's cannon jammed, limiting him to the less powerful machine guns against the enormous Egyptian force. Completing his final pass, Lenart returned to Ekron. Ezer Weizman, one of the other four pilots, was waiting when Lenart arrived. Weizman's cannon had also jammed. Modi Alon then landed, his plane ground-looping and breaking a wing tip as it hit the runway. The fourth plane never returned; it was shot down near an Egyptian airfield further to the south, a field the pilot must have mistaken for Ekron. In one apparently failed mission, the air force had lost one-fifth of its fighter pilots and half of its fighter planes.

But the mission was not the failure it appeared to be. The commander of the Egyptian invasion force was shaken by his first encounter with Israeli fighter planes. He ordered his troops to dig into their positions and radioed Cairo, advising his superiors that he had come under heavy air attack and could not continue northward. It was as close as the Egyptians would ever come to Tel Aviv. With one raid, the air force had potentially altered the course of the war.

After leaving the Negev, Marcus was summoned back to Tel Aviv for a new assignment: relieving the siege of Jewish Jerusalem. In the ten days since the war began, Jerusalem's plight had not improved. The city was still under siege, and there was strict rationing of food and water to prevent mass starvation. Jerusalem was also under constant bombardment from Jordanian forces. On May 16, two days after independence, a young American woman in Jerusalem described life there in a letter to her family, one that would have to wait for the lifting of the siege to be sent: "The incessant shelling all day and most of the night has made Jerusalem literally a ghost town. The shops are mostly closed and the streets are practically empty." There was also no electricity to speak of, and therefore no radios. Jerusalem was a city that ran on rumors.

Ben Gurion feared that Jerusalem could not hold out much longer. Since March, only three convoys had gotten through, all during a several-day period in April when the Haganah launched a full-scale assault on the Arab positions surrounding the Jerusalem-Tel Aviv highway. But the Haganah had been forced to turn its attention elsewhere. After only a few days, it abandoned the positions it had seized, and the Arabs returned to the high ground.

The starting point for the Israeli campaign to release the stranglehold on Jerusalem was a police fortress at the town of Latrun. The Latrun fortress stood on a hill overlooking the Jerusalem-Tel Aviv highway, dominating the approach to Jerusalem. If Israel could capture Latrun, Ben Gurion believed, Jerusalem would be saved. But the Israelis thought the building was lightly defended by Arab irregulars; in fact, heavily armed and well-trained troops of Jordan's Arab Legion manned the fortress.

On May 25, the day before Marcus' return from the Negev, the army made its first raid on Latrun. In the burning desert sun, lightly armed soldiers, many of whom had just come off of immigrant ships, advanced in a direct assault on the fortified Jordanian position. Hundreds of Jewish soldiers were killed or wounded in what would prove to be the worst Israeli defeat of the war. Marcus saw that the raid had cast a pall over the survivors, who knew they would again be called upon to try to dislodge the Arab gunners. A second assault had already been planned on the Latrun fortress before Marcus arrived, and he could do no more than offer words of advice and encouragement, trying by the sheer force of his personality to lift the darkened spirits around him.

Within a few days of his arrival outside Latrun, Marcus was at last formally absorbed into the Israeli Army. On May 28, 1948, Ben Gurion made Marcus the commander of the Jerusalem front and gave him the rank of general – the first general in a Jewish army since Judah Maccabbee. Marcus' appointment was an operational necessity. If, as expected, the Israeli forces broke through to Jerusalem, an overall commander would need to take charge of the three brigades making the assault. That commander needed to be acceptable to the Palmach and British army veterans participating in the attack: Shlomo Shamir, a British army veteran who headed the Seventh Brigade, and Palmach commanders David Elazar and Yitzhak Rabin, who led the Etzioni and Harel Brigades.

When the second attack on Latrun began on May 31, Marcus insisted on riding toward the battle, to a point where he could personally observe the Israeli forces. The second assault also failed, although not nearly at the same cost as the first effort. Marcus felt Latrun could have been taken had the infantry performed better, and he became personally involved in planning a third Latrun assault.

Nothing demonstrated the desperate situation of Jerusalem more than the plight of the Jews of the walled Old City. Since the war began, they had faced the full brunt of the Jordanian attack. Armed with a motley assortment of rifles, handguns, and makeshift explosives, they tried to hold off the Legion's armored assault. If the residents of the New City were under siege, the Jews of the Old City were doubly so. The imposing stone walls of the Old City cut them off not only from the rest of the country, but also from the bulk of Jerusalem's defenders, who were deployed in the New City.

To break through to the Old City, the Haganah would have to penetrate its thick stone walls, or attack one of the city's seven gated entranceways. The Haganah decided to attack Zion Gate, near the Jewish Quarter. David Elazar, the commander of the Etzioni Brigade and later the army's chief of staff, called for volunteers for the dangerous assault. Twenty men and two women stepped forward. One of the volunteers was David Starec, the former *Exodus* crewman. Only four days earlier, Starec had celebrated his twentieth birthday.

Shortly after two o'clock in the morning on May 19, Elazar began the assault with a small mortar barrage. From the wall above, the Arabs fired back with deadly accuracy. As the battle swirled around him, Starec didn't think he would survive. In fighting over the previous few days, he had lost several of his friends, and it seemed as though his turn was coming. Suddenly, Starec felt as though the walls of the Old City were falling on top of him. He felt pain in one leg, an arm, and in his face – all the result of a grenade exploding at close range. But despite his foreboding, it was not Starec's turn to die. He woke up a short while later in a hospital, with a cast on his leg and bandages on his arm and head. Starec's fighting days were over.

The Israelis held their mortar fire briefly, so that two sappers could dash forward and place an explosive charge at the bottom of the gate. The charge blew the gate open, and the remains of Elazar's small assault force charged through to secure the opening, followed by a platoon of Haganah soldiers carrying supplies for the Jewish Quarter's defenders. One Haganah soldier who ran through the Zion Gate that evening was Bostonian Leonard Binder, another of the American Hebrew University students. Binder and the other members of his platoon scurried through the narrow streets of the Armenian Quarter, dodging Arab bullets, until arriving safely in the Jewish Quarter.

But the arrival of Binder's platoon could not alter the fate of the Old City. The poorly armed Jewish fighters were no match for the Jordanians, who quickly reestablished control over Zion Gate, preventing any further reinforcements from arriving. The Jordanians maintained a constant barrage of mortar and artillery fire on the Jewish Quarter. They even managed to maneuver some armored vehicles into the narrow streets of the Old City, where they were able to fire at the Jews at almost point-blank range. On May 28, the Jews of the Old City could hold out no longer. They surrendered to the Legion's forces, who led them through the streets of the Old City to an uncertain future.

The Legion took Binder and the other prisoners to the *kishleh*, an old Turkish prison in the Old City's Arab Quarter. There, the prisoners were paraded before some Arab journalists. One of the newsmen asked in English whether any Americans were in the group. One of the other prisoners whispered to Binder: "What do you think, Lenny? Why don't you tell them?" Binder was torn. If he said yes, his presence might be publicized – a message to his family that he was alive and a guarantee that he would not be killed. But he was also afraid that, as an American, he might be singled out for retribution. "Forget it," he whispered to the other prisoner. Binder kept his nationality a secret. Whether or not for that reason, he would be safely returned to Israel after the war.

As Marcus planned the third Latrun assault, he also directed an alternative effort to break through to Jerusalem. The Haganah had earlier discovered a primitive track running several hundred yards south of the Jerusalem-Tel Aviv highway. The path wound its way up small hillocks and through stone canyons to the holy city. A range of hills lay between the trail and the Latrun fortress, blocking the Jordanian soldiers' view. Marcus became convinced that the alternative road to Jerusalem could be improved sufficiently to accommodate large supply trucks. The road came to be known as the Burma Road, after the route the Allies used in the Second World War to transport supplies to Chiang Kai-shek's beleaguered forces. The work of broadening and improving the Burma Road had to take place at night, so as not to alert the Jordanians. Had they discovered it, the Jordanians could have ended the entire operation with one well-aimed artillery assault.

As the Burma Road neared completion, the third assault on Latrun began to take on a dual purpose. If successful, Israel could reopen the main Jerusalem-Tel Aviv highway and relieve the New City. But even if the raid failed, it would keep the Jordanians pinned down at Latrun and divert their attention from the Burma Road operation. As May turned into June, it became increasingly urgent for Israeli forces to break through to Jerusalem. The U.N. had convinced Israel and the Arabs to accept a four-week truce, to begin on June 11, 1948. For Israel the truce would give its forces the time they needed to rest, reorganize, and absorb the new weapons coming in from Czechoslovakia. But if the road to Jerusalem was not opened before the cease-fire, the continued siege would likely force the New City to surrender. June 11, then, became the deadline for freeing Jerusalem.

On June 8, Israel assaulted Latrun for the third time. For a short while, it appeared that an Israeli success was imminent. The attacking force breached the fortress, but the Jordanians held their ground. Latrun would remain in Arab hands until 1967, when Israel captured it in the Six Day War. After the failure of the third attack, Marcus directed all of his attention to completing the Burma Road.

All three attempts to take Latrun had proceeded without fighter cover. Marcus had requested that the Messerschmitts be used to assault the Jordanian position as part of the third attack. He had even pleaded his case directly to pilot Lou Lenart, telling him a fighter strike on Latrun was necessary to save Jerusalem. In the end, the army directed the precious few Messerschmitts elsewhere.

In the days following its first mission, the fighter squadron had not been idle. On May 30, two of the three planes that survived the first raid made a strafing run against Iraqi columns invading from the northeast. U.S. Air Force veteran Milton Rubenfeld, one of the original group of five pilots but the odd man out for the Ishdud raid, flew as wingman to Ezer Weizman. The Iraqis threw up a barrage of anti-aircraft fire, and Rubenfeld's plane was hit. He soon realized the Me 109 had been severely damaged, and would not make it back to the base at Ekron. Rubenfeld was able to nurse his plane over Israeli territory, to the seaside town of Kfar Vitkin. There he bailed out, landing in the shallow water opposite the town.

The residents of Kfar Vitkin had seen Rubenfeld's Messerschmitt crash. They hurried out to confront what they assumed was an enemy pilot. On only its second day of operations, Israel's fighter squadron was still a well-kept secret – even from the Israelis. As Rubenfeld waded ashore, a group of obviously angry men, some armed with pitchforks, came toward him. Rubenfeld was afraid the men were going to kill him. Unable to speak any Hebrew, he tried to think of a way to communicate the fact that he was a Jew. "Shabbos, Gefilte Fish! Shabbos, Gefilte Fish!" he shouted over and over again, seizing on two Yiddish words he remembered from his youth. The Israelis were convinced, and took Rubenfeld back to the fighter base at Ekron.

More fighter pilots and Messerschmitts continued to arrive from Czechoslovakia. In early June, Giddy Lichtman landed at Ekron in a C-46. Lichtman was delighted to have finally made it to Israel. For once, the hell-raising fighter pilot thought, he would finally be part of something good. He went directly to the Park Hotel in Tel Aviv, where the other fighter pilots were staying. There he met Lenart, Rubenfeld, Alon, and Weizman, members of what would soon come to be formally known as the 101 Squadron.

The Park Hotel was Israel's finest. Located on HaYarkon Street, on the Tel Aviv beach, it was preferred by foreign diplomats and war correspondents. The 101 pilots were housed two to a room, but what interested them more than their living conditions was the nightly party in the hotel bar. Each day, the pilots would make the short trip to Ekron for the day's flying, and then head each night straight for the bar, which by then would already be filling with soldiers and women. The party would continue late into the night. Sometimes, for a change of pace, the pilots would go to other local hang-outs, often to a seaside cafe called the Gallei Yam.

The day after his arrival at the Park Hotel, Lichtman received his introduction to the fighter base at Ekron. At the airfield, he noticed a mechanic lying underneath one of the Messerschmitts, pounding away with a sledgehammer. Clearly, thought Lichtman, the work of assembling the Czech planes was not proceeding smoothly. As a new arrival, Lichtman needed to be checked out before he could be assigned to any operations. He and Lenart each climbed into a plane for the check-out flight. Lenart led the newest member of the squadron through a series of maneuvers, and Lichtman maintained a tight formation with the flight leader. Lenart liked what he saw. He told Lichtman the two would always fly together. "I'll be Lou the Jew and you'll be Gid the Yid," he said to Lichtman.

On June 8, reports reached the fighter base that Egyptian planes were in the Tel Aviv area. Lichtman and Modi Alon were quickly scrambled, and the two men took off in their Messerschmitts for Tel Aviv, with Alon leading the flight. Because the planes did not have radios, the two men had agreed that if Alon spotted anything, he would signal his wingman by waiving his hand in a circular motion and then pointing at the enemy aircraft. Eager to engage the Egyptians, Alon quickly accelerated to full throttle, and climbed at a steep angle toward the sky over Tel Aviv. But Alon's plane was heading directly into the afternoon sun. Lichtman strained to keep his eyes on Alon's cockpit and to maintain formation with the flight leader's rapidly accelerating craft.

After about fifteen minutes, Lichtman thought he saw Alon moving his arm. Alon rolled over into a dive, and Lichtman followed. Below, Lichtman saw four Egyptian Spitfires heading for Tel Aviv. Alon passed through the Egyptian formation first. He let loose with his guns, scattering the Spitfires in different directions. One of the Spits headed south, and Lichtman gave chase. As Lichtman got closer, the Egyptian apparently realized he was being pursued. The Spit went into a series of rolls and steep turns, turning east over the Mediterranean, but Lichtman stayed on the Egyptian's tail. When Lichtman pulled within range he fired. Pieces of debris flew off the Spit's wings. Lichtman fired again, and more pieces of the plane came off. The Egyptian now turned sharply left in an effort to head back to land, but the plane dived down toward the sea, continuing to break apart as it fell. Lichtman was sure the Spit was about to crash, but he couldn't risk staying around to watch. He was low on fuel, so he broke away and headed back to Ekron. The air force later confirmed that the Egyptian crashed, and awarded Lichtman a kill. It was the first time an Israeli fighter plane had downed an enemy fighter.

Back on the Jerusalem front, the Burma Road was nearing completion. On June 10, only one day before the truce, a convoy of trucks made the bumpy, dangerous ride to Jerusalem. It was the first convoy the city had seen since April, and it broke the siege. The Burma Road remained open for the rest of the war.

Marcus was at a Haganah base in the French monastery of Abu Gosh, some ten miles from Jerusalem, the night the first convoy made it through. After celebrating the successful completion of the Burma Road with a group of Palmach soldiers, Marcus retired at 1:00 a.m. A few hours later, Marcus, clad only in a sheet, left his room to relieve himself. He walked out of the monastery, and down a small hill on the northeast side of the base. Although guards surrounded the area, no one saw Marcus leave. At 3:45 a.m., one of the guards, an eighteen-year-old Palmachnick named Eliezer Linski, heard the clatter of rocks in the distance. "*Mi sham?*" ("Who's there?"), he called out. He heard nothing in response, but a few moments later saw a figure clad in a white robe moving in the distance. "*Mi sham?*" the guard shouted a second time. Again there was no response. Linski fired a warning shot, and the person began to run toward the monastery, calling out in a language that sounded like English. The guard shouted again, "*Atsur Ani Yoreh!*" ("Stop or I'll shoot!"). But the figure continued to run, and Linski fired. The unknown intruder stumbled forward for a few more yards before falling over. Linski ran over, trained his flashlight into the face of the intruder, and felt for a pulse. The man was dead. Within a few moments, Linski learned what he had done. He had killed Mickey Marcus.

Ben Gurion ordered an investigation into the circumstances surrounding Marcus' death. As part of that investigation, Linski gave a statement explaining his actions. Linski said he had been unaware that any Americans or Englishmen were staying at Abu Gosh. When he shouted "*Mi sham?*," he was expecting to receive the responding password. When

Linski heard what sounded like English from the figure in the darkness, he thought the intruder was an Arab pretending to be an Englishman in order to sneak into the base. Linski only fired when Marcus – who spoke no Hebrew – failed to give the password, and because Marcus ran toward the monastery instead of stopping and raising his hands. Ironically, the password that night was *"Haderech shelanu"* ("The road is ours").

Six hours after Marcus' death, the U.N.-negotiated cease-fire went into effect. Marcus was one of the last Israeli casualties of the initial round of fighting.

NOTES

[1] Within six months of writing this letter to his parents, Moster was dead. Ironically, his death was not the result of a daring mission against the Egyptians in a Piper Cub. Instead, it happened when Moster was trying to learn how to fly an amphibious plane called a Widgeon. Moster was practicing landings on the Kinneret Sea on December 7, 1948, when the fatal crash took place.

12

THE *ALTALENA*

There were a number of Israeli setbacks during the first weeks of the official war. Most of these were in the fighting with the Jordanians, including the loss of the Old City. In the south, although Israel had stopped the Egyptian advance at Ishdud, the Egyptian army still controlled much of the Negev desert and surrounded the scattered Israeli settlements in the area. And, on the very eve of the truce, the Syrians captured the Jewish settlement of Mishmar Hayarden.

But there were Israeli gains to celebrate, as well. The siege of Jerusalem had been broken in dramatic fashion. The Czechoslovakian airlift was in full swing, beginning the process of evening the balance of power between Israel and its adversaries. Israel's new fighter squadron had thrown the Egyptians off-stride, and started to restore peace to the skies over Tel Aviv. But Israel's greatest accomplishment was that it still survived nearly a month after being invaded by five modern armies. Those invaders had believed they could overrun Israel in a matter of weeks. By surviving that initial assault, the Jewish state had dealt a serious blow to the morale of the Arabs.

The cease-fire carried with it a number of prohibitions on the combatants' activities. They could not bring weapons into the area of the fighting, and men of military age who were not bona fide refugees could not

enter any of the warring countries. To enforce these provisions against
Israel, the U.N. stationed inspectors at Israel's sea ports, and established
an internment camp at Hadera where new immigrants would go for screen-
ing.

Both sides freely disregarded the weapons and manpower prohibitions. The Czech airlift ran throughout the four-week truce, bringing in
weapons, Messerschmitts, and fighter pilots. Foreign military volunteers
continued to enter Israel by sea. To evade the U.N. inspectors, they carried forged papers identifying them as displaced persons. It was clear to
Israel that the truce would not lead to a permanent cessation in the fighting, but would only provide a short breather until the next round. In the
meantime, Israel had to do everything possible to prepare itself.

Stan Andrews and Bob Vickman were two of the new additions to
the 101 Squadron during the truce. Andrews, dark-haired and with a movie
star's good looks, had flown B-25 light bombers in the southwest Pacific
during World War II. Vickman, the tallest member of the squadron at six
feet two, was also a U.S. Air Force veteran, having flown sixty-five aerial
reconnaissance missions in the Pacific Theater during the war. Vickman
and Andrews were best friends, and had come to Israel together from Los
Angeles, where the two had enrolled in art school after the war. As events
in Palestine heated up, the struggle for Jewish independence began to
occupy more and more of their attention. After much discussion, the two
veteran pilots decided to go and fight. As Jews, they wanted to do their
share to ensure the creation of a Jewish state. As artists, they wanted to
illustrate, in photographs and drawings, Israel's rebirth. Before leaving
California, they loaded their suitcases with cameras and painting supplies.

Shortly after arriving in Israel, Vickman and Andrews made their
first contribution to the new squadron. At a bar one night in Tel Aviv, a
group of the fighter pilots decided the 101 Squadron needed a logo. Modi
Alon, one of the squadron's few Israeli pilots, wanted a flying scorpion,
after his RAF unit. Lou Lenart suggested an angel of death, since the air
force's primary foe was the Egyptians and it had been the angel of death
that finally brought Egypt's Pharoah to his knees. Andrews and Vickman
took out pen and paper and began to draw. They fashioned a death's head,
wearing a pair of goggles and a pilot's helmet. That design would be-

come the insignia of the 101 Squadron, and would remain so for the duration of the War of Independence and until the present day.

In early June, another C-46 left Czechoslovakia for Israel, piloted by American Don Kosteff. As usual, the plane carried a full load of ammunition and a disassembled Messerschmitt, all stored in crates marked "Farm Equipment." Two new American fighter pilots flew in the back with the cargo. Aaron "Red" Finkel and Sid Antin had both flown P-47 Thunderbolts for the U.S. Air Force during the war, and had just completed their abbreviated training on the Czech fighter.

As the C-46 made its way south from Zatec to Ajaccio, it climbed above 12,000 feet, passing over the Alps. The altitude caused one of the carburetor's to ice up, and Kosteff became concerned the plane would not make it to Corsica. He needed to make an emergency landing. Kosteff knew exactly where to go. Only a few weeks earlier, ATC pilot Hal Auerbach had been flying a C-46 in the same area when an Italian Spitfire intercepted his plane, forcing it to land at a military airfield outside the town of Treviso, in northern Italy. Auerbach landed his transport, expecting to receive a hostile greeting from the Italians. But the base commander, a colonel in Italy's air force, received the C-46 pilot graciously. The Italian accepted Auerbach's explanation that the flight was bound for South America and was not military in nature, and did not order a search of the C-46. Within a day, Auerbach was permitted to leave Treviso. When he got back to Zatec, he put out the word to all of the ATC crews that if they ever needed a place to land in northern Italy, they should head for Treviso. Kosteff now did so, turning his plane in the direction of the Italian military base.

The C-46 was greeted by the base commander, the same colonel whom Auerbach had found so charming. Kosteff and the colonel exchanged pleasantries, and it seemed as though there would be a repetition of the Auerbach experience. Kosteff advised the colonel that the plane was headed for Nicaragua, via Corsica and Casablanca, and that the purpose of the flight was purely civilian. The two men walked away from the plane to discuss the situation. In the colonel's absence, another soldier approached the plane and looked into the cargo area. He saw the stacks of crates, and pointed a gun at Red Finkel, demanding to know what was inside.

Finkel stalled for a time, refusing to open the crates until the colonel returned. He then went into the cockpit to remove any documents that might give away the plane's true destination. There he came across an envelope among the pilot's papers, and opened it. Inside was a letter from Dr. Felix to the commander of the 101 Squadron. The letter was about Finkel. It read: "Aaron Finkel. Typical American. Oversexed. To be watched." When the colonel returned, he insisted that Finkel obey the soldier's command and open the crate. The crate contained a thirty-caliber Beza machine gun. More soldiers gathered, and it was now clear that the C-46 crew and passengers were not going to get in and out of Treviso cleanly, as Auerbach's group had.

As the crew was led away, Finkel called out to the colonel, asking for permission to make a telephone call. Finkel wanted to alert the Israelis to the capture of the plane and crew. The Italian granted Finkel's request. He called Danny Agronsky, ostensibly the Rome manager of Service Airways and the local representative of LAPSA, but in truth the man in charge of the Haganah's European air operations. After Finkel finished explaining the situation to Agronsky, the Italians started to lead the men to the base jail. Finkel, Kosteff and Antin shouted out indignantly that they were Americans and could not be treated in such fashion. The Italians asked the men if they wanted to see their consul. But, of course, he was the last person they wanted to see. "No, we don't want to bother him," they replied to the surprised Italians. The men would spend nearly two weeks in the Treviso jail before Danny Agronsky succeeded in buying their freedom.

While in jail, the flyers managed to get their hands on an English-language newspaper. There they learned about a disturbing incident that had just taken place on the shore of Tel Aviv, involving a ship called the *Altalena*.

✡ ✡ ✡

When the truce began, Israel had been a state for less than one month. Even as it was trying to hold off the Arab invasion, it also faced the daunting task of organizing the new state's institutions. Its foremost challenge was to unite the different fighting forces – the Haganah, Palmach, Irgun, and

Stern Group – into a unified army. On May 29, the Stern Group voluntarily dismantled itself in all areas outside of Jerusalem. Because the U.N.
partition plan had not assigned Jerusalem to either the Jews or the Arabs,
its legal status was uncertain. As a result, the Stern Group believed it
should be allowed to act independently there. The Irgun took the same
position. Almost immediately after the Stern Group's action, the Haganah
and the Irgun signed an agreement for Irgun members to join the army,
but allowing the Irgun to maintain its own units in Jerusalem. On May
31, the new unified army, the "Israel Defense Force" was officially established.

In the months before independence, Irgun agents outside of Israel,
like those of the Haganah, had been involved in the search for weapons.
In the summer of 1947, the American League for a Free Palestine, the
Irgun's American branch, purchased an old LST (Landing Ship, Tanks)
in Jamestown, New York. U.S. forces had used LST's to land troops during the invasions of Europe and the Pacific islands. The particular vessel
the ALFP bought had been used in the invasion of Normandy. The ALFP
established a fictitious shipping company, "The Three Star Line," to take
ownership of the LST. In order to register the ship, the Irgun had to give
it a name. When it came to Aliyah Bet ships, the Haganah and Irgun had
for security reasons always registered the ship's original name or a name
having no connection with Israel or Judaism. The ship's "Jewish name"
would come later, during the voyage. The Irgun departed from this convention, in a subtle way, with the naming of the new LST. It chose
"*Altalena*," a former pen name of Zionist leader Ze'ev Jabotinsky, the
ideological father of the Irgun. The Irgun believed that the name was so
obscure that it could be used without compromising the ship's true purpose.

As with the Aliyah Bet ship the *Abril/Ben Hecht*, the ALFP recruited
a largely American crew for the *Altalena*. Tall, reed-thin Monroe Fein of
Chicago was one of the early, and most important, hires. A veteran of the
U.S. Navy, Fein served on a number of LST's in the Pacific Theater,
landing troops in the Marshall Islands and at Okinawa. By the end of the
war, he was a skipper. Fein had seen Ben Hecht's propaganda play, *A
Flag is Born*, and for the first time began to think about the situation in
Palestine. Although he knew nothing about Zionism, much less about the

Irgun and Haganah, the Holocaust had deeply troubled him and he wanted to do something to help the Jews of Europe.

In August of 1947, Fein screwed up his courage, and walked into the American League for a Free Palestine's Wells Street office to offer his services. Fein chose the ALFP because of its connection to the Hecht play, and not out of any ideological preference for the Irgun over the Haganah. At the time, he didn't even know there was a Haganah. "If someone from the Haganah had approached me, I'd probably have gone to them," he admitted years later.

"I'd like to volunteer," Fein told the man who ran the ALFP's Chicago office. "Where do you live?" the ALFP representative asked. "On the north side," Fein responded. "How about starting a chapter there?" the man asked Fein. "That's not exactly what I had in mind. I want to go on a ship," Fein announced. By coincidence, Victor Ben Nachum of the ALFP's New York office was in town, and Fein was taken to meet him in a back room. Ben Nachum asked Fein about his wartime experience. "I was the captain of an LST," Fein answered. Ben Nachum's mouth fell open, and his eyes widened with surprise. "We have an LST," he said excitedly. Two days later, Fein received a telegram summoning him to New York.

There, Fein met Abraham Stavsky, David Gutmann's *Abril* recruiter. Stavsky took Fein to the Brooklyn shipping pier, where the LST was moored. Fein was disappointed in the ship. The man who had selected it had served as an engineering officer in the merchant marine during the war, and didn't know anything about LST's. Having worked in engine rooms, he had simply chosen the ship with the cleanest one. But the ship he had selected was one of the oldest available, and with the fewest improvements. Still, Stavsky and Fein established a rapport, and Stavsky hired the Chicagoan as the *Altalena's* first mate. Fein quickly went to work readying the ship.

A long refitting process and a shortage of funds greatly delayed the sailing of the *Altalena*. Originally, the Irgun had planned to use the vessel as an Aliyah Bet ship. With the passage of the U.N. partition resolution in November of 1947 and the announcement by the British that they would leave Palestine on May 14, the Irgun decided it no longer made sense to challenge the British blockade and risk the lives of refugees. Instead, the

ALFP would bide its time, until the end of the British Mandate. During these months of waiting, Stavsky promoted Fein to ship's captain. By then, the two men had grown extremely close. Fein regarded Stavsky, who had been involved with Aliyah Bet since before World War II, as "one of the greatest men I ever met."

After making a number of merchant runs to raise money, the *Altalena* arrived in the French city of Port du Bouc in early May of 1948. The Irgun decided to use the *Altalena* to bring arms and recruits to Palestine. In anticipation of the ship's departure, units of Irgun soldiers began making their way to France from all over the world. Men and women came from Italy, Austria, Germany, North Africa, Britain, and even Cuba. Ultimately, the *Altalena* would sail with more than eight hundred passengers from fifteen different countries. The search for weapons initially proceeded more slowly. By May 14, when Ben Gurion declared Israel's independence and the war officially began, the Irgun had still only collected a handful of personal weapons.

In late May, Fein and Stavsky met in Fein's cabin with the local Haganah representative, to find out if the Haganah wanted to use the ship jointly with the Irgun. The agent asked Fein how many passengers the ship could carry, and also asked about cargo space. Although unspoken, Fein assumed that the "cargo" the Haganah had in mind was weapons. Ultimately, the Haganah decided against sharing the *Altalena* with the Irgun.

The breakthrough in the search for heavy weapons came on May 23, 1948. That day, the French government agreed to provide the Irgun, without charge, six half-tracks, hundreds of Bren and Spandau heavy machine guns, five thousand Enfield rifles, four million rounds of ammunition, mortar and artillery pieces, and military uniforms. As the weapons were being loaded, the first truce was agreed to, and it seemed that the ship would have to wait out the cease-fire in France. But the French government, concerned that its role in arming the Israelis would be discovered, wanted the *Altalena* to depart as soon as the weapons were on board. At dusk on June 11, the day the truce went into effect and, under French pressure, the *Altalena* left Port de Bouc, bound for Israel. As the ship pulled away, the nearly nine hundred men and women on board sang "*Hatikvah*."

With the truce in effect, Fein was uncertain whether the ship would sail directly to Israel. The crew had loaded enough provisions for a thirty-day voyage, long enough to wait out the cease-fire. If they needed to stay at sea that long, Fein planned to stay out of sight by spending the month sailing among the Greek islands. Once the *Altalena* reached Israel, he would sail the ship directly to Tel Aviv, and beach the ship there. An LST could not be landed on just any beach, though. It needed a steep beach for its landings. The LST's hull was angled, so the stern could float while the bow rested on the shore, allowing it to back off after unloading its troops. To ensure the ship could land on the Tel Aviv beach, Fein had gotten photographs of the landing site and a hydrographic survey of the area. He determined that a location opposite the Kaete Dan Hotel suited the ship perfectly.

As it turned out, there would be no need to hide in the Greek islands before continuing on to Israel. On the sixth day of the voyage, the *Altalena* received instructions to head directly to Israel, and to land at "Gray Two." Gray Two was the code name for Kfar Vitkin, a small settlement located to the north of Tel Aviv and a stronghold of Mapai, Ben Gurion's left-leaning political party. The change of location to Kfar Vitkin came about as a result of negotiations in Israel between the Irgun and Haganah to divide the *Altalena's* weapons. Initially, the Haganah had insisted that the Irgun turn over all of the weapons and the ship to the government. The Irgun was willing to give the Haganah most of the arms, but it wanted a percentage allocated to Irgun units operating independently in Jerusalem, and to Irgun units that had been absorbed into the army and that were fighting in other parts of the country. The Irgun and Haganah finally agreed that eighty percent of the weapons would go to the army with no restriction on their allocation, while twenty percent would go to Jerusalem. At the Haganah's insistence, the landing site was changed from Tel Aviv to Kfar Vitkin.

On the evening of June 19, the *Altalena* cruised along the coast of Israel, searching in vain for the two vertical red lights that were the agreed signal for the landing area at Kfar Vitkin. Nervous the operation might be discovered, the troops at the landing site had dimmed the lights so low they could not be seen from more than one hundred yards away. At one point, as the *Altalena* sailed opposite Tel Aviv, Fein sent several crewman ashore in the launch to clarify their location. The sailors borrowed the telephone of the night watchman at Tel Aviv's Reading power plant, to contact the army and advise it of the *Altalena's* arrival. They also radioed the ship to clarify its position. A few hours later, Fein spotted the two red lights, and tried to beach the LST. But the Kfar Vitkin beach was not suited for an LST landing, and the ship could get no closer than three hundred yards from shore.

Everyone agreed that the passengers and arms should be unloaded at night, to keep the landing secret from U.N. inspectors enforcing the truce provisions. But by the time the *Altalena* finally reached Kfar Vitkin, dawn was fast approaching and there was no time to offload the passengers. The *Altalena* had to put back out to sea for the daylight hours. The next night it returned and, by three in the morning, all but fifty of the passengers were ashore. Those fifty stayed on the *Altalena* to defend the ship against an air attack from the Egyptian air force, using Bren guns mounted around the deck. At three-thirty a.m., the Irgun and Haganah began unloading the ship's enormous cargo of weapons. Everyone pitched in to help: soldiers guarding the site, the crew, and even residents of Kfar Vitkin, who had historically been hostile to the Irgun. There was singing, and the settlers brought refreshments. Amidst the celebration, it seemed that all of the simmering hostility between the two rival forces had been forgotten.

As news of the *Altalena's* arrival spread, Irgun members began to make their way to Kfar Vitkin. Some had left their units without permission, desperate to be part of the Irgun's great achievement. The Irgun's high command also reached the scene, anxious to see for themselves the fruit of their efforts. At one point, Stavsky called Fein over. "I want to introduce you to somebody," he told the captain, and presented Irgun leader and future Israeli Prime Minister Menachem Begin. Slowly, as the afternoon wore on, the crew noticed a change in the atmosphere around the ship. The singing stopped, and the settlers began to move away from the unloading site. Unbeknownst to the men remaining on the ship, the army had been sealing off the approaches to Kfar Vitkin, preparing to seize the *Altalena* and its cargo.

At about two-thirty in the afternoon, two former Aliyah Bet ships – the Canadian corvettes *Wedgewood* and *Haganah* – approached the

Altalena. The *Wedgewood* commander was Paul Shulman, the chief of naval operations. Fein was glad to see the ships. He had been expecting all along to receive naval protection for the unloading. A small launch brought Shulman close to the *Altalena*, and he called out to Fein. "Do you have orders to fire on me?" Shulman asked. Fein was incredulous. "I don't know what you're talking about. But if we did, do you think you'd still be sitting there," he responded. Shulman returned to his vessel.

Fein tried to find out what was going on from the Irgunists, but nobody seemed to know. At about five-thirty, he heard the sound of machine gun fire. His first thought was that Arabs must be attacking. Just then, Stavsky, who had taken the launch to the beach with some of the other crewmen, called Fein on the walkie talkie: "We've got some trouble on the beach. We want to come back to the ship."

"I'm going back out to sea," Fein responded. "You follow me further out to sea," he instructed Stavsky. At that point, only one-fifth of the *Altalena's* five hundred tons of weapons had been unloaded. As Fein began to turn the ship's bow around, one of the navy vessels opened fire.[1] Fein maneuvered the LST between the launch and the navy ships to protect the small boat.

The *Altalena* crew quickly pulled the launch aboard, and headed south for Tel Aviv at full speed. Begin believed that Ben Gurion would not dare to order another attack in full view of Tel Aviv's crowded beach. The *Wedgewood* and the *Haganah* followed close behind. Fein hugged the shoreline, taking advantage of the much shallower draft of the LST to stay away from the pursuing corvettes. The navy radioed the *Altalena*, ordering it to turn away from Israel's shores. Fein disregarded the order. He believed that in the open sea, the *Altalena* would be at the mercy of the Israeli ships. Instead, Fein continued toward Tel Aviv, hoping to land the LST on the city's crowded beach at the original landing site opposite the Kaete Dan Hotel. Near midnight, the *Altalena* reached the waters off Tel Aviv, just ahead of the Navy vessels. For a moment, it appeared that Fein might succeed in getting the vessel ashore. But in the shallow water only a few hundred yards from the beach, the LST ground to a halt on the wreckage of the *Tiger Hill*, an Aliyah Bet ship from the 1930's. In the darkness, the crew had not seen the obstruction. Stavsky couldn't believe it. "We're stuck on top of my ship," he cried out. It was Stavsky who had purchased and sent the *Tiger Hill* on its pre-World War II voyage to Palestine.

The *Wedgewood* and the *Haganah* took positions near the *Altalena*, and the three ships waited for daybreak. The next morning, Begin broadcasted from the ship's loudspeaker to the crowds that had gathered on the beach, telling them the Irgun had purchased weapons for Israel, but the government was preventing them from coming ashore. Around one o'clock, army units and Irgun soldiers began to fill the Tel Aviv beach opposite the ship. Irgunists seized control of many of the waterfront shops and hotels. Within a few hours, the two groups began trading gunfire on the shore and on the streets of Tel Aviv. The army also fired directly on the *Altalena*, hitting some of the crew. One of the wounded was Stavsky, who was shot in the knee. When Fein heard Stavsky had been hit, he left the bridge to see how his friend was doing. In obvious pain, Stavsky looked up at Fein. "Do you think they'll have to take it off?" he asked, pointing to his leg. "It's only a nick," Fein lied, trying to calm Stavsky before returning to the bridge. Begin became hysterical as the shooting continued. He could not believe that Jews were killing Jews.

The fighting went on for most of the day. As it intensified, casualties on board the LST began to mount. On his own authority, Fein decided to surrender the ship. He lowered the Israeli flag and ran up the white flag. But his communication of surrender was ignored. At four o'clock in the afternoon, an artillery shell fired from the beach scored a direct hit on the *Altalena*. The blast ignited the uniforms in the cargo hold, and the blaze quickly spread. There were not enough crewman on board to run the *Altalena's* sprinkler system and put out the fire. Fein realized that the four hundred tons of weapons could explode at any moment. He ordered the passengers and crew to abandon ship, jumping into the water with two other crewmen after everyone else had left. Before Fein reached the shore, the LST began to explode. The fire and explosions consumed much of the *Altalena* and destroyed its remaining cargo of weapons.

Fourteen lives were lost in the battles at Kfar Vitkin and Tel Aviv. One of these was Stavsky, who bled to death from the gunshot wound to his knee. But there would be no full-scale civil war. In an emotional and bitter speech on the Irgun's radio station that evening, Begin called on his followers to refrain from any acts of violence against the army or the government. Fein followed Begin, speaking for ten minutes about what had happened to the *Altalena*. For the remainder of the War of Independence, the burned-out hulk remained where it had run aground, a monument to the young nation's brief civil war.

The fighting could have been even more bloody. At one point, the Haganah tried to mobilize the air force to become involved in the fray. It was there that the American and other foreign volunteers, whose ranks accounted for most of the air force's pilots, drew the line. They refused to take part in fighting between Jews, then or ever. At an angry meeting between the air force's deputy chief of staff and the air crews, 101 pilot Stan Andrews expressed the sentiments of most of the foreign flyers: "Without us, those airplanes can't be flown. And nobody can make us fly them. I for one refuse to participate in a civil war, and I refuse to lift a finger against other Jews." Israel ultimately decided not to force the issue, and the air force stayed out of the fighting.

Andrews' stance was influenced by an experience he had the day before. He and Bob Vickman, cameras in tow, had worked their way down to the beach area, anxious to photograph and film the burning ship. Again and again Irgun soldiers stopped them, demanding identification. On each occasion, they explained they were Haganah pilots, and each time the Irgunists let them pass. Several times, the Irgunists cautioned the Americans to be careful, telling the new arrivals that there were too few pilots in the country. The concern the Irgun showed for the safety of two men who were, after all, Haganah members, deeply affected the two pilots.

There has been considerable debate over the years over who was to blame for the tragedy. Some Irgun supporters suspect the Haganah concealed from Ben Gurion that an agreement for the allocation of the arms had been reached. Believing there was no agreement, he suspected the worst when he learned of Irgun soldiers racing to Kfar Vitkin to meet the ship. To him, such actions showed the Irgun was preparing to seize power. Those who defend the government's attack on the *Altalena* believe that, distasteful as it might have been, it was necessary to unify the nation and its fighting forces. Even some who sailed on the *Altalena* feel that, in the end, good came out of the tragic episode. Still, it is difficult to imagine that this salutary purpose could not have been accomplished without the terrible loss of life.

Before the next round of fighting, there would be a dramatic effort to heal the wounds of the *Altalena* incident. Fein requested a meeting with Paul Shulman. The two met secretly in an apartment between Tel Aviv and Jaffa. Fein and some of the other *Altalena* crew wanted to volunteer for the Israeli Navy. According to Fein, most of the crew knew nothing of Israeli politics. Instead, they had simply seen an advertisement and volunteered their services to help the Jewish state. For himself, Fein wanted the opportunity to command a ship. Shulman was receptive. He bore no ill will toward Fein or his crew. Shulman felt the navy had met "the hardest test of devotion and loyalty to a 'one state' government" when it intercepted the *Altalena*, but he had derived no pleasure from his role in the affair. "No task could have been more painful," he later wrote. Shulman returned to Haifa to plead Fein's case with the navy. But despite Shulman's efforts, the navy refused to give Fein a command, or to allow the *Altalena* crew to join en masse. Dejected, Fein left the country in September. Although some of the crew were allowed to join the navy as individuals, an opportunity for a more fitting epilogue to the *Altalena* affair was lost.

✡ ✡ ✡

As the *Altalena* lay smoldering opposite Tel Aviv, another ship sailed toward the city. The *Marie Annick* was a small fishing vessel whose decks were overflowing with some one hundred and fifty displaced persons. Ironically, the *Marie Annick* had sailed from France on the same evening as the *Altalena*. A much slower vessel, it arrived several days after the ill-fated LST first landed at Kfar Vitkin.

Not all of the small ship's passengers were truly refugees. There were also thirty or so Canadians on board, carrying false documents that identified them as DP's. As the *Marie Annick* sailed toward the Tel Aviv port, the passengers strained to see the cause of the smoke on the horizon. Some of the Canadians feared the worst, thinking the Arabs must have just attacked Tel Aviv.

The Canadian group included Art Goldberg, Lionel Druker's old friend from Vancouver, and one of the early Canadian recruiters. After passing through a U.N.-run internment camp near the town of Hadera, the Canadians made their way to the Tel Letvinsky recruiting camp. Only a few months before, Tel Letvinsky had been a British army base. Now under the control of the Israeli army, it was a sort of clearinghouse, where new recruits went for assignment. The process was hardly an orderly one. Officers desperately in need of men would raid the base, grabbing new recruits before they received assignment to another unit through the normal process.

One of the new Canadian arrivals was Harvey Sirulnikoff, a veteran of the Canadian army. Sirulnikoff was assigned to an artillery unit. But Sirulnikoff had been trained as an infantryman, and he wanted to go to the infantry. He refused the assignment. As he was standing around the base, trying to decide what to do next, a truck pulled up and a soldier jumped out. The soldier, a native English-speaker, told Sirulnikoff that his unit needed men. Sirulnikoff asked what type of unit the soldier belonged to. "It's secret stuff," the soldier responded. "That's for me," exclaimed Sirulnikoff, who jumped on board. The truck headed out of the camp, and drove to an old winery outside the seaside town of Herzliya. Sirulnikoff went inside, and there he saw the unit's weapons – six antiquated seventy-five-millimeter anti-aircraft guns. The "secret stuff" was artillery.

An Australian named Michael Landshut commanded the artillery unit. Landshut was a member of Britain's forces in Palestine who had joined the Haganah, bringing with him the new army's first twenty-five pounder artillery piece. Landshut had handpicked a group of English speakers to man his guns. Sirulnikoff was not the only *Marie Annick* passenger to join. Arthur Goldberg, also seduced by the promise of "secret stuff," came on board as well. Maurice Loeb, who like Goldberg haled from Vancouver, was another recruit. Yale Joffe, a resident of Calgary who left his studies at the University of British Columbia to take part in the fighting, also joined the unit. The men trained on the old guns for only a week before heading north to face the Syrians at Mishmar Hayarden.

The government regarded the Canadians who arrived on the *Marie Annick* as "*Machal*," an acronym for "*Mitnadvei Chutz L'Aretz*" ("Volunteers from outside of the land"). The Machal designation was reserved for men and women who came to Israel from the democracies of the west to join in the fighting. That included Americans, Canadians, South Africans, Brits, and Frenchmen. As the flow of such volunteers increased, the army established an office in Tel Aviv to cater to the special needs of Machal soldiers.

Israel needed the truce period to organize its army, a task that took on even greater urgency following the *Altalena* incident. As the Israel Defense Force replaced the pre-state underground forces, it was decided that all of the nation's soldiers should take an oath of allegiance to the new army. The oath would formalize the transition from the underground to the IDF, and would provide an opportunity for former Irgunists to demonstrate their loyalty.

The Americans were concerned about the oath. In principle, they had no problem declaring their allegiance to Israel, but were afraid they would jeopardize their U.S. citizenship by doing so. Herbert Hordes, the University of Michigan student who had fought with the Carmeli Brigade in Haifa and Acre, approached the brigade's welfare officer, together with some other Americans, to seek guidance. The welfare officer was aware of the problem. "There is a special swearing-in ceremony for the Americans. You will go to Tel Aviv to the Machal office and they'll make arrangements for you," he advised Hordes and the others. But Hordes would be present for the unit's swearing-in, and asked the welfare officer how he should conduct himself during that ceremony. "When they call your name to swear, you say you do not swear," he told Hordes.

A few days later, Hordes and other members of the 22nd Battalion of the Carmeli Brigade were brought together for the swearing-in. Moshe Carmeli, the commander of the Carmeli Brigade and the architect of the capture of Acre, conducted the ceremony. Carmeli, who had taken as his last name the name of his brigade, was a fiercely dedicated soldier. He ordered the men to attention, and one-by-one, called out the soldiers' names. Each soldier responded with a loud cry of *"Ani nishbah"* ("I swear"). When Hordes heard his name, he called out *"Eyneni nishba"* ("I do not swear"), as directed by the welfare officer. Carmeli was infuriated. His face a bright crimson, he turned to two MP's and ordered them to immediately arrest Hordes. As the MP's marched Hordes off, he tried to explain that he had only been following the welfare officer's instructions. It didn't help. The MP's locked him up in a former British army jail.

For his meals, Hordes had to be escorted from his jail cell to the mess. There, soldiers and officers alike waited in line, cafeteria style, reflecting the Haganah's democratic spirit. There was one exception. Regulations provided that prisoners were not to wait in line. Instead, the MP's were to interrupt service, and take the prisoner directly to the front. The MP's walked Hordes into the mess. By this point, the other members of the unit, including the MP's, knew why Hordes had refused to take the oath. They were greatly amused by the episode, and the MP's decided to have some fun at Carmeli's expense. They waited until the brigade commander was about to be served, and then surged forward with Hordes. Carmeli's face again turned bright red as he was forced to wait while Hordes received his meal first. The next day, the welfare officer straightened things out, and Hordes was released from jail.

The swearing-in issue also caused problems for David Gutmann. The former *Abril* and *Paducah* crewman had joined the Palmach's naval arm after being released from the detention camps of Xylotymbu and Atlit. With the formation of the Israeli Navy, Gutmann signed on as an engineering officer. He was posted to the former Aliyah Bet ship the *Haganah*. The ship's captain was Moka Limon, the same man who had commanded the *Paducah*. At the beginning of the official war, the navy assigned political officers to each of its ships, a practice that offended the American seamen who encountered it. The *Haganah's* political officer insisted that the ship's crew swear allegiance to the IDF. Gutmann and three other Americans refused, explaining that the oath could cost them their citizenship. The political officer ordered the Americans to stand in shame at the ship's stern. "What are you, Americans or Jews," he chided them. "I hope both," answered Gutmann. As soon as Limon learned what had happened, he intervened on behalf of the Americans. Gutmann later transferred to the *Pan York*, another former Aliyah Bet ship. Together with Heavy Greaves, who the British finally released from Cyprus, he made several more runs between Europe and Israel, bringing in thousands more refugees.

NOTES

[1] That initial attack on the Altalena was not as intense as it might have been. One of the Navy's gunners was Jerry Gross, a veteran of the dismantled Canadian Platoon. Gross decided that he could not fire on fellow Jews. He quietly removed the firing pins from his guns.

13

THE TEN DAYS FIGHTING

The four-week truce was set to expire on July 9. In anticipation of the renewed fighting, the IDF General Staff established several goals. Jerusalem occupied much of the attention of Israel's military planners. To free the New City from the threat posed by the Jordanians, the army identified four targets: the towns of Latrun, Ramallah, Lydda and Ramle. In the north, the IDF sought to encircle the Syrian bridgehead at Mishmar Hayarden, and to destroy those forces. In the Galilee, the army was ranged against the ragtag Arab Liberation Army, an irregular Arab force headed by Fawzi El Kaukji. Kaukji's forces had infiltrated into the Galilee through Syrian lines in the waning days of the Mandate. To consolidate Israeli control over the Galilee, the IDF would have to attack Kaukji's strongholds, particularly the one at Nazareth. And in the south, the army needed to break through Egyptian lines, to establish an overland link to the encircled Israeli settlements in the Negev.

The army hoped to launch the second round of fighting with a string of surprise air attacks on the Syrian, Jordanian and Egyptian forces. In the south, the 101 Squadron would attack the Egyptian air base at El Arish, to destroy Egypt's Spitfires on the ground. On July 9, four American pilots readied themselves for the El Arish raid: Lou Lenart, new arrival Bill Pomerantz, and Stan Andrews and Bob Vickman, the two art students who came together from California. Lenart, the flight leader, took off first, to be followed by Andrews. But Andrews' Me 109 ground-looped on take-off. Andrews was uninjured, but his plane blocked the runway. As Lenart circled above and Vickman and Pomerantz waited on the runway, ground crews took more than twenty minutes to right Andrews' plane and get it out of the way. The other two planes then joined Lenart, and the three Me 109's headed south for El Arish.

Soon Lenart realized he had used up too much fuel circling the field. He didn't have enough left to make it to El Arish. He ordered everyone to turn around over Gaza. As they headed back to base, he noticed an Arab ship unloading at the Gaza port. Lenart dove down, bombing and strafing the ship. Vickman was close behind. Lenart pulled out of the strafing run and returned to base. When Lenart landed, he met Pomerantz, who had also made it back to the base safely. Vickman, however, was not there. He would never return. Somewhere between Gaza and Ekron his plane had been lost. The army never found either the wreckage of Vickman's Me 109 or his body.

Stan Andrews was devastated by his friend's death. The air force grew increasingly concerned about Andrews' mental state, and soon decided to ground him. But Andrews would have the last word on the subject.

Operation Dani was the code name for the offensive against Latrun, Ramallah, Lydda, and Ramle. The Eighth Brigade, an all-armored force, took part in the operation against the Jordanian Legion. Lionel Druker, the former commander of the Canadian Platoon, was one of the early recruits to the Eighth. Druker was hand-picked by the legendary Palmach commander Yitzach Sadeh, the grey-bearded, barrel-chested soldier who would later be regarded as the father of Israel's armored corps. Sadeh had learned of Druker's extensive tank training in the Canadian army, and gave him command of a decrepit, World War II surplus Sherman tank the Haganah had found before the British left the country. That Sherman would become the first tank in Israel's arsenal.

But when Druker first saw the Sherman, he was concerned. Many of its parts were missing, including the main gun and engine. The army would find replacements for most of the missing parts, but not a new main gun. In its place, the army installed a long pipe to act as a dummy gun, hoping it would at least inspire fear on the battlefield. Druker's lone Sherman was soon joined by two Cromwell tanks driven by former British soldiers who had deserted their units and thrown in with the Israelis for the fighting against the Arabs. Sadeh placed Druker in command of the three-tank force.

On July 10, the Eighth Brigade and a jeep-born commando unit from another brigade attacked Lydda, the site of a former British airfield. Druker's tanks took part in the fighting, the first time the Israeli Army had deployed tanks in combat. Israel wanted to capture the Lydda field intact, so Druker was careful to direct his tank's fire away from the runways and control tower. In the end, the Eighth would not play a meaningful role in the battle. But the attack on Ramle would be one of the most dramatic Israeli victories of the war. In a lightning raid spearheaded by the commando unit – led by a dashing, one-eyed soldier named Moshe Dayan – Lydda was captured in less than a day. Dayan would also lead the assault the next day on the neighboring town of Ramle, an action that produced another dazzling Israeli victory. Those raids would later do much to create Dayan's legend.

Israel immediately began to make use of the Lydda field. The first plane to land was an Auster piloted by Tennessean Jerry Renov, whose drawl quickly gave away his Southern roots. Another of the American Hebrew University students, Renov was a religious Jew. He wore a skullcap during his missions, a practice that earned him the nickname *"HaKippah HaMe'offefet"* (the "Flying Kippah"). As events heated up following the partition resolution, Renov joined the Haganah, later transferring to its air service. During the siege of Jerusalem, Renov had regularly flown between Tel Aviv and Jerusalem, carrying small amounts of much-needed supplies in his tiny plane. He had a special reason to fly those missions. His wife Bea was one of the city's besieged residents. Ultimately, Renov would receive permission to fly his wife out of Jerusalem. But before that happened, he made sure to provide her with some special relief from the hunger plaguing the city.

One day during the siege, Bea Renov was chatting with her friend Ruth Gutman in the living room of Bea's ground floor apartment. Gutman's husband had also been a student at the university. Suddenly, the women heard the sound of a plane diving on the building, and ducked under the furniture for cover. They heard no explosions, and the two cautiously peered out the window to see what had happened. Just then, the plane flew low for a second pass, this time dropping a small package right into the yard behind Bea Renov's building. The two women ran out to retrieve it. They were surprised and delighted by what they found – a kosher salami, courtesy of Jerry Renov.

Shortly after the army captured Lydda and Ramle, it pulled Druker out of the fighting. During the end of his service in the Canadian army, Druker had been a tank instructor. It was that experience the IDF now wanted to tap. Druker relinquished his tank to a young South African, and reported for duty as the chief instructor for a new school to train armored officers. The school was in Sarafand, another former British military base, this one located outside of Tel Aviv. Using a translator, Druker now devoted all of his energy to communicating his knowledge of the intricacies of tank warfare to the Israelis.

Although the chief, and initially the only, armored warfare instructor, Druker was not the highest-ranking Canadian soldier at Sarafand. That distinction fell to Joe Weiner, a red-headed, former captain in the Canadian army and the brainchild behind the Sarafand school. Weiner's decision to come to Israel had been an unusual one. In effect, his father made it for him, bluntly asking one night: "When are you going to Israel?" Despite his father's encouragement, it was still a difficult decision for Weiner. Unlike virtually all of the other Canadians in Israel, Weiner was a professional soldier, with particular expertise in artillery and armor. Weiner's career had begun as an enlisted man, and he had worked his way through the ranks to become a captain. When his father asked him about Israel, Weiner was still in the Canadian army, and had been told to expect a promotion to major. But Weiner thought over his father's request, and decided to forego the promotion and go to Israel. Like Druker, Weiner also saw combat before the assignment to Sarafand.

Toward the end of the truce, Weiner had been approached by Ben Dunkelman, the strapping Canadian major who had dreamed of leading a brigade of Canadian soldiers against the Arabs. With the dismantling of the Canadian Platoon, a much smaller force than the one Dunkelman envisioned, his dream would not be realized. He got the next best thing, though – a command of an Israeli brigade. Dunkelman was placed in charge of a reconstituted Seventh. The Seventh had led all three failed attacks at Latrun. By the time the truce went into effect, its manpower was severely depleted and its morale was at a nadir. When the truce ended, Dunkelman was to command a new Seventh, organized into three battalions, the 71st, 72nd and 79th. Eventually the Seventh would become home to most of the Americans and Canadians who were not in the air force. The 79th Battalion was armored and Dunkelman, whose only experience was in the infantry, asked Weiner to command the 79th. With only a few days left before the expiration of the truce, Dunkelman and Weiner scrambled to organize and train the brigade.

A dedicated military man whose only experience came from the Royal Canadian Armored Forces, Weiner was shocked by the primitive Israeli attitude toward armored combat. The Israelis viewed armored units as a place to send men who couldn't adapt to the rigors of the infantry. From their point of view, a man who couldn't march into combat could at least ride to the fighting in an armored car. With this in mind, they sent Weiner a concentration camp survivor whose shin had been broken in two places. The wound had never healed properly, and the soldier's leg bent like a rubber stick when he walked. There was another, even less likely soldier in the unit. The Israelis had sent to the 79th a seven-foot Ethiopian Jew. The Ethiopian had walked barefoot from his native land, across Egypt, to join in the fighting. But there were no shoes in Israel that would fit the enormous Ethiopian, and thus no place for him in the infantry. There was a problem the Israelis had not anticipated, however. The seven-foot Jew couldn't fit into an armored car.

The story of the giant Ethiopian didn't end there. Unfit for combat, he was instead given the task of sweeping around the base. But Weiner felt badly as he watched the gentle giant walking barefoot, sometimes over the camp's rock-strewn paths. One day, the unit came across a warehouse of British army supplies in a newly-captured Arab village. One of the soldiers found a giant pair of boots which he thought might fit the Ethiopian, and he brought them to Weiner. Weiner gave the boots to the young Ethiopian, who could not believe his bounty. His eyes wide with delight, he fell to his feet and began to kiss the hands of his embarrassed commander. A few days later, Weiner ran into the Ethiopian again. There were the boots, laces neatly tied, polished to a bright sheen – hanging around the soldier's neck. Regarding the boots as a present of great value, he refused to wear them on his feet.

Left: Californian Stan Andrews attended art school in Los Angeles with his best friend Bob Vickman before the pair joined Israel's fighter squadron. The two created the 101 Squadron's angel of death logo. Andrews was killed during the bombing of the Iraq El Sueidan Fortress. *(Courtesy of Red Finkel) Right:* The logo of the 101 Squadron. *(Courtesy of Red Finkel)*

This picture was taken in Italy shortly after the crew and passengers of Don Kosteff's C-46 were released from jail. C-46 pilot Don Kosteff *(standing, first from left)* and fighter pilots Red Finkel *(in front)* and Sid Antin *(first from right)* are ready to continue their journey to Israel. *(Courtesy of Red Finkel)*

Navigator/bombardier Jules Cuburnek (*fifth from left*) with his U.S. Air Force B-17 crew before their twenty-fifth and final mission of the war, on March 8, 1944. (*Courtesy of Jules Cuburnek*)

Pilot Ray Kurtz (*second from left*) and Jules Cuburnek (*first from left*) stand under their C-46 with the rest of the crew during a stopover in Ajaccio, Corsica. The group was making a transport flight from Zatec to Israel, in June of 1948. (*Courtesy of Jules Cuburnek*)

Ray Kurtz (*right*). Kurtz was the mission leader for the first and only bombing of Cairo during the War of Independence. (*Courtesy of Jules Cuburnek*)

Captain of the ill-fated *Altalena*, Monroe Fein stands on deck before the ship departs Port du Bouc for Tel Aviv. (*Courtesy of David Gen*)

Captain Monroe Fein (*second from right*) and Abraham Stavsky (*fourth from right*) examine some of the weapons on board the *Altalena*. *(Courtesy of David Gen)*

The *Altalena* sailed with more than eight-hundred passengers from fifteen different countries. *(Courtesy of David Gen)*

The *Altalena* on fire. To the left, Irgunists on rafts are seen paddling out to pick up survivors. *(Courtesy of David Gen)*

The *Marie Annick*, crowded with refugees and Canadian volunteers, makes its way to Israel. The *Altalena* was still burning when the *Marie Annick* arrived. *(Courtesy of Leib Shanas)*

The Canadians on board the *Marie Annick*. Arthur Goldberg is standing, hands clasped, in the center. *(Courtesy of Leib Shanas)*

Lionel Druker, commander of Israel's first tank, astride his Sherman. *(Courtesy of Lionel Druker)*

The two British Cromwells that joined Druker's Sherman. The British tank commanders are on the Cromwell on the left. (*Courtesy of Lionel Druker*)

Yitzhak Sadeh (*left*), the father of Israel's armored corps. Sadeh made Druker Israel's first tank commander. (*Courtesy of Lionel Druker*)

White flag raised, the Arabs of Nazareth surrender after the Seventh Brigade captured the city. The capture was spearheaded by Joe Weiner's 79th Armored Battalion. (*Courtesy of Jules Cuburnek*)

A group of foreign military volunteers. Lester Gorn, the American infantry officer who commanded the Fourth Anti-Tank Squad, stands on the far left. Canadian Harvey Sirulnikoff (*standing, second from right*) served in Michael Landshut's artillery unit, and later in the Palmach. *(Courtesy of Leib Shanas)*

Hank Greenspun, after his adventures in Hawaii and Mexico, being congratulated by Prime Minister David Ben Gurion. *(Courtesy of Las Vegas Sun)*

Rudy Augarten flew over ninety missions in his P-47 Thunderbolt during World War II, earning the Distinguished Flying Cross. *(Courtesy of Rudy Augarten)*

Augarten stands in front of the Egyptian Spitfire he downed on the second day of Operation Yoav – the first of four aerial victories. *(Courtesy of Rudy Augarten)*

This World War II publicity photo features the men of the Black Sheep Squadron. The aces, including 101 Squadron pilot Chris Magee (*first from left*) and Pappy Boyington (*fourth from left*) stand in front. The caps and bats were a gift from the St. Louis Cardinals. *(Courtesy of National Archives)*

Chris Magee (*kneeling center*) a recipient of the coveted Navy Cross, poses with other members of the Black Sheep in January of 1944. *(Courtesy of National Archives)*

Training in Czechoslovakia on the Me 109. *First, second, and fourth from left:* Chris Magee, George Lichter, and Rudy Augarten. *(Courtesy of Red Finkel)*

The 101 Fighter Squadron. *Standing, first, fourth, sixth, ninth, eleventh, thirteenth, and fifteenth from left:* George Lichter, Lou Lenart, Sid Antin, Stan Andrews, Rudy Augarten, Leo Nomis, and Bill Pomerantz. *Kneeling, first, second, third, and fifth from left:* Coleman Goldstein, Giddy Lichtman, Chris Magee and Red Finkel. An Me 109 is in the background. *(Courtesy of Rudy Augarten)*

101 fighter pilots standing in front of a Spitfire. T*op row first from right:* Red Finkel. *Middle row on plane, first and third from left*: Bill Pomerantz and Sid Antin. *Standing, second, third, fourth, and fifth from left*: Chris Magee, Giddy Lichtman, Leon Frankel, and Leo Nomis. Note the Squadron logo near the propeller. *(Courtesy of Red Finkel)*

Prime Minister David Ben Gurion *(center)* with former Black Sheep Chris Magee *(right)*, during a visit to the 101 Squadron. *(Courtesy of Eddy Kaplansky, Sonny Wosk)*

Members of the 103 Squadron. *Standing, fourth and seventh from left:* Sam Boshes and Trygve Maseng. *(Courtesy of Alisa Poskanzer)*

This photo was taken only minutes before the three B-17's left Zatec for the Cairo raid. This is Norm Moonitz's (*standing, third from left*) crew, standing in front of their B-17. *(Courtesy of Norm Moonitz)*

The three B-17's on a bombing run. *(Courtesy of Jules Cuburnek)*

A B-17 in flight. *(Courtesy of Arieh Jacoby)*

A B-17 drops its bombs. American Arieh Jacoby took these photos out of a waist gun position on the B-17. *(Courtesy of Arieh Jacoby)*

Royal Canadian Air Force veteran Jack Goldstein was the radio operator for the B-17 raid on Cairo. *(Courtesy of Jack Goldstein)*

Spencer Boyd, only a day or so after arriving in Israel. Boyd was murdered after the Miles Aerovan he was piloting crash-landed in Arab territory. *(Courtesy of Eddy Kaplanksy, Red Finkel)*

Prime Minster David Ben-Gurion gets a close look at a B-17. *(Courtesy of Arieh Jacoby)*

The Seventh Brigade, together with a unit of the Carmeli Brigade, received the task of clearing the Arab Liberation Army from the eastern part of the Galilee. The Liberation Army forces were concentrated most heavily in Nazareth. That hilltop village was the biggest plum of Operation Dekel, as the Galilee campaign was called. The planning for the assault on Nazareth did not go well, however. Weiner was concerned that an attack on Nazareth, with its British-built stone fortress, could turn into a bloodbath if not planned properly. Dunkelman advocated a plan that the IDF's newly organized Northern Command had foisted upon him, which called for the infantry to capture two neighboring Arab towns before leading an attack that same night on Nazareth. Weiner's armored battalion would join the infantry for the assault on Nazareth. Weiner was certain the plan, which in his view reflected a lack of understanding of armor, would be a "fiasco." The two headstrong Canadians argued at length, neither convincing the other of his position. But Dunkelman had the higher rank, and the last word. He relieved Weiner of his command.

When Weiner's unit learned of their commander's dismissal, they were furious. Weiner's assistant Baruch Ezer advised Weiner that if he did not participate in the assault, neither would the rest of the unit. Meanwhile, the budding mutiny came to Dunkelman's attention, who sent soldiers to arrest Weiner's men. The situation threatened to spiral out of control. But Weiner diffused the crisis, announcing he would participate in the battle as a private. Whatever his formal position in the army, it was clear that Weiner would lead the armor into battle at Nazareth, despite his misgivings.

On July 16, only a few hours after midnight, an armored column from the 79th arrived at a small olive grove outside of Nazareth, the agreed rallying point. But Weiner had been right. The infantry failed to arrive as scheduled. Day broke, and Weiner's thinly disguised force was spotted. Snipers from Nazareth fired upon the Israeli vehicles, and Weiner had to decide whether to attack or retreat. The decision was not a simple one. To reach its position outside of Nazareth, the column had fought its way through a number of smaller Arab villages, all under the control of the Liberation Army. If the 79th retreated, there was no guarantee it could return to Nazareth. Weiner decided to move forward, with a modified plan. He would make a rapid thrust into Nazareth, and try to secure the high point in the town. Assuming he was successful, the infantry, once it arrived, could then move in and secure the rest of the area.

The Canadian pulled four vehicles out of the column, three make-shift armored cars and a half-track mounted with a twenty-millimeter anti-tank gun. He gathered the crews and laid out his plan. Earlier, Weiner had observed two Liberation Army armored cars advance over a hill a short distance out of Nazareth, probing in the direction of the olive grove where the 79th's vehicles were hiding. After a short time, the Liberation Army cars pulled back behind the hill. Weiner became convinced a large armored force was waiting in ambush on the other side of the hill. From his knowledge of British armor tactics, which it seemed clear the Liberation Army was employing, Weiner thought the Liberation Army intended to allow the Jewish force to pass over the hill toward Nazareth. Then, when the last car had cleared the top of the hill, the Liberation Army would fire on the end of the column, blocking the others from retreating. Weiner had a solution.

"Go up the road," he ordered, "and when you get to the top there'll be a roadblock there. I don't know what it is, but, as soon as you see it, front car, you open fire, move to the left, second open fire, move to the right, third to the left, and that will leave a passage in between the three armored cars for the twenty-millimeter to fire through." Weiner tried to relax the men as they prepared to head out to battle. "Now don't rush. Just take it easy, as if you were going to a picnic." The twenty-millimeter was the secret weapon. It was the only gun the four vehicles had that could penetrate an armored car. It would be protected, until the last possible moment, by the three homemade armored cars in front.

The attack went better than Weiner could have hoped. As he had forecast, a large Liberation Army force lay in wait on the other side of hill. There were nine Arab vehicles in total, two in front and seven more behind the first pair. The lead Israeli armored vehicles, in turn, fired and moved into position, giving way to the half-track with its twenty-milli-meter gun. The half-track fired at one of the lead Arab armored cars, hitting the turret and damaging it, freezing the vehicle's main gun in place. The Israeli gunners fired their machine guns at the now helpless Arab vehicle. The bullets pinged off harmlessly, but the hail of gunfire pan-icked the Liberation Army crew. They jumped from the safe confines of their vehicle and ran. They were sitting ducks for the Israeli gunners.

The Israelis then fired on the second lead armored car. They scored a direct hit on a pair of hand grenades hanging over the driver's seat. The grenades exploded, killing everyone inside the armored car. Next, an Israeli bullet hit the undercarriage of a third armored car, locking the wheels. The driver couldn't turn the damaged vehicle, and it tumbled down the hill. The remaining vehicles in the Liberation Army column retreated. The road to Nazareth was open.

The 79th roared into the city, taking up positions from which to shell the Liberation Army strongholds. By this time, the infantry arrived, bolstering Weiner's force. At 6:15 p.m., less than two hours after Weiner launched the attack on the column outside the town, Nazareth surrendered.

Weiner's experience with the 79th convinced him the Israelis desperately needed more formal training in armor tactics. He pleaded his case, first to Chaim Laskov of the IDF's Northern Command. "They've just learned the little bit I've told them and the little bit that they've picked up," he complained to Laskov. "You've got to teach them more." Laskov carried the fight to the next level. He convinced Chief of Staff Yaakov Dori that Israel needed an armored warfare school. There were two candidates to command the school, Weiner, and a former colonel in the Russian army whom the Palmach favored. Dori interviewed both officers, and asked each why he should receive command. Weiner gave his pitch: "I'm trained under British tactics as used by the Canadian army, which is a small army and it's the type of army that I hope someday that Israel will be able to support, where you have a lot of reservists and a small permanent force." Dori chose Weiner, and sent him to Sarafand with Lionel Druker to establish the school.

The second round of fighting was not just a tale of dazzling Israeli victories. In the north, the IDF was unable to dislodge the Syrians from Mishmar Hayarden. But largely due to Michael Landshut's artillery unit, the army at least stopped the Syrians from breaking out of the bridgehead and taking further territory. The most dramatic moment came on the morning of July 10, when Landshut's Anglo-Saxon gunners single-handedly drove back five Syrian tanks that had tried to rush from Mishmar Hayarden to the country's north-south highway. Had the Syrian tanks succeeded in reaching the highway, many Jewish settlements in the north would have been isolated from the rest of the country.

Despite their success against the Syrians, the Canadian and other members of the Landshut unit were disappointed in the French guns. They were unreliable and, perhaps worse, dangerous to the men who fired them. On one occasion, Harvey Sirulnikoff, the Canadian who had come to the unit looking for "secret stuff," fired one of the guns. As he did, something zinged by his face. The object caught another soldier, who had been standing nearby, in the chest, inflicting a minor flesh wound. Sirulnikoff soon realized what had happened. The rim of the shell, which dated back to World War I, had broken away during firing and knocked off the blast shield. It was the flying shield that had nearly decapitated Sirulnikoff. During the unit's existence, some half of its thirty or so soldiers would be injured, in nearly every case by the unit's own malfunctioning French guns.

But there were lighter moments as well. On one occasion, as the unit traded fire with the Syrians, Arthur Goldberg noticed Maurice Lobe, another Canadian and the unit medic, running from one gun position to the other. Lobe seemed oblivious to the Syrian shells exploding around him. Goldberg could not imagine why the medic was acting so crazily. But Lobe had his reasons. It was a hot summer day, and one of Lobe's responsibilities was to give the soldiers salt tablets, little blue sugar and salt pills, that were supposed to ward off dehydration. Before the shooting began that day, Lobe had forgotten to hand out the pills. So around he raced, giving out the little tablets and reminding each soldier, "Don't forget to take your salt pill."

After the fall of Lydda and Ramle in the first few days of the renewed fighting, the British moved quickly in the United Nations for another cease-fire. The British maintained close relations with the Jordanians and Egyptians, and were anxious to spare the Arabs any further humiliating defeats. On July 15, the U.N. agreed to order another truce, to take effect on July 17. Britain's action, coming only a week after the fighting resumed, left Israel precious few days to build on its earlier victories. Still, there would be enough time for one more Israeli surprise before the guns fell silent.

Al Schwimmer had not been idle since organizing the purchase of the C-46's and Constellations, the planes that now formed the backbone of the Czech airlift. In the months following the departure of those planes from the U.S., Schwimmer hunted for bigger prey – the B-17 Flying Fortress. The B-17 had been one of the U.S. Air Force's front-line heavy bombers during World War II, and many of the planes, with their military hardware removed, were available for purchase. Ultimately, Schwimmer bought four of the huge planes from different airfields throughout the U.S. As with the transport planes, Schwimmer hired crews to try to put the B-17's in flying shape. At the same time, Schwimmer struggled to keep one step ahead of the federal agents who were tracking the operation's every move.

On June 12, 1948, Schwimmer managed to get three of the heavy bombers out of the U.S., flying them with full crews from Miami to San Juan, Puerto Rico. Charles Winters, a non-Jewish Miami businessman who had sold two of the planes to Schwimmer, flew one of the B-17's personally. Winters would later pay a heavy price for helping the Jewish state. From San Juan, the bombers flew to the Azores. During the long trip across the Atlantic, the air crews started to learn, more concretely, about the shortcomings of the surplus planes. When the U.S. stripped the planes of their military gear, they also removed much of the navigational equipment. Without proper navigation instruments, the crews had to improvise. At intervals during the long flight, the crew would remove one of the plexiglass windows at the top of the plane. The navigator, held by other members of the crew, would poke his head through the opening and into the slipstream to confirm the plane's heading against the position of the sun.

Disaster nearly struck one of the planes. The B-17 had originally been fitted with a plexiglass window on the floor of the plane, near the navigator's station. That window allowed the navigator to determine drift by constantly checking the plane's position against landmarks on the ground below. On one of the B-17's, that plexiglass window had been removed, and replaced with a thin piece of plywood. American Eli Cohen, the navigator on that flight, inadvertently stepped on the plywood. It snapped, and Cohen fell through the opening until only his arms, shoulders, neck and head were still in the plane. He shouted for help, but had difficulty making himself heard above the roar of the B-17's four engines. The co-pilot finally heard Cohen's frantic shouts. He and the other crew members rushed over and tried to drag Cohen back into the plane. The pull of the outside air on Cohen's body was too great, and the crew could not lift him back inside. Finally, one crewman grabbed a piece of rubber hose hanging on the wall, looped it under Cohen's arms, and the crew finally was able to pull the bruised and battered American into the plane.

From the Azores, the B-17's flew directly to Zatec, arriving during the truce. In Czechoslovakia, the hard work of refitting the planes for military use began immediately. The ground crews installed bomb racks, gun sights, and gun positions. In many cases, they couldn't find the original equipment, and there was a lot of improvising. Instead of the fifty-caliber machine guns the B-17's originally carried, the crews installed thirty-caliber Beza machine guns. The crews also installed British bomb sights, unable to find the American model. Creating new bomb racks proved the most difficult challenge. Without even a similar system, a whole new rack and bombing system had to be fashioned.

Finding crews for the B-17's was a less difficult process. Many of the men flying Israel's C-46's had B-17 experience. Four of the ATC flyers, Norm Moonitz, Ray Kurtz, Al Raisin and Bill Katz, had been B-17 pilots. (Katz, exercising the captain's prerogative during the naming of his World War II plane, had called it "Katz and his Kittens.") The emerging B-17 squadron also took navigators and bombardiers from the ATC, including Jules Cuburnek, a veteran of twenty-five B-17 missions over Europe as a navigator/bombardier. A call also went out within Israel for experienced air gunners, and these men, mostly South Africans and Americans, were pulled from their units and flown to Czechoslovakia.

As the first three B-17's were being readied, efforts were underway to bring the fourth to Czechoslovakia as well. On July 11, Swifty Schindler, the man behind Service Airways, was at the controls of the last B-17 as it left Tulsa, Oklahoma, bound for New York. He flew the plane east to a small, suburban airport at Westchester, New York. Schindler hoped only to make a brief refueling stop in Westchester before continuing on to the Azores, and from their to Zatec. But one engine developed an oil leak on the way, forcing a layover at the small airport, while a Schwimmer crew repaired the engine. The presence of the heavy bomber in upstate New

York did not go unnoticed. The *Herald Tribune* chartered a plane and sent three reporters to Westchester to investigate. Schindler and his crew refused to talk to the reporters, quickly finishing the repairs and taking off for the Azores – with the *Herald Tribune* plane in tow.

But the repairs had eaten up most of the daylight hours. Schindler's B-17 suffered from the same lack of navigational equipment as the other three planes, and he worried he might get lost over the ocean at night. As Schindler passed over the Canadian coast, he headed for Halifax, receiving permission to land at a Royal Canadian Air Force base. Although Schindler told the Canadians he had been on a training flight, they became suspicious and notified the American government. The U.S. State Department asked them to find a pretext to hold the plane. It was now clear to everyone that the B-17 was bound for Israel.

Absent a formal request from the Americans, the Canadians were not willing to hold the B-17 indefinitely. For its part, the U.S. had not had time to prepare such a request, yet still did not want to see the plane leave for Israel. On July 17, the Canadians solved the dilemma by releasing the plane with just enough fuel to return to Westchester. But Schindler fooled all of them. He convinced the Canadian in charge of fueling his plane that his auxiliary tanks were empty, when in fact they were nearly full. With the fuel he needed, and flying low out of Halifax to avoid radar and conceal his destination, Schindler made the next leg of his journey to the Azores. But there his luck ran out. The American consul learned of the B-17's arrival and notified Washington. The U.S. convinced the Portuguese to detain the plane and crew, and Schindler and the others were returned to the U.S. to face charges. There would only be three planes in Israel's heavy bomber squadron.

Originally, Israel planned to send all three of the refurbished bombers directly from Zatec to Israel, and from there to begin bombing operations. But Ray Kurtz had other ideas. From the beginning of the war, the Egyptians had bombed Tel Aviv, Israel's largest city, without opposition. Initially, the Egyptians had used Dakotas that had been modified to carry bombs. The unopposed raids of even these makeshift bombers had been devastating to the morale of Tel Aviv's residents. They had also been deadly. On May 17, forty-two Israelis were killed in an air raid on Tel Aviv's central bus station. On June 3, an Israeli member of the 101 Squadron shot down two of the Egyptian bombers over Tel Aviv, putting an end to the Dakota raids. But the Egyptian Spits continued to attack the city.

It was during one of Kurtz's layovers in Tel Aviv that the seed was sown for an idea to stop the Tel Aviv bombings. An Israeli had complained to Kurtz about the Egyptian raids. "Why don't you go bomb Cairo?" demanded the Israeli, not understanding that the C-46's flown by the ATC were transport planes, not bombers. But with the arrival of the B-17's, Kurtz had his bombers.

When Kurtz learned of the plan to fly the B-17's directly to Israel, he refused. "No way! We're going to bomb Cairo on the way in," he insisted. Initially, the air force rejected Kurtz's scheme, fearing the loss of the valuable planes in a raid on Egypt's capital city. Ultimately there was a compromise. One plane would go to Cairo, while the other two would hit the Egyptian army at Gaza and El Arish. Kurtz would command the mission.

As the planes were being readied for their first bombing run, the crews planned the details of the raid. They plotted courses to the targets and times for the assault. For the Cairo raid, there was an added precaution. The ATC located an airline schedule, and decided to fly into Cairo between two arriving flights, and thus at a time when large planes would be expected to come over the city.

The B-17 was a high-altitude bomber. In its original incarnation, before the U.S. military released it for sale, it was fitted with an oxygen system. But that system, like much of the rest of the B-17's non-essential flying equipment, had been removed. Without oxygen, the B-17's would have to bomb from lower, more vulnerable altitudes. Using cylinders of welder's oxygen, the ground crew at Zatec succeeded in creating one makeshift system. The B-17 with that system would be the one to attack Cairo.

Then came the matter of assigning the pilots to the different planes and targets. Bill Katz, as it turned out, had more B-17 experience than any of the other pilots. Kurtz assigned Katz the B-17 that would hit Cairo. Kurtz would fly co-pilot for that flight. Moonitz would go to Gaza, and Raisin to El Arish.

On the morning of July 15, the crews gathered on the field at Zatec. Recognizing the historical significance of Israel's first heavy bomber raid, the men posed for pictures in front of their planes. Then, at 10:00 a.m., they took off for the long, non-stop flight to the Middle East. Each plane carried twelve five-hundred-pound bombs. The formation flew south, passing over the Alps and then over the coastline of Yugoslavia. From there, the planes continued along the Albanian coast. Katz suddenly noticed puffs of black smoke to the left of his plane. It had been several years since Katz had flown a combat mission, and it was a few moments before it dawned on him that the Albanians were firing on the B-17's. He and the others turned further out to sea to avoid the fire. A short while later, the three bombers split up for the rest of the flight. Katz's B-17 flew over the Mediterranean, before turning east over Egypt. As dusk approached, he flew toward Cairo airport from the west. Jack Goldstein, the co-pilot on the first C-46 to see action in Israel, was the radio operator for the raid. Goldstein tuned the radio to the control tower's frequency, and listened. The tower had spotted the large plane approaching, and asked it to identify itself. Several times the tower repeated the request. Finally, with no answer forthcoming, and likely assuming that the plane's radio was not working, the Egyptians radioed permission to land. Below, at the airport, a green light flashed, confirming the tower's communication. The ruse worked, the Egyptians mistook the B-17 for a commercial plane.

Katz turned away from the airport, on the outskirts of Cairo, and headed toward the main city. With darkness falling, the city's lights were beginning to come on. To the crew, the lights of Cairo were a beautiful sight, all the more so because they made targeting easier. Over the city, the plane headed for the aiming point – King Farouk's palace at Cairo's center. As it came into view, the bombardier opened the bomb bays and released the entire load. Katz then turned sharply to the north for Israel. The raid had been entirely unopposed. Within less than an hour, Katz landed safely at Ekron. There, Katz's plane joined the other two B-17's.

Moonitz's and Raisin's planes had had a more difficult time. Gaza and El Arish were in the war zone, and were blacked out. The two pilots couldn't find their primary targets, so they headed farther south, and dropped their bombs on Rafah, an Egyptian town in northern Sinai. The raid triggered heavy ground fire, but the flak did not find its mark. All three B-17's came through their first mission unscathed.

Israelis were ecstatic that their fledgling air force had struck back at the Egyptians in such dramatic fashion. "It was like we had dropped the atomic bomb," recalled Jack Goldstein. This, despite the fact that the physical damage inflicted on Cairo was not great. The bombs missed the palace, falling just outside of its grounds. But the mission had elevated Israeli morale and communicated to the Egyptian military that Tel Aviv was not the only civilian center vulnerable to attack. Raids on Tel Aviv all but ceased following the Cairo mission.

Years later, in a bizarre twist of fate, Goldstein learned more about the effect of the bombing. He found himself seated at a wedding in Canada with an Egyptian who had lived in Cairo during the War of Independence. The groom had mentioned to the Egyptian before the wedding that Goldstein had served in the Israeli Army during the war. The Egyptian asked Goldstein whether he had any connection with the B-17 raid on Cairo. Flustered, Goldstein responded, "What if I did?" The Egyptian, it turned out, had been standing on a Cairo street when the attack took place. He told Goldstein how the people had screamed and run in panic as the bombs fell. To the residents of Cairo, a city not previously bombed during the fighting or even during the Second World War, it had felt as though the world was coming to an end.

There were other consequences from the Cairo raid. The Egyptian military was furious that the Israelis had succeeded in bombing Cairo without opposition, and took a number of steps to prevent another attack. Robert Fine, Bill Malpine and the other POW's at Cairo's Albassia prison would learn firsthand about the Egyptian response. The prison's commander was Major Abdul Mohammed El Chasab, a professional soldier and the son-in-law of the army's commander-in-chief. Shortly after the raid, the Americans witnessed a meeting between Chasab and an Egyptian brigadier general. The brigadier, who was responsible for Cairo's air defenses, had been dismissed for failing to prevent the Cairo raid. Weeping, the brigadier pleaded with Chasab to intervene on his behalf with Chasab's father-in-law.

Sacking the air defense commander was not the only Egyptian response to the air raid. During the first part of the war, the Egyptians had used powerful eighty-eight-millimeter guns mounted on rails against Israel. Fearing the Cairo raid was the beginning of an air campaign against their capital city, the Egyptians moved the eighty-eight's to Cairo. But

Israel never hit Cairo again, and those powerful guns were lost to the Egyptian army for the rest of the war.

After briefly considering basing the B-17's in Zatec and flying raids from there, the air force decided to keep the bombers in Israel. They were housed at the Ramat David airfield, a former RAF base in the north, near Haifa. Over the next few days, the B-17's flew more missions, bombing the Syrians at Mishmar Hayarden, and the Egyptians at El Arish and Majdal. The planes also formally became a squadron, with Ray Kurtz as the first commander. The air force asked the squadron to choose a number by which it should be designated. The men settled on sixty-nine, a number that had obvious significance to the squadron's many carousers. Informally, the sixty-ninth became known as the "Hammer Squadron."

✡ ✡ ✡

On July 17, with the second truce about to take effect, Spencer Boyd climbed into a Miles Aerovan, a twin-engine passenger plane, for a brief flight from Tel Aviv to Sodom, near the Dead Sea. Boyd, a non-Jew, had already served in two air forces before coming to Israel. At the beginning of the Second World War, he left his home in Chicago to enlist in the RCAF, where he served as a navigator. He transferred to the American air force after the U.S. entered the war. In Israel, Boyd was a member of the No. 1 Squadron, which flew mostly communications, light transport, and ambulance missions. At Sodom, Boyd picked up seven passengers for the return flight to Tel Aviv.

Unlike most of the foreign volunteers, Boyd made a special effort to learn Hebrew. He was concerned that he might one day be forced to land near a kibbutz, and wanted to be able to quickly identify himself as a member of the Israeli Air Force. He explained his thinking to Joseph Heckelman, another American volunteer. Heckelman asked what Boyd would do if he was forced down near an Arab settlement. "In that case, it's all over," Boyd responded.

Late in the evening of July 17, Boyd headed back to Tel Aviv. There was an air raid alert as Boyd reached the city, and he banked his plane away to look for another airfield. A short while later, the Aerovan ran out of fuel. Boyd made a forced landing in the desert, and the plane caught fire as it skidded to a stop. But Boyd and his passengers were lucky. They managed to scramble free of the burning plane. Unsure when help might arrive, the group decided to split up. Boyd and five of the passengers stayed with the plane, while the remaining two passengers hiked into the desert to look for help. Boyd gave those two his pistol, the only weapon on board.

Within hours, the two searchers ran into an Israeli patrol. With the soldiers, they returned to the plane, anxious about the six people left behind. A gruesome sight awaited them. An Arab gang had stumbled across the crash survivors. The Arabs killed Boyd and four of the other five passengers. The fifth passenger was badly wounded, but survived the massacre by playing dead. Boyd's comment to Heckelman had been cruelly prophetic.

✡ ✡ ✡

On July 18, three days after the Cairo raid, the second truce went into effect. The Ten Days fighting, as that second round of fighting would later come to be known, saw dramatic Israeli victories at Lydda and Ramle, and in the eastern Galilee against Kaukji's Arab Liberation Army. While there were no similar successes against the Syrians or Egyptians, Israel was at least able to prevent further Arab advances on those fronts. Although not yet of obvious military significance, the Cairo raid and the arrival of the Hammer Squadron signaled an important increase in Israeli firepower. With both a fighter squadron and a heavy bomber squadron, the IDF was becoming a modern fighting force.

14

THE SECOND TRUCE

The second truce, which the British had pushed through the U.N. Security Council, did not herald a permanent end to the fighting. The Arabs continued to reject a Jewish state of any size. Israel, for its part, still had not established control over all of the territory allocated it under the partition resolution. It wanted to free the encircled Jewish settlements of the Negev, drive the Arab Liberation Army from the rest of the Galilee, and push the Syrians back across the border in the north. The Israelis greeted the cessation of hostilities with a redoubled effort to purchase weapons and increase the army's manpower.

Like the first cease-fire, the second placed an embargo on the warring countries, prohibiting them from importing weapons or admitting men of military age who were not bona fide refugees. The U.N. hoped to more effectively enforce these restrictions than it had during the prior truce. It deployed a three-hundred-officer monitoring force in the region, made up of soldiers from the U.S., Belgium, France, and Sweden. The force was backed by a fleet of planes, ships, jeeps, and trucks.

While the Israelis and Arabs expected another round of fighting, the U.N. had other ideas. Count Folke Bernadotte, a Swede whom the U.N. appointed special mediator, advanced a series of plans for a permanent peace in the region. All of these heavily favored the Arabs. Initially, Bernadotte proposed a tiny, semi-autonomous Jewish state, linked in a political and economic union with Jordan. This plan also called for the U.N. Economic and Social Council to regulate future Jewish immigration. Bernadotte's later proposals, while slightly more favorable to Israel, still won him no admirers there. And yet, rejecting as they did any Jewish state in Palestine, the Arabs also opposed Bernadotte's plans. They still hoped, even after two rounds of fighting, to wipe Israel off the map.

The Czech airlift continued in the first weeks of the truce. But the Czechs had come under increased pressure from the Americans to shut down the Zatec base. Throughout the conflict, the American government had aggressively worked to stop the flow of arms to Israel from any and all sources. Although President Truman had recognized the Jewish state shortly after Ben Gurion's Declaration of Independence, the American government remained ambivalent toward Israel. The State Department, which had opposed Truman's grant of recognition, remained hostile to Israel, and its view gradually became the dominant one within the administration. The U.S. expressed its hostility from the beginning of the war by its refusal to sell weapons to Israel, and its efforts to block the departure of Schwimmer's planes. For months, the Czech operation had been an open secret, and the Americans were determined to stop this clear violation of the truce terms.

Israel knew the clock was ticking, and increased the pace of ATC flights from Czechoslovakia. By early August, the last of the Me 109's had been flown to Ekron, and only a small supply of Czech weapons remained at Zatec for transport to Israel. On August 12, the Czechs formally notified Israel it had twenty-four hours to evacuate Zatec. The crews were awakened in the middle of the night and told to get ready to leave immediately. The men hurriedly packed their belongings and jumped into cabs for the ride out to the airfield.

One of the American ground crewmen was devastated by news of the sudden departure. He had become seriously involved with a Czech woman, and the two hoped one day to marry. But with his departure, she would be stranded behind the Iron Curtain, and the two might never see each other again. The mechanic discussed his plight with the others, and they came up with a plan. They dressed the young woman as a flyer and, with a group of ATC crewmen, she climbed onto one of the planes. The Czech guards watching over the departure failed to realize what was happening. When the C-46's took off for the final time from Zatec, the woman was on board.

Meanwhile, the IDF began planning the next round of fighting. Everyone agreed that most of the army's attention should be focused on the Egyptians. The Jordanians had achieved their main objective, the capture of the Old City of Jerusalem, and seemed content to reinforce their position there. The Syrian, Lebanese and Iraqi forces, the weakest of the Arab armies, had already been more or less contained.

But before the IDF would be in a position to strike effectively at the Egyptians, it needed to accomplish a number of things. The soldiers of the Negev Brigade, the "Wild Beasts of the Negev" with whom Marcus fought during the war's first week, had been the front line of defense against the Egyptians for nearly four months. They were exhausted and their ranks depleted. The Negev Brigade was in no position to spearhead an assault. A fresh brigade, fully equipped with jeeps, heavy guns, and half-tracks, had to replace it. The replacement brigade, with its equipment, would have to be transported to the Israeli areas of the Negev.

These tasks were complicated by the fact that the Egyptian army encircled Israel's Negev settlements. In the past, Israel had maintained a limited stream of supplies with nighttime patrols across Egyptian lines, and using the single-engine Piper Cubs and Austers of Ralph Moster's Negev Squadron. But now a larger-scale effort would be needed.

In early August, Ben Gurion called a meeting of his top military advisers. Ben Gurion asked Yigal Yadin, the Southern Front commander, whether it was possible to open a corridor through Egyptian lines. Yadin thought Israeli forces could break through, but did not believe the passage could be maintained for more than ten or fifteen hours. That might not provide enough time to move the two brigades, and would only allow the supply trucks a one-way trip south.

Ben Gurion then asked Aharon Remez whether the air force could resupply the Negev. It was a moment the air force commander had long awaited. From the beginning of the war, he had sought to convince the IDF of the benefits of air power. In his view, the IDF had not yet fully utilized the air force. Remez believed the army could have avoided tragedies like the deaths of the thirty-five Haganah soldiers sent to relieve the Etzion bloc, if only it had involved the air force in more of its operations.

Remez told Ben Gurion that the air force could accomplish all of the IDF's goals for resupplying the Negev, and in a short period of time. Remez's only concern was a shortage of fuel. There was probably enough to carry out the airlift, but unless more was found, the air force might not be in a position to conduct operations following the resupply effort. Aware that plans were underway to locate more fuel, Ben Gurion assigned the Negev resupply to the air force.

The air force, in turn, assigned the mission to the newly arrived ATC. After leaving Zatec, the ATC had relocated its operation to Ekron. Fresh from the Hotel Stalingrad and the Zlaty Lev, the transport crews were now housed in the Bristol, a ramshackle, three-story hotel in downtown Tel Aviv. Little more than a week after completing the Czech airlift, the ATC would begin a new one.

But the ATC's C-46's, giant planes by Israel's standards, could not fly into the Negev until there was an airstrip long enough to accommodate them. Leo Gardner, one of Schwimmer's early hires, helped select a site near the settlement of Ruhama. There, Israeli bulldozers flattened two nearly mile-long strips in the desert sand, one for landing and one for take-off. There was no time to pave the makeshift runways, however. When the first C-46 arrived for a test landing, its engines kicked up an enormous cloud of desert sand, enveloping the nearly two-story plane. Leo Gardner, the pilot for that first trip, immediately suggested the airlift be designated Operation Dust. The name stuck.

For security reasons, the air force decided that Operation Dust flights would be flown during the night only. In the darkness, the huge planes would be less vulnerable to Egyptian ground fire. Also, by keeping the C-46's out of the encircled Negev during the daylight, those planes would not be exposed to the Spitfires of Egypt's air force. Even flying only at night, though, the air force was confident it could complete the airlift in only a matter of weeks. The flying time between Ekron and Ruhama was less than thirty minutes, allowing the same plane and crew to fly as many as three or four missions in a single night.

The ATC wanted to place someone at Ruhama, to command over the new base and help coordinate the airlift from the Negev side. It sent Canadian Bill Novick, one of the C-46 pilots. Novick, who had originally been recruited by Syd Shulemson, had been on one of the crews that brought the three B-17's from Florida to Zatec.

With everything in place, the airlift began on August 23. The routine was always the same. The planes would take off from Ekron and climb quickly to 5,000 feet for the flight south. As the C-46 neared Ruhama, the radio operator would contact Novick, who then ordered the lighting of a line of flare pots between the strips. Those flare pots, which were immediately extinguished once the transport plane had touched down, were Ruhama's only runway lights. Invariably, the Egyptians would fire on the approaching planes, sending up waves of inaccurate and ultimately harmless tracer fire. Once the plane had landed and the dust settled, the work of unloading men and equipment began, followed immediately by the loading of departing members of the Negev Brigade. For the return flight, the plane would again climb quickly for the short flight over Egyptian forces back to Ekron.

Harvey Sirulnikoff, one of the original members of Michael Landshut's artillery unit, took one of these flights out of the Negev. Sirulnikoff had been a reluctant recruit to artillery from the start, and during the second truce had slipped away from his unit and joined the Palmach. It was a measure of the casualness of the new Israeli army that Sirulnikoff's action was not unusual – nor was it considered improper. In fact, Sirulnikoff had considered another offer before hooking up with the Palmach, one from a fellow Canadian named Leo Heaps.

Heaps spent World War II in the British army, rising to the rank of major. He had been part of a joint American, British, and Polish force that parachuted into occupied Holland in September 1944. The goal of that operation had been to capture five major bridges behind enemy lines. The fifth bridge, Arnhem, eluded the Allies' grasp. Casualties were staggering, exceeding those of the D-Day invasion. (The mission was the subject of the movie *A Bridge Too Far*, starring Robert Redford.) Hundreds of soldiers were captured by the Germans, including Heaps. He escaped his German captors by jumping out of a train, and made his way back to Allied lines. He then returned to Holland, where he helped two hundred fifty men from the original assault force escape. Heaps' actions won him the Military Cross.

In Israel, Heaps tried to establish a jeep-born commando unit – "Heaps Jeeps." He had some grand schemes, most of which were never realized, including a crossing into Jordan to assassinate King Abdullah. Sirulnikoff declined the invitation to join Heaps Jeeps, and set his sights on the Palmach.

The Palmach assigned Sirulnikoff to the Negev Brigade. Together with a group of thirty other Palmachnicks, Sirulnikoff infiltrated across Egyptian lines into the Negev to join the rest of the brigade. The group was lightly armed. In fact, only about half of the men carried rifles. In the event of a firefight, those who were unarmed were to take weapons from those who were armed – as they fell. Compounding their difficulties, few of Sirulnikoff's new comrades had ever received formal military training. As a result, they did not know how to remain silent during the nighttime infiltration across Egyptian lines, and their noisy passage drew Egyptian gunfire. The fire was not accurate, though, and Sirulnikoff's group passed through without incident.

In late August, Sirulnikoff's unit waited at Ruhama to be airlifted out of the Negev. It would be the first plane ride in Sirulnikoff's life, and for nearly all of the other soldiers. As the men prepared to board the plane, the pilot, an American, stood before them. "If anyone needs to throw up," he announced, "do it now. I don't want anyone messing up my plane."

Unlike the first truce, which had only been scheduled to last four weeks, the second cease-fire was open-ended. As a result, Israel did not know when the next round of fighting might begin. The air force was therefore desperate to complete the airlift as quickly as possible. There were flights seven days a week, including on the Sabbath. Yom Kippur, the holiest day in the Jewish year, fell during Operation Dust. But the airlift took precedence, and that night Norm Moonitz piloted a C-46 down to Ruhama.

As he had done many times before, Moonitz gently guided his plane over Egyptian lines, the darkness pierced only by the flashes of tracer fire below. He banked the plane toward the makeshift runway, waited for the flare pots to be lit, and landed. Moonitz continued up the dirt runway toward the unloading area. He cut the engine, and waited.

Normally, before the propellers had even stopped turning, soldiers were at the plane's door ready to unload its precious cargo of arms. This time, though, there was no one to meet Moonitz's plane. He climbed out of the C-46 and walked over to the primitive wooden shack that was the only building at the airstrip. One man was on duty inside. "Where is everybody?" demanded Moonitz. "Everyone is in synagogue for Yom Kippur" came the reply. Moonitz was furious. "I'm as Jewish as they are. If they are not here in ten minutes to unload this plane, I'm going to kick all of this crap out onto the runway." It was a threat that Moonitz would not have to carry out.

On one occasion, a C-46 became stranded at Ruhama. At Ekron, the plane had been loaded with a pumping station. But no one had thought about how the giant piece of equipment might be unloaded in the primitive conditions at Ruhama. All night, soldiers worked to try to get the pumping station off, until finally someone came up with a solution. A truck was loaded with large drums, and then backed up to the doors of the C-46. The tops of the drums were level with the floor of the transport plane, and the pumping station was pulled out of the plane and onto the drums. But it was dawn before the equipment was finally extracted, and the plane was exposed. The army was worried that the Egyptians might try to strafe the valuable plane. Novick volunteered to fly it back. At the normal airlift altitude of 5,000 feet, the C-46 would be a sitting duck for the Egyptian gunners. Novick therefore decided to fly just above the tree tops in a mad sprint back to Ekron. On his way north, he passed over an Egyptian gun emplacement, and could see the sleeping soldiers. By the time they had roused themselves, Novick was already out of range. He made it to Ekron unscathed, the only daytime flight during the airlift.

The air force did not let Ben Gurion down. In little more than two weeks, the ATC flew over four hundred sorties, bringing in more than 2,200 tons of weapons and supplies, removing one entire brigade and flying in its replacement. By September 9, Operation Dust was complete.

The Negev airlift was not the only thing occupying the air force during that second truce. It now had a heavy bomber squadron and transport squadron to assimilate. At the same time, the air force needed to organize its other squadrons with their hodgepodge collection of aircraft, and to deploy those squadrons in airfields throughout the country.

At the beginning of the truce, the 101 Squadron was in a deplorable state. Of its complement of eight Me 109's, only one was in flying condition. The Czech plane had been nearly a complete disaster. Crack-ups on take-offs and landings were nearly daily occurrences. Its most serious drawback was only discovered weeks after the first Me 109's arrived in

Israel. The plane's two nose-mounted machine guns were supposed to be synchronized with the revolutions of the propeller. This allowed the pilot to fire the guns between the prop blades. But several pilots who test-fired their guns found holes in the blades when they landed. The guns didn't stay in synch. The pilots believed the problem with the guns cost Bob Vickman his life, theorizing that he must have shotdown his own plane during the aborted raid on El Arish.

The plane functioned so badly that a rumor began to make the rounds. There were those who believed that the factory where the planes were made – the same factory previously used by the Germans to make Messerschmitts – had been purposefully sabotaged during the war by Czechs who were hostile to the Nazis. Whatever the cause, the unpredictability of the plane took a substantial toll on the morale of the fighter pilots. Some quietly transferred out of the squadron, or left the air force altogether.

In July, a solution to the Messerschmitt problem began to take shape. In addition to the Me 109, the Czech air force also had in its arsenal more than fifty Spitfires. The Spits had been flown during the war by Czech pilots in the RAF. After the war, the British had allowed the Czechs to take the planes back to their homeland. But the Czechs were phasing in Russian fighters, and the Spitfires were available. On July 15, the Czechs agreed to sell fifty of the Spits to Israel. The deal allowed Israel to visit the different Czech bases where Spits were deployed, and to select the planes that were in the best condition. There had not been time, though, for Israel to choose the planes, much less transport them to Zatec or dismantle them for transport, before the Israelis were expelled from the country. Both sides were still prepared to go forward with the sale, and Israel looked for another way to bring the planes over.

Shortly after the Czech deal was signed, the first Spitfire began service with the 101 Squadron. That plane, though, had not come from behind the Iron Curtain. When, on the first day of the war, Max Alper had shot down an Egyptian Spit that was attacking the Tel Aviv airfield, the pilot of that plane had managed to crash land on the Tel Aviv shore. The plane was not flyable – a wing had been torn off and the propeller badly damaged – but much of it was intact. From that day, the Israelis held out hope that the plane could be repaired and pressed into service on Israel's side.

For that purpose, the air force called on David Panar, a professor of engineering at the University of Alberta who had come over after grading exams for the spring 1948 semester. Panar, who had been recruited by Ben Dunkelman, had been with the British Air Commission during the war. The air commission was a civilian arm of the RAF. As part of his work, Panar had worked on many of the different planes flown by the British during the Second World War, including Hawker Hurricanes, Hamdon bombers, and Heath Canucks. Panar, the air force believed, could help repair the Spit. "There was only one little itty bitty thing they forgot to check," recalls Panar. "I had never seen a Spitfire in my life."

Panar quickly disabused the Israelis of the notion that the plane could simply be repaired and flown again. The Spit had suffered too much damage in the crash. At a minimum, the wings, propeller, and engine would have to be replaced. The Israelis claimed to have spare parts available, something Panar initially found hard to believe. But they took him to an old British supply base where, to Panar's surprise, he found ten acres of aircraft parts and spares that the British had abandoned. On closer examination, though, Panar realized that much of the material was unserviceable. In fact, some of the equipment had been obviously sabotaged by the departing British. There were propellers with blades hacked off, and Rolls Royce engines, the type used in the Spitfire, with their crank cases smashed. "It's too bad the British damaged all the crank cases," Panar commented to his Israeli companions. Because the crank case in the Egyptian Spit had also been damaged beyond repair, there would be no way to run the plane's motor. "Wait," they told the engineer, "we have another field."

And so they went to another former British base. The second site also had a dump filled with aircraft parts, including Rolls Royce engines. These engines had also been sabotaged, but the British had not coordinated their efforts at the two bases. The magneto on every engine was destroyed, rendering them unserviceable, but the crank cases had not been touched. It would be a simple matter to take an engine from the second field, replace the magneto with one from an engine at the first field, and piece together one working engine. The search had also yielded a replacement wing assembly, and the process of piecing together the Spitfire began to get underway in earnest on June 15.

The work proceeded over the next few weeks. Panar was aided by a former RAF rigger and some Spitfire manuals that the air force had scrounged up. By mid-July, it seemed as though the plane might actually get off the ground. It was then that Panar approached the air force for guidance on a critical decision regarding the plane's configuration. The wings were from a Mark IX, a fighter version of the Spit. The fuselage, though, had come from a Mark XII, a photo-reconnaissance model. "What do you want," asked Panar, "we obviously can't have both."

"Why not?," asked the Israelis. They felt there would be great value in a plane that could both fight and take pictures. And so it was. Panar's crew installed fifty-millimeter cannons in the wings, and a Fairchild photo-reconnaissance camera in the fuselage. On July 23, Panar's twenty-second birthday, the Spit took off on its first test flight. It flew, and remained in service for the rest of the war.

But the 101 Squadron would require more than Panar's hybrid Spit to be an effective fighting force. The Czech Spits were clearly still needed. A way would have to be found to get them out of Czechoslovakia without the C-46's. The air force assigned Sam Pomerantz, a gifted aeronautical engineer and pilot, to the project. Pomerantz, married and the father of two children, was older than most of the other volunteers. He was devoted to his family, and brought them over to Israel shortly after his own arrival.

Pomerantz travelled to Czechoslovakia with Dave Panar and another volunteer to select the planes that Israel would purchase, and determine the best way to bring them to the Middle East. The Czechs took the three men to the different airfields where the Spitfires were based. There they examined log books to determine which planes had the least flying time. Of these planes, they paid particular attention to the condition of the tires and propellers – parts that could not be repaired or replaced in Israel.

With the selection of the Spitfires completed, Pomerantz turned his attention to the problem of getting them to Israel. At first, it did not seem that the planes could simply be flown to their destination. The range of the Spitfire was limited, and the U.N.-imposed arms embargo made it impossible for Israel to secure landing permission for the many refueling stops that would be needed between Czechoslovakia and Israel. But reviewing literature on the Spitfire, Pomerantz learned that they had occasionally been fixed with long-range tanks during World War II for ferry flights over great distances. In fact, the Spitfire that Buzz Beurling had flown to Malta had been customized in this fashion. Long-range Spitfire tanks, however, were not available. Pomerantz came up with an alternative. He thought Messerschmitt tanks could be attached to the wings of the Spitfire, and that a pumping mechanism could be fashioned to deliver the fuel from the auxiliary tanks to the plane's main tank during flight. The additional tanks, alone, would not be enough to guarantee that the fighters could cover the more than fifteen hundred miles that separated Czechoslovakia and Israel. Fuel efficiency would have to be increased by stripping the planes of all non-essential equipment, including radio compasses. Even that would not allow a non-stop flight to Israel, however. There would still have to be one refueling stop along the way. The issue of securing permission for the planes to land for refueling was one for the government to resolve.

Pomerantz and Panar went to work modifying a first group of Spits, and by late September six planes were ready for the first flight. That flight would essentially be a test run. If it worked, the Czechs would allow the Israelis to transport more planes in the same manner. Otherwise, Israel would likely be forced to transport the planes by sea, a time-consuming process that might not allow the fighters to arrive before the end of the war. In the meantime, the Yugoslavians agreed to allow the Spitfires to refuel at an airfield at Podgorica. There, an Israeli Constellation would greet them. The Constellation would then, like a giant mother bird, guide the fighter planes for the remainder of the flight to Israel. Without their radio compasses, the Spitfires would have no chance of navigating themselves. To avoid any political entanglements, the Yugoslavians insisted that the Spitfires be unmarked, and that the Constellation be painted with a Soviet red star on its side.

The air force gave the ferry operation an official name. For reasons that seem to have been lost to history, it chose the name Velveeta – after the cheese of the same name. The pilots for Operation Velveeta were a mixture of Americans, South Africans, and an Israeli. Pomerantz, unwilling to impose risks on others that he was not prepared to assume himself, insisted on flying one of the modified planes. On September 22, the Spits left for Yugoslavia. There, one plane was damaged when its landing gear failed to deploy, and had to be left behind. On the second leg of the journey, two of the remaining five planes landed at Rhodes – too low on fuel to make it all of the way to Israel. The Greeks seized those Spitfires. But three of the planes, including the one piloted by Sam Pomerantz, made the long journey safely, proving it could be done. Operation Velveeta was a success. There would be another ferry flight.

After Velveeta, the 101 Squadron suddenly had four Spitfires in its arsenal, with the promise of more to come. 101 pilots who had never flown the British fighter quickly checked out on the new plane. Most found it easy to handle – a dramatic improvement over the unpredictable Me 109. In the same month that the Velveeta Spits landed, a group of three Canadian fighter pilots, all with extensive experience on the Spit, also arrived in Israel. The timing could not have been better. John McElroy, Denny Wilson, and Jack Doyle would accomplish great things in the new fighters.

Of the three new additions to the squadron, McElroy was the biggest catch. With the death of Beurling, McElroy would be the most accomplished fighter pilot to fly for Israel. His lightly-scarred face, the result of one of his two wartime crash landings, gave some hint of his extensive combat experience. McElroy's eleven and one-half aerial victories made him Canada's eighth leading ace of the war. Most of those victories were in Malta, where for a time McElroy and Beurling flew in the same squadron. Like Beurling, McElroy was a hard worker. During his initial flight training, he rose hours earlier than the other trainees, to squeeze in two extra flights before the other men ate breakfast. McElroy's involvement with Israel began in May 1948. He was living in Vancouver at the time, when two Jewish acquaintances approached him about helping to recruit flyers for Israel. Over the next few months, he contacted more than forty of his acquaintances from the air force – all non-Jews – many of whom agreed to fly for Israel. One of McElroy's recruits was Len Fitchett from Victoria, who would prove to be a spectacular pilot. One night, the police paid a visit to McElroy's wife, inquiring about her husband's activities. McElroy's contacts thought it best for him to get out of the country until things quieted down, and he headed out to Israel to join in the flying himself.

In Geneva, on his way to Israel, McElroy ran into two other Canadians who were also making their way to Israel. The two Canadians, Jack Doyle and Denny Wilson, had also flown Spitfires during the war. Doyle, a swaggering fighter pilot who had shot down two enemy planes at Anzio before being shot down himself, had initially signed on to train Israeli pilots in Italy. Later, he too decided to continue on to Israel as a pilot. For the final leg of their journey to Israel, the Canadians flew from Rome to Haifa. They were joined on that flight by American Wayne Peake, a former P-51 Mustang pilot from North Carolina. At the Haifa airport, the four fighter pilots presented themselves to an American officer who was part of the U.N.'s truce supervision force. The Canadians were armed with false identification. Doyle, of Irish descent, was given the name "Yochanan Ha'Iree" ("John the Irishman"). Peake didn't have fake papers. Instead, he had prepared a cover story to explain his visit to the war-torn, Mediterranean country. "I'm a fur salesman," he explained to the startled American officer. "Oh, God, you don't expect me to believe that one," the officer told Peake. "Oh, yes," Peake assured him, "I'm selling all sorts of furs." They all passed through the inspection without incident.

The success of Peake and the three Canadians in getting past the American truce monitor had little to do with the quality of their forged papers or Peake's story. By this time, the monitor was well aware that Americans and Canadians were entering the country to join the fighting. He had no desire, though, to interfere with this process. Once, he was confronted with a group of new arrivals, all of them obviously military volunteers. "Do any of you speak English?" he asked. "No," they responded. Nevertheless, he explained that if any of them were of military age, they were not allowed into the country. The men all shrugged their shoulders as if they didn't understand. "Off the record, does anyone need a ride into Haifa?" he asked. "Sure, we all do," one of the Americans answered. The U.N. monitor drove them to town.

There were other new arrivals to the 101 Squadron during the truce. One of these was test pilot Chalmers "Slick" Goodlin, a giant figure in American aviation. As an employee of Bell Aircraft, he had flown the famed X-1 experimental jet to the threshold of the sound barrier. Millions of Americans knew his face from Gillette ads that featured the dashing young pilot – the fastest man alive. But with Goodlin on the brink of making aviation history, the air force decided to take the project in-house, and to assign one of its own to the history-making flight. A short while later, Chuck Yeager replaced Goodlin, and stepped into the pages of aviation history as the first human to travel faster than the speed of sound. At the suggestion of a Jewish friend, a Hollywood producer named Joseph Berg, Goodlin agreed to fly for the Israelis.

Leo Nomis, an American Indian, also joined the 101 Squadron during the second truce. Nomis had enlisted in the RAF at the beginning of World War II, not willing to wait for the U.S. to get into the fighting. He served with the RAF on Malta, for a time in the same squadron as Buzz Beurling. Like the Canadian pilots, he brought a wealth of Spitfire experience to the 101 Squadron.

With the new planes and pilots came a change of scenery for the air force's only fighter squadron. Aharon Remez, the air force commander, decided to move the 101 out of the Ekron field, crowded now with the fleet of newly-arrived ATC planes. Ekron was within range of the Egyptian guns, and, perhaps more ominously, the Spitfires of the Egyptian air force. Remez wanted to move the 101 north, away from the Egyptian threat. A new field was established in the orange groves outside of Herzliya, more than ten miles northeast of Tel Aviv. The pilots moved from their hotels in Tel Aviv to the Falk Pension, a small residential hotel in the nearby town of Kfar Shmaryahu.

As more planes and pilots entered the country, the air force now had the opportunity to more formally organize itself. At the Ramat David airfield in the north, the same base where the B-17's of the Hammer Squadron were located, the air force deployed another new squadron – the 103rd. The 103 was a medium bomber squadron. Its fleet of planes included four Bristol Beaufighters, twin-engine attack bombers that had been smuggled into the country in a particularly ingenious way. The war surplus planes had been purchased in Britain through a front company. Israeli agents then established a film production company, which leased the planes from the front to make a film about the exploits of New Zealand Beaufighter pilots during the Second World War. On August 1, 1948, the planes took off with the cameras rolling and vanished – reappearing hours later in Israel after a refueling stop in Corsica.

The Beaufighters were in terrible condition, though. Over time, one of the four would have to be cannibalized for parts, in order to keep the other three in the air. They were still regarded as death traps, and some of the flyers privately wondered whether the person behind the purchase of the planes had been more interested in making money than in helping Israel. Many of the 103 Squadron's flyers were South Africans, although its ranks included several American pilots. Sam Boshes was one of these.

Boshes had flown a B-26 bomber during the Second World War. That plane was considered so dangerous to fly that it came to be known as the "Widow Maker." Boshes flew sixty combat missions over Europe with the 450th Bombardment Squadron. The five-foot-seven-inch New Yorker was highly regarded by his crew, who referred to him affectionately as "The little Jew from Jew York." When an injury prevented him from flying for several weeks, Boshes' men refused to go up with another pilot. They had good reason to be loyal. Time and again, he proved himself a cool-headed, resourceful pilot. One such occasion was on July 18, 1944, during a mission over Paris. According to the laconic entry in Boshes' flight log: "Heavy flak - received a direct hit on right side of plane - top turret smashed - windshield splintered - nose wheel hit - right tire flat - right engine on fire - co-pilots headset wire cut two inches from head - rear gunner wounded in leg - came back on single engine - left engine sputtered and cut out, crash landed on English coast." And there was another flight, this one on April 21, 1944, over St. Pol, France: "Severe damage - left engine hit - front ammo box hit, fire started - almost bailed out - bombardier put out the fire - left formation and came home alone - wing flaps were riddled, caused bad trim."

Tryg Maseng, the blond Norwegian-American who had left his studies at Columbia to join the ATC, was another 103 Squadron pilot. Maseng had begun the war as a non-Jewish volunteer, but he did not finish it that way. While stationed at Ramat David, he decided to convert to Judaism. Maseng had not been circumcised as an infant, and Jewish law required him to undergo the procedure as part of the conversion ritual. Maseng was undaunted. "If Arabs can do it at the age of thirteen, I can do it as an adult," he announced. He arranged for the ceremony to be performed at Ramat David, and all of the pilots attended.

Boshes' and Maseng's new squadron also flew Dakota transports, which Israel modified to fly bombing missions. To turn the Dakotas into bombers, ground crews pulled or propped open the cargo and emergency doors, and partitioned the floor with two-by-fours into a small checkerboard. Fifty-kilo bombs were placed in the spaces created by the partitions. One of the great military specialties of the War of Independence was that of "bombchucker." That title applied to those who flew in the cargo area of the Dakotas during bombing runs. On a signal from the pilot, a bombchucker would lift a bomb from the floor. The bomb would then be passed from one bombchucker to another, until finally it reached a bombchucker who was straddling the open doorway, secured to the plane with a safety rope. That last man would pull the pin from the bomb and push it through his legs and out the door, like a football center hiking the ball to the quarterback.

The Hammer Squadron underwent some reorganization during the truce. Ray Kurtz, the commander of the Cairo raid and the 69th's first squadron leader, left to return to the ATC. Bill Katz took his place. Other crewmen, borrowed from the ATC for the first B-17 raids, returned with Kurtz to the transport squadron. Brooklyn fireman Norm Moonitz was one of those who went with Kurtz.

Moonitz and Kurtz were always a pair. One night, the two walked into the Park Hotel bar in Tel Aviv. It was filled with members of the air force, including Aharon Remez, the air force commander. "Norman and I decided we're going to inaugurate the official salute of the Israeli Air Force," Kurtz announced. A hush fell over the room. All eyes were on the two former firemen. "In the American air force, we salute like this," Kurtz continued, and he and Moonitz executed razor-sharp American salutes. "In the English air force, they salute like this," Kurtz went on, and he and Moonitz performed the open-palmed British salute. "We'll show you what the Israeli Air Force is going to do." Kurtz and Moonitz walked to opposite sides of the bar. They turned, and walked toward each other. When they were only a few feet apart, they stopped and clicked their heels. Each man then slapped his forehead with an open hand, and called out "Oy Vey!" It was a hit.

Under Bill Katz's command, ground crews continued to work on the heavy bombers throughout the lull in fighting, completing the hasty refitting work that had begun in Czechoslovakia. In addition to restoring the B-17's as much as possible to their original condition, an attempt was made to add a distinctively Israeli touch to the planes. Scientists at the Weizman Institute developed what they thought would be an extremely potent psychological weapon. They built an octagonal shaped ball, large enough to be seen from hundreds of feet below the plane but small enough to be deployed from the back of a B-17 through the tail gunner's position. The surface of the ball was dotted with different-colored lights. There were also vents, through which smoke would escape from inside of the ball. The idea was to release the ball, which was tethered to the plane by a cable, out of the back of the bomber during a low pass over Arab positions. The ball's flashing, multi-colored lights and billowing smoke were supposed to simulate missile fire, making the Arabs think that Israel had obtained some of these advanced weapons. In the words of Max Cohen, the flight engineer for the first test flight, "It was supposed to scare the hell out of the Arabs."

On the appointed day, American Jim McConville climbed into the pilot's seat of the B-17. Cohen was in the back of the plane, manning the cable. McConville took off, and swung the giant plane out over the Mediterranean for the test. He signaled Cohen, and the flight engineer released the ball. Immediately, the whole plane started to whip violently back and forth as the ball reached its full extension. Afraid the pilot was about to lose control of the plane, Cohen quickly grabbed a pair of wire cutters, and severed the cable linking the experimental device to the plane. The B-17's would not carry the simulated missiles.

Not all of Israel's efforts during the truce were devoted to offbeat projects. Israel also used the truce period to add other, more conventional weapons, to its arsenal. But these additions were, on occasion, made in distinctively non-conventional ways.

15

THE *LINO* AND THE *KEFALOS*

The motive for the Czech government to sell arms to Israel remains a mystery. Some believe the Czechs needed hard currency for their post-war recovery. Most suspect the Soviets were behind the arrangement, trying to undermine Britain's interests in the Middle East by helping Israel. The Russians may also have hoped that, after the war, Israel would ally itself with the East rather than the West, given the fact that many in Israel's ruling party were socialists. It may be that the truth is some combination of these.

One episode suggests the Czechs may have been motivated more by money than ideology. In the spring of 1948, before Israel's independence, the Haganah learned the Czechs had agreed to sell the Syrians an enormous quantity of weapons. The arms were to travel to Syria on an Italian ship called the *Lino*. The deal included 10,000 rifles, eight million bullets, hand grenades, and explosives. It was an amount of firepower roughly equal to the entire arsenal of the Haganah. Ben Gurion was determined to prevent the arms from reaching their destination.

On March 28, the Haganah decided to bomb the *Lino* as it sailed south through the Adriatic. The "bomber" for the mission would be the lone C-46 that Leo Gardner and Steve Schwartz had flown to Italy a few weeks earlier. The Haganah wanted Gardner to fly the transport plane low over the *Lino*, so that a crew in the back of the plane could roll a fifty-kilo bomb onto the ship below. Despite his misgivings about what was clearly a risky, desperate mission, Gardner and Schwartz dutifully took off with the bomb on board to look for the *Lino*. Not surprisingly, they were unable to find the arms ship in the open sea. They aborted the mission and returned to Italy.

Fortuitously, the *Lino* experienced engine trouble, forcing it to dock at an Italian port. The Haganah's contacts were particularly strong with the Italian authorities. With their connivance, the *Lino* was moved to the port of Bari, where the Haganah would have a better chance of blowing up the ship. But before the Haganah could attack, it had to confirm that the ship was carrying weapons. Steve Schwartz still had a role to play in the *Lino* saga.

One day shortly after the ship arrived at Bari, Schwartz was having a beer in a cafe near the port. Schwartz offered an American cigarette to a stranger sitting next to him. With American cigarettes in great demand in post-war Italy, the stranger was extremely grateful. The two men began to talk, and the Italian mentioned that he was a port official. Schwartz handed over the rest of the pack of cigarettes. He told the port official that, as a former marine radio officer, he was curious what the radio room looked like on the *Lino*. "No problem," the Italian told him. He took Schwartz aboard the ship and introduced him to its radio operator. While on board, Schwartz confirmed that the *Lino* was carrying weapons. With that information, the Haganah sent a team of frogmen to blow up the ship. The team planted a limpid mine on the hull. The charge blew a hole in the ship's bottom, sending the *Lino* and its cargo of arms to the bottom of the harbor. But the story didn't end there.

A few months later, after Israel's independence, the Syrians sent an army officer to Italy to salvage the *Lino*. Israeli agents, with the help of the Italians, kept close tabs on the Syrian operation. Israel had no desire, however, to foil the Syrians at this stage. It had other plans. The Syrians would need to hire another Italian ship to transport the salvaged cargo, and the Israelis secretly arranged for them to obtain the *Argiro*. Unbeknownst to the Syrians, two of the engineers on the *Argiro* were Israeli agents. When the ship passed beyond Italy's territorial waters, the two engineers stopped the engines. A short while later, a small fishing boat with two men in Syrian army uniforms pulled alongside. They advised the Italian captain that the ship was in danger of being attacked. The officers explained that they would stay on board for the duration of the voyage, using communication equipment they had brought along to stay in touch with Syrian authorities.

The Syrian officers, in fact, were Israeli agents. They promptly began radioing to a second ship, a yacht Israel had recently purchased and sent to Italy for refitting. On board the yacht were a dozen armed Israeli agents. One of these was Aaron Lebow, a former Aliyah Bet crewman from New York. Lebow had sailed to Israel on the *Northland*, the *Paducah's* companion ship. He had avoided deportation to Cyprus by hiding with Jack Yeriel in the ship's water tank.

The Israeli yacht pulled alongside the *Argiro*. Lebow and the other members of the boarding party clambered aboard. There was no resistance from the unarmed crew, and control over the arms ship was quickly established. One of the Israelis took the wheel of the Italian vessel, and the two ships sailed to Haifa. There, the *Argiro's* cargo, some eighty percent of the original Czech shipment, was unloaded. Operation Pirate, as the mission had been known, was a complete success.

The seizure of the Syrian arms was not the oddest chapter in the story of Israel's arms procurement effort. That honor belonged to the *Kefalos*. The saga of the *Kefalos*, like that of the *Lino*, began before Israel became a state. In April of 1948, the Haganah asked Al Schwimmer to follow up on a tip that it might be possible to buy spare airplane engines and parts from a dealer in Hawaii. For the inspection trip to Hawaii, Schwimmer recruited Hank Greenspun, a tall, rugged man who had served as an ordinance officer on General Patton's staff. Greenspun was living in Las Vegas, trying to launch a new radio station. But when Schwimmer explained why he was needed, Greenspun couldn't say no. With no time even to say goodbye to his wife and two young children, he flew immediately to Los Angeles, and from there on to Hawaii.

When he reached Oahu, Greenspun contacted Nathan Liff, the owner of the Universal Airplane Salvage Company. It was Liff's call to Service Airways that had prompted Greenspun's trip. Liff took Greenspun on a tour of the salvage company's grounds. Among the hundreds of acres of junk, all of which would eventually be melted down by Liff's company, Greenspun saw the crated airplane engines. But the former ordinance officer, who knew nothing about planes and engines, was more interested in the hundreds of machine guns that littered the area. Although used, a quick inspection of their actions showed the guns still worked. Even more exciting to Greenspun was a sea of new machine guns, barrels and gun mounts – all located in a second field a mere fifty feet beyond Liff's. The adjacent yard was a United States Naval Depot, and the weapons there belonged to the U.S. government.

Greenspun quickly established a rapport with the gray-haired Liff, who spoke English with a strong Yiddish accent. Both men had been affected deeply by the Holocaust, a subject they discussed briefly at the beginning of the tour. Feeling that he could trust the older man, Greenspun explained the true purpose of his trip. He was not really in Hawaii to buy spare engines and airplane parts for a civilian airline. Instead, he needed the materials for the Jews of Palestine, who soon would be fighting for survival against the Arabs. Greenspun wanted the run of the salvage yard to take whatever he needed, and he asked Liff for his help. Liff was quiet for a moment, and then looked into Greenspun's eyes: "This is God's honest truth, Greenspun?" "It is, Mr. Liff," came the reply. Liff didn't hesitate. "Take what you need. Forget about money. It's all yours."

Greenspun learned how to operate a forklift, and each night loaded the used machine guns into crates. As a former ordinance officer, he knew that gun barrels would need to be replaced during battle. The new barrels sitting in the adjacent naval depot yard were too tempting to resist. But the navy was not simply giving them away. The depot had a pair of marine guards who patrolled at night in opposite directions between the two fields. Undaunted, Greenspun observed that every two hours, there was an eight-minute span when both guards were far enough away to allow a dash across with the forklift. Night after night, Greenspun grabbed cases of new barrels to add to his increasing haul of guns from Liff's yard.

He soon realized, though, that he could not select the proper aircraft engines without help. He sent a message to Schwimmer, asking for assistance. Schwimmer dispatched Willie Sosnow, another of the original Service Airways volunteers. "Are you out of your mind?" asked Sosnow, when Greenspun told him about the gun barrels from the navy yard. But Greenspun was not to be deterred. At the end of each night's work, the two packed the engines, guns, and barrels into engine crates. After a few weeks, they had amassed forty-two crates with airplane engines, and sixteen more with machine guns and barrels. These would now have to be shipped to California. From there, the plan was to take them by boat to Mexico, where they could be loaded onto the Service Airways C-46's as they headed south on their way to Panama.

But the first of many problems presented itself. It would cost six thousand seven hundred dollars to ship the crates to California. It was money that Greenspun simply didn't have. Liff and Greenspun, whom the older man had come to refer to affectionately as "Hankela," had by this time grown extremely close. Greenspun again took Liff into his confidence. The salvage company owner didn't have all of the funds himself but, at Greenspun's request, he invited twelve local Jewish businessman to a gathering at Liff's apartment. Both men spoke briefly, and cryptically, to the gathering about their need for money. After being introduced by Liff, Greenspun said only: "It's simply this. Are the Jewish people going to live or are they going to die?" Liff announced he would give the first seventeen hundred dollars, and asked the businessmen to come up with the other five thousand. Within five minutes, and without asking any questions, the twelve guests put together the rest of the money.

Relieved his adventure was over, Greenspun flew back to Las Vegas. But a week later, he learned the authorities in Hawaii had been asking questions about the shipment. The Haganah was concerned that the guns, which had just arrived at the port in Wilmington, California, might be seized. Greenspun flew out to California immediately.

Greenspun decided to get the guns out of the dock warehouse before the federal authorities could act. With a borrowed truck and a group of volunteers the Haganah recruited, he separated the sixteen boxes from the rest of the shipment and transported them to a Los Angeles warehouse owned by a surplus dealer sympathetic to the cause. The next day, as the Haganah had feared, agents of the U.S. Customs Bureau arrived at the Wilmington dock, armed with a seizure order for the entire Hawaiian shipment. But when the warehouse was opened, they were annoyed to find that sixteen of the forty-eight boxes had disappeared. The F.B.I. joined in the search for the missing crates.

It now became imperative to get the guns out of the U.S. as quickly as possible. With the federal authorities hot on the trail, the surplus dealer whose warehouse now held the missing crates got cold feet, and demanded that they be removed immediately. Greenspun decided the only option was to get the guns onto a boat for Acapulco – it was too risky to simply transfer them to another warehouse. From Acapulco they could be transported overland to Mexico City, as originally planned.

But before the weapons could travel to Mexico, they would have to be readied for the voyage. The guns needed to be taken from their crates, smeared with cosmoline preservative for protection against moisture, and wrapped in tarpaulins. Film producer Bernie Fineman found volunteers who were able to prepare the guns for shipment. Lenny Cohen, a UCLA student, was one of the volunteers. Cohen's father had recently passed away after a long illness. As his father lay on his deathbed, Cohen asked whether he thought a Jewish state might be created in Palestine. "In my lifetime it never happened, and in your lifetime it never will either. But the least you can do is send money," the elder Cohen told his son. Cohen wanted to do more than send money, and helping to prepare the Hawaiian weapons for shipment was a good first step. Later, he would travel to Israel to join the fighting himself.

The search for a boat for the Acapulco trip took nearly a week. After much effort, Greenspun found the *Idalia*, a sixty-foot yacht owned by Lee Lewis, a young Jewish captain who was sympathetic to the Haganah. Lewis agreed to take the guns to Acapulco, asking only for expenses. It was a decision he would soon regret.

The *Idalia* was moored at a Wilmington yacht club, directly across the bay from an enormous lumberyard. Greenspun did some reconnaissance. He noticed that trucks entered its grounds all day long, but were only checked upon departing. Better still, the huge stacks of lumber that covered its grounds provided ample space for a truck to hide, so that its continued presence would go unnoticed at closing time. Greenspun decided the safest method of loading the boat was to truck the guns into the lumberyard before closing, hide the truck among the lumber stacks, and then load the guns at night onto the *Idalia* – which would sail over from the yacht club across the bay.

On the appointed day, the weapons truck drove into the lumberyard. Its load included one hundred fifty canvas tarps filled with guns and barrels, each tarp weighing nearly two hundred pounds. After night fell, twenty-four volunteers snuck into the yard to transfer the weapons from the truck to the boat. The process was more difficult than anyone imagined. The battery on Lewis' boat died, forcing Lewis and Greenspun to borrow another boat in the middle of the night to ferry the heavy sacks of guns from the lumberyard to the yacht club. Back at the club, the sacks had to be moved again, this time to the *Idalia*. During the final transfer to the yacht, the gangway and then the boat's guardrail were broken, infuriating Lewis. Worse, the weight of the guns caused the yacht to ride so low that the closed portholes were barely visible above the water line.

The next morning, with all of the guns loaded and the volunteers gone, Lewis confronted Greenspun. "Get your stuff off my boat," he demanded. "What are you talking about?" a shocked Greenspun responded. "The *Idalia* can't take the load. She'll be at the bottom before we clear the breakwater," Lewis insisted. Greenspun was equally adamant. "Forget it. I don't have the time, the men, or any place to put the stuff." The men argued, with Lewis at one time suggesting that Greenspun simply buy the boat and make the run himself. But the operation had always been run on the cheap. In Hawaii, he had been forced to improvise to raise the money needed to ship the guns to California. Lewis wanted nearly three times that amount for his yacht, and Greenspun had no hope of coming up with the funds on such short notice, particularly with the federal authorities on the trail of the weapons. Finally, Lewis left the boat for a few hours, forcing Greenspun to choose between purchasing the boat or taking the guns off.

Greenspun quickly made up his mind. With Lewis gone, he called Bernie Fineman, asking the film producer to immediately dispatch a cook, a navigator and an engineer to the pier. When Lewis returned, Greenspun told him he had arranged for a second boat to meet the *Idalia* off Catalina Island. There, the weapons would be transferred, and the second boat would make the long voyage to Mexico. Lewis was suspicious, but reluctantly agreed to make the short voyage for four thousand dollars.

Greenspun's crew arrived that night. The engineer was Nat Ratner, who had sailed as a crewman on the *Exodus* nearly a year earlier. Al Ellis, the navigator, had earned two purple hearts on Okinawa. This would be his first mission for the Haganah.

Just before midnight, the yacht headed out of the port, bound for nearby Catalina Island. As the ship passed the breakwater on the way to the open sea, Greenspun moved toward Lewis. "There's no boat waiting for us at Catalina, Lee," he admitted. "The *Idalia* is going all the way to Acapulco and it's taking the guns with it." Under the circumstances, Greenspun advised, Lewis should simply go through with the original deal to sail the weapons to Acapulco for payment. "And if I don't?" challenged Lewis. Greenspun had prepared for the confrontation. He pulled a Mauser from his pocket, and pointed it at Lewis. "I'll blow your brains out and heave you over the side," he told the yachtsman. But Lewis, who didn't believe the threat, wasn't ready to give in. Greenspun brought the gun to Lewis' temple. "Will you take us to Acapulco, Lee? You have five seconds to answer, yes or no." Greenspun counted off, "one, two, three, four," but Lewis remained silent. Greenspun released the safety. "Five," he announced, and moved his finger to the trigger. "Yes!" gasped Lewis. Greenspun put the gun back into his pocket and walked away, relieved that Lewis had not forced him to shoot.

The boat continued toward Acapulco. In the Gulf of California, opposite Mazatlan, it ran into a powerful storm. Rain and wind pounded the ship, and it was buffeted by huge waves. Lewis instructed the crew to move to the rear of the yacht. He hoped their combined weight would lift the *Idalia's* bow over the approaching waves. But the maneuver didn't work. "We'll have to lighten ship! She'll go down if we don't dump at least half of the guns," he shouted over the roar of the storm. This time, Lewis had an ally in the ship's cook, who also urged Greenspun to throw some of the heavy guns overboard. Again Greenspun refused to budge. Having made it this far, he wasn't simply going to throw the guns away. Lewis was forced to continue fighting the crashing waves in the overloaded boat. The storm finally abated, and the yacht made it all the way to Acapulco.

At the Mexican port city, Greenspun left the *Idalia* to make arrangements to ship the weapons overland to Mexico City. The others stayed on board the yacht to await his return. Frank Morgan, a minor film star, was sitting on his yacht when the *Idalia* pulled in. Morgan knew the ship and her captain; he also noticed how low the yacht was riding in the water. A few days before, the American consul had asked Morgan and the other boat captains in port if they knew about a boat that had left Wilmington with a cargo of contraband. That boat, Morgan was now convinced, was the *Idalia*. He summoned Lewis to his boat, and urged him to report the matter to the American authorities. Lewis took Morgan's advice to heart. Without Greenspun's or the crew's knowledge, he went ashore and contacted the consul. Lewis disclosed that his boat was the one the U.S. authorities had been searching for. The consul thanked Lewis for the information, but told him that the U.S. couldn't act against the *Idalia* or her crew while she was in Mexican waters. Unaware of Lewis' actions, Greenspun completed the arrangements for the transshipment of the weapons to Mexico City, where they would be loaded onto Schwimmer's C-46's when they passed through on the way to Panama. Again, Greenspun thought his work was done.

The Haganah decided otherwise. It had been impressed with Greenspun's abilities as an operative. It abandoned the plan of loading the *Idalia's* weapons onto the transport planes. Instead, the Haganah dispatched an old freighter called the *Kefalos* to Tampico Bay, a port city a few hours north of Mexico City. The Haganah wanted Greenspun to purchase more arms in Mexico and South America – enough to fill, together with the weapons from the *Idalia*, the cavernous holds of the *Kefalos*. Greenspun immediately plunged into his new assignment. In the first week alone, he purchased thousands of Springfield rifles, together with ammunition; thirty- and fifty-caliber machine guns; aerial bombs; seventy-five -millimeter howitzers, and even several old cannons from the days of Pancho Villa. Those weapons alone cost more than one million dollars. Greenspun also bought two thousand tons of airplane fuel, enough to replace that used for the Operation Dust airlift. Slowly, the ship began to fill with Greenspun's purchases.

But then the operation began to fall apart. The *Kefalos'* destination and cargo had become open secrets, and local Arabs demonstrated against the ship. The pressure on the Mexican government was not just internal. The U.S. and Great Britain also weighed in, demanding that the Mexicans not become a party to a violation of the arms embargo. Greenspun needed to act quickly. He told his Mexican contacts that the arms were actually being purchased on behalf of Chiang Kai-shek's Nationalist Chinese Army. Their sale, therefore, would not violate the U.N. embargo.

The story was not meant to fool the government, but only to give it a face-saving way to allow the weapons purchases and loading to proceed. At one point, trying to further muddy the waters, Greenspun told a writer from the weekly *La Semana* that he was actually buying arms for the Arabs.

The pressure continued to build on the Mexican government. Finally, it told Greenspun the ship could sail only if he provided documents proving the *Kefalos* was carrying arms for Nationalist China. That Sunday, Greenspun walked through the streets of Mexico City with Willie Sosnow, trying to decide what to do next. Greenspun noticed a sign for the Chinese Embassy. The gate was open, and the two men walked in. Inside they found the second deputy consul in an otherwise empty building. The two Americans feigned an interest in investing in Taiwan, and the consul excused himself to retrieve some literature from another office. Greenspun sent Sosnow after the consul, and quickly raced through the building. He found an unoccupied office, and started looking through the desk. He grabbed some stationery and matching envelopes, as well as large metal seals and stamp pads. Greenspun stuffed the materials in his pockets, and went back out to the entranceway. A few moments later Sosnow and the consul reappeared, and Greenspun quickly pulled Sosnow outside.

Greenspun arranged to have the *Kefalos'* inventory of weapons typed onto the Chinese stationary, and then embossed the pages with the seals. He delivered them to his contacts in the Mexican government, and waited. By now, the ship was fully loaded, and ready to leave the moment it got clearance. Saturday evening, less than a week after Greenspun's visit to the Chinese Embassy, one of his contacts tipped him off that at eight a.m. Monday morning, the government would issue an order to unload the ship and seize its cargo. Greenspun raced to the airport, and chartered a plane for Tampico. There he headed to the docks and tracked down the chief customs inspector, one of the men who had to clear the ship before it could leave. Greenspun told the inspector the government had given its permission for the ship to depart, showing him the false Chinese documents and slipping the official a large bribe. The inspector then summoned immigration officials, who also needed to clear the ship. Greenspun bribed them as well. Greenspun then met with an army major in charge of a contingent of troops guarding the ship. Greenspun convinced him the ship had been cleared, and the major agreed to remove his soldiers from the *Kefalos*.

Everything was in place. Greenspun needed only to instruct the captain to set sail before eight a.m. on Monday. But the captain was in no mood to comply with Greenspun's order. Devoted to Israel, the sailor hadn't known what to make of the stories that the guns he would be carrying were really bound for the Chinese – or the Arabs. He also didn't like Greenspun, who for several months had been entertaining prominent Mexican officials in a luxury hotel in Mexico City while the captain and his wife languished in the squalor of the Mexican port town. "I give the orders around here," he shouted at Greenspun. "Now get the hell off my ship." The two men argued further, but the captain wouldn't budge. Finally, Greenspun pulled out his Mauser. "Get ready to leave Tampico," he told the captain. "If you don't, I'll take over this stinking tub and sail her all the way to Haifa without you." The captain hesitated for a moment, and then relented. The next morning, with Greenspun watching from the shore and Ratner and Ellis on board, the *Kefalos* sailed out of Tampico.

Oddly, after everything that had happened in Hawaii, California, and Mexico, nothing further interfered with Greenspun's mission. Neither the British nor the Arabs attempted to confront the ship at sea. It simply pulled into Haifa Bay toward the end of the second truce, and unloaded its valuable cargo.

Israel did not use the second truce solely for purposes of rearming. As the weapons of the *Argiro* and *Kefalos* made their way to Israel, so did large numbers of Americans and Canadians. In the end, most of the foreign volunteers would arrive during these months of relative quiet on the battlefield.

16

AND STILL THEY COME

"Better that you should die in Palestine," Dr. Sternhill pronounced, completing his medical exam. Tiny Balkin laughed. In fact, Tiny wasn't tiny at all. The dark-haired, stocky ex-marine stood six feet tall and weighed over two hundred pounds. He had volunteered to fight for Israel, and needed the Los Angeles doctor's medical clearance before he could make the trip overseas with the other volunteers. During the physical, the doctor discovered that Tiny had high blood pressure. But Doctor Sternhill, a Jew, was sympathetic to the former marine's desire to go to Israel to fight, and gave him a clean bill of health.

Tiny's decision to volunteer had come to him suddenly. One night in 1947, Tiny and his mother went to see *Monsieur Beaucaire*, starring Bob Hope, at the Paramount Theater in downtown Los Angeles. Before the movie, a newsreel showed the British dragging Jewish refugees off of an Aliyah Bet ship. He turned to his mother and said simply, "I'm going."

A few days later, he went to the Los Angeles offices of Land and Labor for Palestine to volunteer. Within several months of Tiny's physical, Land and Labor put him and another local volunteer on a train to New York. There, Land and Labor hid the two Californians in a large summer home in Peekskill, New York, until transport could be arranged across the ocean to France. The organization used the Peekskill home as a hideout, to keep American volunteers out of the city and away from the FBI's prying eyes until the next stage of their journey to Israel.

Tiny and his travelling companion were not the only future Israeli soldiers billeted in Peekskill. When they arrived, they found another dozen or so already staying there. One of the first new faces Tiny encountered was that of Bostonian George Tzizik, who had been assigned to bunk with Tiny. That first day, Tiny was sitting on his bed, chatting with Tzizik who was unpacking his bag. A woolen cap caught Tiny's attention. "It's hot over there. You're not going to need a stocking cap," he chided Tzizik. "It's a stump cap," responded Tzizik. As he looked down, Tiny caught a glimpse of wood in the space between Tzizik's right pant leg and sock. Tzizik had a wooden leg.

He told Tiny how it happened. Tzizik had been a member of an infantry unit that was advancing on German lines near the Ruhr River on November 16, 1944, a few months after D-Day. As Tzizik's platoon of twenty-seven men neared the German positions, they spotted a farmhouse and concealed themselves in its courtyard. The men fired the platoon's four mortars at the Germans. The Germans fired back, but the rock walls of the courtyard shielded the platoon from the German artillery.

Just then, American bombers from the Eighth Air Force passed overhead, on their way to attack the German positions. Tzizik wasn't impressed. He was sure the platoon's mortar fire was inflicting more damage than the air force's heavy bombers. The presence of the bombers also made Tzizik uneasy. More than he feared the enemy, he worried about the danger of friendly fire. He was afraid that some green pilot would lose his nerve at the first sign of anti-aircraft fire and drop his bombs early, hitting the troops he was supposed to be helping. But the bombers passed over without incident. The men continued to fire their mortars as fast as they could be loaded. One of the mortars became so heated from the firing that it bent, trapping a live shell in the tube. They discarded the useless mortar, firing the other three even faster.

All of a sudden, Tzizik heard the sound of an incoming shell. It was from a 105 Howitzer, an American gun. After spending months on the front line, it had become second nature for Tzizik to identify an artillery piece from the sound of its shell. As the whistle of the shell drew nearer, the men scrambled for cover. There was nowhere to go. The rock walls, which had so effectively protected the men from the Germans, now created a killing zone. The Howitzer shell hit the courtyard, spraying shrapnel in every direction. Screams and moans filled the air as shrapnel ricocheted off the walls, ruthlessly cutting down Tzizik's platoon. Tzizik felt a terrible pain in his right leg and fell to the ground, losing consciousness to the sound of his comrades dying around him. Of the twenty-seven men in the courtyard, only Tzizik and two others came out alive.

Tzizik's survival came at a steep price. His wound was serious, and the doctors had to amputate his right leg just below the knee. Infection set in following the operation, and he was not expected to live. Tzizik fought back, and the loss of a leg was not enough to keep him from travelling to Israel to fight.

Tiny soon discovered that he and Tzizik were not the only ones at Peckskill with physical ailments that should have disqualified them from military service. George Baler had terrible eyesight, and was virtually blind at night. His glasses were so thick that Tiny thought they looked like the bottoms of milk bottles. Baler's vision kept him out of World War II, but now he wanted to do his part for Israel. Only twenty-two, Baler was the oldest volunteer at the summer home.

Not everyone in Peekskill was in bad shape. Mort Levinson, another Boston native, was there with his brother Fred. A college football player, Mort was lean and muscular. Fred had just finished serving with the U.S. Army, and was also fit for military service. But the Levinson brothers stood out for a different reason. While most parents were doing everything they could to keep their sons from fighting for Israel, Mort and Fred's mother wanted her sons to go. "She felt that we should try to make a contribution to the establishment of the State of Israel," recalled Mort. She did, however, have one request of her two sons. She feared losing both of them, and asked them to serve in separate units to minimize the risk.

The time in Peekskill passed slowly. There was little to occupy the men, other than a basic Hebrew class taught by a young, red-haired Israeli woman. Otherwise, they sat around and talked, or strolled in the woods surrounding the summer home. The men grew bored and restless, and were anxious to continue on to Israel. Finally, after about a week, they received word they would be moving out to Europe. Their adventure was about to begin.

The Peekskill group traveled to the offices of Land and Labor in New York City for a briefing before continuing on their journey. Ehud Avriel, one of the Haganah's top operatives in the United States, addressed the men. He told them they would be traveling from New York to France on the *Marine Falcon*, a converted World War II liberty ship. Avriel then turned to a discussion of security measures required for the voyage. He told the Americans to board the *Marine Falcon* one at a time, not to talk to each other during the trip, and not to talk with anyone else on the ship about Israel. "Everybody is listening," he cautioned them. Avriel also instructed the Americans to come up with cover stories to explain why they were travelling from New York to France. When the *Marine Falcon* arrived at the French port of Le Havre, he continued, the men would be met by a local Haganah representative. They would recognize him by the pipe he was carrying in one hand, and by the Yiddish newspaper rolled up under his other arm. Tiny thoroughly enjoyed the briefing. "Fantastic," he thought. This was the adventure he had been looking for.

After boarding the ship and settling in, it soon became obvious the men would not be able to strictly follow their instructions. The *Marine Falcon* retained much of its military design. Instead of private cabins, the passengers were berthed in men's and women's dormitories. Each dormitory housed twenty to thirty passengers in bunk beds that were four tiers high. For whatever reason, Tiny's entire group was assigned to the same dormitory.

Still, Tiny took seriously what he heard in New York. By coincidence, a group of his friends from California, members of the Zionist youth group *Habonim*, were also travelling on the *Marine Falcon*. They were heading to Israel to form a new kibbutz, and were quick to engage Tiny in conversation about the situation in Israel. He gave the group his cover story. He was going to Paris to study art. They tried to interest him in Israel and Zionism, but the ex-marine wouldn't budge. "I live for my art," he told them.

As the ship pulled into the harbor at Le Havre, Tiny and the others scanned the dock, looking for their contact. Soon, they spotted someone with a pipe and Yiddish paper. "This is so silly," thought Tiny, "this guy stands out like a sore thumb." Just then, to the amazement of Tiny and the others, the man shouted in the direction of the group, "Hey, are you the guys going to Palestine?" But no one at the dock seemed to notice or care what the group of Americans was up to. The men gathered around the French Haganah representative for instructions on the next leg of their journey.

From the port city of Le Havre, Tiny and the others went by train to Paris, where they spent their first night in France. Before heading to their hotel, the group went to a secret Haganah office near the Champs Elysees, where each man received 1,000 francs to cover his expenses during the stay in France. The group then split up for the rest of the evening. Near-sighted George Baler took his money and headed for the closest French bakery. Most of the others behaved in a fashion more typical of young men going off to war. They went to enjoy themselves in Pigale, Paris' red light district.

After a few nights at a small hotel in Paris, the men took a second train ride, this time to Marseilles in the south of France. There were a number of Jewish displaced persons camps in the Marseilles area. The Haganah used the DP camps as assembly points, where refugees and fu-ture soldiers were brought together for transport to Israel. Tiny's group headed to the San Jerome DP camp.

San Jerome was a sprawling, dusty facility with a mixture of bar-racks and tents to house the hundreds of Jewish refugees living there. Barbed wire surrounded its grounds. It was a closed camp, and the DP's could not leave without permission. Next to the camp was a hospital for the criminally insane. As they went to bed each night, the DP's, many of whom had survived the Holocaust, were subjected to the crazed laughter of the hospital's inhabitants.

While most of the residents of San Jerome were survivors, there were also Jews from Morocco and other North African countries. They had been expelled from their homelands as revenge for Israel's Declaration of Independence on May 14, 1948. Whatever their backgrounds, all of the DP's shared one thing in common. They had a fervent desire to live in the one country that wanted them. Together, the residents of San Jerome waited to go to Israel.

Tiny's group chafed at being stuck in the camp, until one of the men discovered a hole in the camp fence. One day, a few of the men snuck into Marseilles in search of a decent meal, only to learn later that the beef they thought they had eaten had actually been horse meat. Whenever they went into Marseilles, the men were careful not to attract the attention of British agents attempting to keep tabs on Israel's activity in the area.

The Americans had been in the camp nearly a week when Haganah agents woke them in the middle of the night and told them to get ready to leave immediately for Israel. The agents instructed the men to speak only Yiddish or, if they didn't know Yiddish, not to speak at all during the journey. That subterfuge, together with forged documents identifying the Americans as DPs, was supposed to fool the United Nations inspectors at the port of Haifa.

Together with some three hundred camp residents, Tiny and the others rode on trucks to the nearby beach. From there, they walked several miles, until they saw a one-hundred-twenty-foot fishing boat moored offshore. After looking it over, George Baler reassured himself that this little boat would take the passengers to a ship, which would then transport the group to Israel.

The fishing boat, however, turned out to be the ship that was to take the Americans and the refugees all the way from France to Israel. Formerly an Italian vessel, the Haganah renamed it the *"Mishmar Ha'Emek"* in honor of a kibbutz of the same name. After purchasing the ship and hiring its Italian crew, the Haganah modified it to accommodate four hundred passengers. Below deck in the ship's hold, the Haganah created two levels, each with three rows of shelving to serve as beds. The beds were designed to occupy as little space as possible. They were three feet wide by six feet long, with only three feet of space separating each bed from the one above it. Oil lamps lit the crowded sleeping area.

But the living quarters were not the worst part about travelling on the *Mishmar Ha'Emek*. For toilets, the Haganah constructed two platforms adjacent to the ship's deck. A passenger needing to go to the bathroom had to stand on one of these platforms, literally over the open sea, and relieve himself through a hole in the bottom of the makeshift latrine. The small boat also lacked cooking facilities for such a large load of passengers. With no room to install a proper galley, workmen had taken several large barbecues and bolted them to the ship's wooden deck.

While the Italian crew was in charge of sailing the ship and the Haganah had overall command, it was the job of the Americans to try to make the voyage go as smoothly as possible for the DP's. For most of the volunteers, the time spent in the camp and on the ship represented their first contact with either Holocaust survivors or Jews from North Africa. Both groups of passengers made an impression on the Americans.

The survivors' stories haunted Tiny. One man told how he and other prisoners in his camp were forced to crawl through the snow in the middle of the night, as the guards beat them with sticks to speed them along. As he crawled, the survivor heard a man cry out in pain, and immediately recognized the voice as his father's. The survivor could do nothing to help. Instead, he had to continue crawling in the snow, until the German guards let the prisoners return in their tracks to the barracks. On the way back, he found his father lying in the snow, blood pouring from a gaping head wound. The son packed the wound with snow and dragged his father back inside, saving his life.

The North Africans made a different kind of impression on George Baler. They apparently thought all Americans were like those they had seen in Hollywood movies. These refugees did not speak English, but whenever they would see one of the Americans, they would sing "Hey bob-a-re-bob," or point an imaginary Tommy gun and say, "Ra-ta-ta-ta-tat, Chi-ca-go."

The trip to Haifa took eleven days. At one point a British warship appeared on the horizon. The Israeli crew feared the British might attempt to interfere with the ship's passage, and ordered all of the passengers below decks. The conditions below were hardly comfortable. It was a hot September day and there was little ventilation in the hold, but the passengers only had to stay out of sight for a few hours. The two ships passed each other without incident.

Other than the episode with the warship, the most trying part of the voyage was the food. The passengers received little to eat – mostly tea and biscuits. Several of the Americans felt the need to supplement this meager diet, and ate the leftover pasta the Italian crew had thrown in the garbage. The Italians were not on the same subsistence diet as the passengers.

The approach to Haifa was emotional for passengers and crew alike. As the city came into view, all of the passengers gathered on deck. Everyone seemed alone with their thoughts, and there was total silence on the overcrowded vessel. As the boat entered Israel's territorial waters, the crew replaced the Italian flag with an Israeli flag. An Israeli agent on board punctuated the ceremony by firing a few shots from a Sten gun into the air. Then, almost in unison, the passengers broke into "*Hatikvah*," the anthem of their new state.

After arriving in Israel, Tiny and the others left the ship for an old British base in Hadera. There, the men were given physicals. Tzizik's turn came first. He was ordered to remove his shirt, and responded to a number of routine questions regarding his health. Everything seemed to be in order, and Tzizik put his shirt back on and turned to walk away from the doctor. "Wait," said the doctor. "What's wrong with your leg?" The doctor had noticed Tzizik's slight limp.

Having made it this far, Tzizik was determined not to be turned back. "I twisted my ankle. It's okay now," he told the doctor. To illustrate the point, Tzizik placed a chair in the middle of the room, took a running start, and leapt over it. The doctor was convinced, and cleared Tzizik to join a unit.

Tiny wasn't as lucky. The doctor took Tiny's blood pressure. After rechecking the absurdly high reading, he decided to send the former marine for further testing at the Weizman Institute. In vain, Tiny tried to convince the doctor to let him continue with the other men who had passed their physicals. The doctor would not be swayed, his decision seemingly ending any chance Tiny had of participating in the fighting. Tiny was not alone in his predicament. The doctor also suspected that a British volunteer had a heart ailment, and ordered more testing for the Brit as well. The other new recruits were given clean bills of health and were ordered to proceed to the main recruitment base at Tel Letvinsky, where they would receive their assignments.

Tiny was not ready to give up. He and the British volunteer snuck onto the bus to Tel Letvinsky, with everyone who had passed their physicals. The two took seats near the back, while two smaller recruits hid under the rear seat. Before the bus was cleared to depart, a soldier climbed on board, carrying a list of the men who were to report to Tel Letvinsky. He called out each name, and Tiny answered for the recruit whose place Tiny had taken. Sensing something might be amiss, the soldier asked

Tiny his father's name. "He's dead," said Tiny, as the real recruit frantically whispered, "Shmulik, Shmulik!" The soldier was satisfied, and didn't hear the whispers of the real recruit. The bus moved out.

At Tel Letvinsky, the men heard rumors about the Fourth Anti-Tank Squad. It was said to be a special unit run on democratic principles. Heading the Fourth was Lester Gorn, the former U.S. infantry officer who modeled the unit after Carlson's raiders. Tiny liked what he heard, and joined the unit. The Fourth would play an important role in the coming fighting.

The others who had traveled with Tiny were scattered among other units. Tzizik joined a naval unit based at the port at Atlit. Tzizik's unit – "*Chayl Ha'Nachita*" ("Landing Corps") – had been created by Amnon Lin and Ahia Ben Ami, two Israelis who wanted to pattern their unit after the United States Marines. Tzizik was assigned to train new recruits. When he arrived at Atlit, he and other members of the unit lined up before their commander, an Israeli veteran of the British army. The commander asked if any of the men had any infirmities. Having made it past the doctor at Hadera, Tzizik felt emboldened. "Well, I've got a wooden leg," he announced. The commander looked at him for a moment, and then laughed. "Come on, I know you Americans have a good sense of humor." Tzizik couldn't resist the challenge. He hitched up his pants and rapped his knuckles against the wooden leg. The sound was unmistakable. Stunned, the commander shouted, "What the hell are you doing here?" "What the hell do you think I'm doing here?" responded Tzizik, who launched into an impassioned speech about Zionism and the need to fight to establish a Jewish state and restore Jewish honor lost during the Holocaust. Tzizik's emotion convinced the commander. "Well, all right, you'll probably do the best of all of them," he said finally. Tzizik remained with the unit.

Mort and Fred Levinson honored their mother's request that they join different units. Fred went to the military police, where he would become the only American M.P. Mort followed the trail of many Americans and Canadians before him. He went to the Seventh Brigade, commanded by Canadian Ben Dunkelman. Before Tiny's group arrived in Israel, Ben Gurion and Chief of Staff Yaakov Dori decided to concentrate all of the American and Canadian infantry volunteers into Dunkelman's

Seventh Brigade, and in particular to its 72nd Battalion. Over time, the 72nd became known as the "Anglo-Saxon Battalion." Mort was assigned to the Seventh, although not to the 72nd Battalion. Instead, he ended up in the 79th Armored Battalion, the battalion formerly commanded by Joe Weiner and the home to far fewer Anglo-Saxons than the 72nd.

Tel Letvinsky's commander wanted to put George Baler and Mike Rubin into the Seventh as well. Neither wanted to go. Before coming to Israel, Rubin had studied Hebrew at the Hebrew Teacher's College in Boston, and he wanted to join an all-Israeli unit so he could add to his knowledge of Hebrew and become absorbed into the country. Baler felt the same way, and the two jointly expressed their preference to the base commander. But he was adamant, "You have to go to the Seventh. I'm giving you a command." The men stood their ground. "We're not going," they responded. This continued for a while, with neither side backing down. Finally, the commander offered the men a choice. He said, "Look, if you tell me you're religious, we'll send you to a religious unit. If you tell me you're communists, I'll send you to the Palmach."

For Baler and Rubin, the choice was easy. They could not pass up a chance to get into the elite unit. They told the commander they were communists, and were immediately taken to Palmach headquarters by jeep. The men received assignment to the Ninth Battalion of the Negev Brigade, the "Wild Beasts of the Negev" who had just been airlifted north during Operation Dust. There they would join Canadian Harvey Surilnikoff, whose own circuitous route to the Palmach had first taken him through Michael Landshut's artillery unit.

Things continued to move quickly for the new communists. After joining the Ninth in the south at Beer Yaakov, they received their basic training. They each fired three shots from a Sten gun and drove a makeshift armored car for one half-hour through the empty streets of the recently-captured Arab towns of Lydda and Ramle. When new Spandau and Beza machines guns arrived a few days later, Baler and Rubin also learned how to assemble and disassemble those weapons. That was the extent of their training.

The Ninth was an armored unit or, at least, it had what passed for armored cars in the Israeli Army. To construct each armored car, the army had taken an open command car, surrounded it with tin or plywood, and filled in the gap with gravel and sand to stop bullets. Outside of this, the army placed two thin metal sheets. In this respect, the armored cars were like the "sandwiches" the Haganah had used in its efforts to transport supplies to besieged Jerusalem. But these vehicles had more military trappings than the Haganah's convoy vehicles. The army installed a rotating turret with a light machine gun on the top, and placed a fixed turret with a light machine gun in the front. Four soldiers traveled in each armored car: a driver, a radio operator, a machine gunner for the top turret and a machine gunner for the front turret. Rubin and Baler were assigned to different cars, and each became a machine gunner.

While Tiny's fellow crewmen from the *Mishmar Ha'Emek* were settling into their new units, the small boat returned to France to bring over another group of DP's and soldiers. That voyage would turn out to be its last.

At the French port of Toulon, several hundred DP's and eight American military volunteers boarded the *Mishmar Ha'Emek*. The refugees were nearly all North Africans. Only about thirty-five of the ship's three hundred passengers were Europeans. Most of these were Holocaust survivors. One of the American volunteers for this trip was Lee Silverman, a U.S. Navy veteran who had left his studies at UCLA to join the fighting. Silverman was also a gifted basketball player. He had been a member of UCLA's freshman basketball team, a team coached by John Wooden, the man who would later become the greatest coach in the history of college basketball. Another member of this second group was Joe Becker. Becker was blind in one eye, the result of a childhood disease. Like Tzizik and Tiny before him, Becker hoped to hide his infirmity from Israel's military doctors.

There was a third American at Toulon that day who would inextricably link the last two voyages of the *Mishmar Ha'Emek*. Twenty-year-old Phil Balkin was Tiny Balkin's younger brother. Phil had always looked up to his older brother, and wanted to be like the combat-hardened former marine. After Tiny left California for the long trip to Israel, Phil began to think about joining him. The two corresponded, and Tiny did his best to convince his younger brother not to follow. In the end, and without telling Tiny, Phil rejected his older brother's advice.

The first four days of the voyage to Israel proceeded without incident. But then, without warning, a violent storm struck the *Mishmar Ha'Emek*. Gusting winds and enormous waves tossed the small fishing boat. At one point during the storm, Silverman stood on deck near the fantail and looked straight up at what should have been the sky. He saw only a sheet of water, spray from one of the giant waves crashing over the ship. Soon, the crew realized that the boat was taking on water.

The *Mishmar Ha'Emek* was in danger of sinking. The Israeli radio operator sent out S.O.S. calls, but there was no reply. Frantically, the crew tried to remove the seawater from the ship, but the water pumps failed. The passengers began to panic. There was only one lifeboat, and it could hold no more than forty people. Silverman and the other crewmen went to check on its condition. They found that it was already filled with the thirty-five Europeans. The Moroccans stood next to the lifeboat, screaming, "Save the children! Save the children!" The Europeans would not give up their seats. The Holocaust had honed their survival skills to a fine edge. The crew tried, in vain, to get them to budge, but finally gave up and went to tend to the ship. But then, as quickly as it arrived, the storm abated. The pumps were repaired and, for the next two days, the ship drifted as the crew pumped and bailed water out of the holds. Finally, it resumed its course for Haifa.

In addition to the usual difficulties of life aboard a crowded refugee ship, the passengers faced another problem. The Israelis always tried to place medical personnel on these ships. The assignment for this voyage of the *Mishmar Ha'Emek* was given to a Russian doctor. But the choice was a poor one, as Lee Silverman and many of the passengers were to discover. Bothered by a sore throat, Silverman visited the doctor, who gave him some peroxide to gargle. But what the doctor neglected to tell him was that the peroxide was concentrated. Silverman sustained severe burns over his mouth, lips and tongue when he tried to gargle with it. That act of malpractice paled in contrast to the Russian's other activities on the boat. The doctor gave the wrong medicine to three pregnant women who came for assistance during the trip. All three miscarried.

As the voyage continued, the passengers faced yet another problem. The crew had not anticipated the two days of drifting, and the supply of food was running dangerously low. Rationing was implemented. But soon it became clear that, even with the rationing, they could not make it to Haifa on the remaining supplies. The crew decided to dock at Crete, to purchase food for the remainder of the journey. As Crete came into sight on the horizon, however, another storm struck. Giant waves began propelling the *Mishmar Ha'Emek* toward a cluster of rocks that jutted out near the shore. The Italian captain, a graying man in his mid-sixties and a veteran of the sea, desperately tried to maneuver the ship away from the rocks. The ship's only engine churned furiously against the force of the storm. Without warning, the engine gave out under the strain. Nothing, it seemed, could stop the ship from being smashed. Overcome with fear, and helpless to prevent the impending disaster, the captain passed out. For the second time in six days, Silverman, Balkin, Becker and the others were convinced their end was at hand. But just as quickly as the first storm abated, this one too turned out of the path of the little ship. The *Mishmar Ha'Emek* came to rest fifty yards from the rocks.

There was still the matter of food. Once revived, the captain took the ship's lifeboat into port and returned a short time later with six live mountain goats. The *Mishmar Ha'Emek* resumed its course towards Haifa as the Americans set to work preparing the goats. While others primed the barbecues, Silverman slit the throats of three of the animals. But the galley had not been used in days, and a large grease fire erupted. The fire needed to be put out immediately, before it threatened the ship. With no fire extinguishing equipment available, the crew tore the barbecues from the deck and pushed the burning galley into the sea.

The *Mishmar Ha'Emek* reached Haifa port fifteen days after leaving San Jerome. During the trip, none of the Americans had showered, shaved, or changed clothes. As the ship docked, Lee Silverman peeled off each filthy piece of clothing from his body and walked off the ship stark naked. Some of the other crewmen did the same. Together, they walked into a warehouse where they were sprayed with DDT and given fresh clothes. Within a week of the *Mishmar Ha'Emek's* arrival, it sank in the still water of the port, never to sail again.

The Americans passed through the U.N. camp at Hadera, and then on to Tel Letvinsky. Like Tiny, Becker found his way to Lester Gorn's Fourth Anti-Tank unit. Phil decided to chart a course independent of his brother. Instead of going to the Fourth, he joined the 89th Battalion of the

Eighth Brigade, an armored unit composed mainly of South Africans.

On a leave from his unit, Tiny was walking in Tel Aviv when someone came up from behind and slapped him on the back. Tiny turned, and found himself face-to-face with Phil. Tiny had mixed feelings as he greeted his brother. He was happy to see him again, but disappointed that Phil had not followed his advice and stayed away from the fighting. Tiny now faced a dilemma. He couldn't decide whether to ask his brother to join the Fourth so he could keep an eye out for him, or let him fight with a different unit. Given the freewheeling structure of the army, Tiny could have easily arranged Phil's assignment to the Fourth. But the danger was obvious. If the unit was hit hard, both brothers could be killed. Tiny decided to let Phil go elsewhere.

It took Silverman a few weeks to find an assignment. For a time, he thought about joining a tank unit, but then he ran into a fraternity brother from UCLA. The fellow Bruin worked at air force headquarters. He told Silverman that he and many other Americans worked for air force intelligence, and that Silverman should join as well. Silverman took his friend's advice, and reported to the air force. When he arrived at air force headquarters in the Hayarkon Hotel in Tel Aviv, Silverman found an American ghetto. The intelligence branch was headed by American Nat Cohen, and nearly all of its personnel were Americans.

The Haryarkon Hotel also housed the air force's photo-reconnaissance unit. Americans Arieh Jacoby, another Hebrew University student, and Lee Goodwin, a non-Jew who arrived after the war began, established the unit. During the second truce, Yale Joffe, one of the Canadian members of Michael Landshut's artillery unit, had moved to photo-reconnaissance. The members of the photo-reconnaissance unit had varied responsibilities. They mounted cameras in several of the 101 Squadron's fighters, including the hybrid Spit that David Panar had assembled. Sometimes Joffe and the others had to take the pictures themselves, flying in a two-seater plane or tagging along on bombing missions in a B-17. For the B-17 shots, Joffe would stand in one of the waist gunner's positions. With another crewman holding Joffe to keep him from getting sucked out of the plane, he would extend his camera into the slipstream to photograph the bombs as they fell.

Tiny Balkin, Lee Silverman, and the others were part of a small flood of North American volunteers who came during the second truce. As the flow of volunteers increased, the army struggled to deal with their special needs. Few of the Americans spoke Hebrew, and most had no close relatives in the country. In other respects as well, their situation differed from that of the Israeli citizens with whom they served. The Israelis were required to be in the military. They couldn't simply leave when they decided they'd had enough. But the foreign volunteers were afforded this luxury. The Israelis resented it. And for some of the Americans, it made them less willing to submit to military discipline.

The army took a number of steps to ease the plight of the North American volunteers. The army agreed that the foreign volunteers should receive a supplement to their regular army pay, recognizing that these soldiers lacked the support structure that the Israelis had. Lee Harris, an American who had come in 1947 to work for the Palestine Economic Corporation, ultimately became responsible for distributing that supplemental pay to the Americans and Canadians. The money distributed by Harris was raised by the American and Canadian Jewish communities. The army also requisitioned the San Remo Hotel on Hayarkon Street in Tel Aviv, to serve as a recreation center for all of the foreign volunteers.

There were other efforts. The army distributed an English language pamphlet, "How to Get Along," that was intended to explain to the Anglo-Saxon volunteers some of the peculiarities of life in Israel. It had sections on such things as hygiene ("Don't touch unwashed fruit, street vendor's wares, or any food of whose freshness you are suspicious") and hotels ("If you go to a hotel, don't expect a room to yourself"). The pamphlet tried to prepare the English speakers for their first contacts with Israelis: "Boys and girls born here are fittingly enough called Sabras (cactus) - like the fruit of that name, prickly without and sweet within. You'll find that the equality of the sexes has gone further here than perhaps anywhere in the world. For example, girls have been serving in the front-lines with the men; they are without prudery and quick on the comeback."

The army also put one of the American volunteers, Harold Schiffrin, to work creating a military newspaper for the English-speaking soldiers. During World War II, he had been an editor of *Stars and Stripes*. The result of Schiffrin's efforts was *Frontline*, a high-quality paper with stories about some of the volunteers, news about the fighting, cartoons, and articles about Israel. There was even the occasional poem, like one called "Truce Without End" by an American volunteer named Judah Stampfer:

> *The pools of our minds are long since covered with leaves,*
> *And our backs are learning the decay of ripe fruit,*
> *Here in the trenches, behind green netting, on beds of pine needles,*
> *The pungent rosins stinging through our blankets,*
> *The dark comes swaying on the bars of branches,*
> *Gnats swarming through the tangled beards of roots,*
> *Ant patrols tickling across our wrists,*
> *Mornings it's pleasant oiling our rifles after we brush our teeth,*
> *And to shave, propping our pocket mirrors against the sandbags.*
> *Nights we stroll the lanes between the mine fields.*
> *Otherwise we read paper novels, and sing love songs to each other.*
> *Somewhere there was a war;*
> *And somewhere there was a peace.*
> *But that was long ago,*
> *And many insects have intervened.*

Despite the different efforts to help the foreign volunteers, some found the extended period of quiet too difficult to bear. Chris Magee was among them. A marine pilot during World War II, Magee had been a member of Pappy Boyington's legendary Black Sheep Squadron. With the Black Sheep, Magee had flown his combat missions wearing a bandanna, a tradition he continued when flying in the 101 Squadron. He was among the elite of the Black Sheep, with nine kills to his credit, the second highest total in the squadron behind Pappy Boyington. Magee received the coveted Navy Cross for a solo attack on a force of fifteen Japanese dive bombers.

Magee was not Jewish. But, like many of the Jewish volunteers, he had been moved by the Holocaust. Even before World War II, he had been troubled by the plight of the *St. Louis*, a ship loaded with Jewish refugees that had escaped Europe, only to sail back after no country – including the U.S. – would accept its passengers. When the fighting started in Israel, Magee's wife had commented to him: "It's a wonder you aren't involved in the Israeli thing." Soon, Magee was. He signed up at the Land and Labor office in Chicago in May 1948, and went to Czechoslovakia for training on the Me 109. Magee arrived in Israel in June, and stayed until October – returning when it seemed clear the fighting would not resume.

But Magee was wrong.

17

OPERATION YOAV

During the second truce, the Israeli General Staff carefully crafted its next move. Initially dubbed Operation Ten Plagues, the general staff changed the name of the planned offensive against the Egyptians to Operation Yoav to honor a fallen Palmach commander. The goals of the operation were to relieve the isolation of Israel's Negev settlements and to drive Egyptian forces from the area. The scattered Jewish settlements were surrounded by the Egyptians and thus physically separated from the rest of Israel. Political factors played an important role in launching Operation Yoav, as well. The Arabs were arguing they should receive the Negev, and had succeeded in persuading former U.N. Mediator Count Folke Bernadotte of their position. Before his assassination by dissident Jewish forces in Jerusalem, Bernadotte had made known his view that, in any final drawing of borders, the Negev should be Arab. Israel needed to occupy the Negev if it was to claim it.

The main headquarters of Egypt's Negev forces were in the towns of Gaza, Majdal, and Faluja. Operation Yoav's primary targets were these towns, as well as Iraq El Manshie and Iraq Suweidan, two strategic hilltop villages in the region separating the Egyptian and Israeli forces. At Iraq Suweidan, most of the Egyptian defenders were concentrated in the seemingly impregnable British-built fortress known to the Israelis as the "Monster on the Hill."

In September, as Rudy Augarten and the other fighter pilots waited for their chance, the ATC completed Operation Dust. Operation Dust laid the groundwork for Operation Yoav. With everything in position for the offensive against the Egyptians, Israel looked for a way to attack without violating the U.N.-sponsored truce that had been in effect since the last round of fighting ended in July. The terms of the truce permitted Israel to bring supplies to the besieged Jewish settlements of the Negev. Nevertheless, Egypt had been preventing Israeli convoys from passing through Egyptian lines. This was to be the trigger for Operation Yoav. At midday on October 15, 1948, Israel notified U.N. Truce Supervision Headquarters that an Israeli convoy was on its way to the Negev. As Israel expected, the Egyptians fired on the convoy, in full view of the U.N. observers. With Egypt firing the first shot, Israel was able to launch Operation Yoav without violating the truce.

As the sun set over the Negev only a few hours later, Israeli fighter planes and medium bombers swooped in to attack the Egyptian air base at El Arish. They caught the Egyptians completely by surprise. The Israeli planes shot up the air base, destroying four Egyptian Spitfires on the ground and demolishing the main hangar. That same evening, Israeli heavy and medium bombers attacked Egyptian troop concentrations at Gaza, Majdal, Bet Hanun, and Beersheba.

The air attacks were intended to aid the ground assault, which was set to begin several hours later. The combined air and ground operations represented an evolution in Israel's military strategy. Before Operation Yoav, Israel's ground and air forces had essentially fought separate wars. While the ground forces tried to enlarge the borders of the new state and defend areas under attack, the air force sought to neutralize the threat posed by the Arab air forces, and to ferry supplies and wounded soldiers. Beginning with Operation Yoav, the air and ground forces would regularly operate in coordination.

American Lou Lenart, one of the first members of the 101 Squadron, was excited about the prospect of increased air and ground coordination. That had been Lenart's specialty when he flew Corsairs with the marines in World War II. Lenart had pushed the concept to Aharon Remez, the air force commander, and Remez responded favorably. Lenart then had a crew customize a jeep to act as a command post in preparation for Operation Yoav. They armed the jeep by mounting a Spandau machine gun on the hood and a Beza machine gun on the back. The crew also installed radio equipment and hooked up a trailer with a generator. Lenart assembled a squad consisting of a radio operator and some gunners, and made final preparations to rendezvous in the south with the ground forces. His hope was to use the mobile command post to control the planes when they were over the battlefield, so they could immediately be assigned new missions depending on the flow of the battle.

Everything seemed set, when Lenart realized he had overlooked one thing. A bullet hole in one of the jeep's tires would cripple the whole operation. Lenart decided to pick up two spare tires, and he and fellow 101 pilot Coleman Goldstein went over to supply. Lenart asked the clerk for the tires, but the clerk refused. He told Lenart a written request was needed. It was already past five o'clock, and both men knew there was no way to get a written request until the next morning. By then it would be too late. Looking past the clerk, Lenart could see there were stacks of tires available. The two men argued back and forth, with Lenart becoming increasingly frustrated and angry. After all he had gone through in lobbying Remez and assembling a command post, Lenart was not about to give up. He grabbed a rifle, chambered a round, and placed the end of the gun between the eyes of the supply clerk. "Okay, you son of a bitch, you've got ten seconds to give me the tires or I'm going to blow you're fucking brains out." Goldstein, watching all of this, turned white. Lenart didn't have to count to ten. The clerk handed over the tires, and Lenart headed south to rendezvous with the ground troops.

On October 16, the second day of Operation Yoav, fighter pilot Rudy Augarten finally got his chance to fly. That was the mission on which he encountered the two Egyptian Spits, downing one before returning to base. Fellow 101 pilot Leon Frankel, who was also in the air that day and witnessed the battle, crashed a short time later, ending his career with the fighter squadron. Although the 101st had added to its arsenal the Operation Velveeta Spitfires and the one assembled by David Panar, the Me 109 continued to see action during this third round of fighting. Augarten was one of the few pilots who flew the unpredictable plane without mishap.

Like most of the volunteer fighter pilots, Augarten had flown combat missions in World War II. But he had an experience during the war that set him apart from the others. He was shot down over German-occupied territory, and was missing in action behind enemy lines for sixty-three days.

✡ ✡ ✡

It began on June 10, 1944, soon after D-Day. Leaving from a base in southern England, Augarten was on a search-and-destroy patrol in a flight of four P-47 Thunderbolts. The sky was overcast, and the planes came down through the clouds over the French town of Caen. Below, a battle raged between the Germans and the Allies. Caen was well-defended by the Germans, and anti-aircraft fire started to rock the planes. The pilots quickly pulled up to avoid the German flak. Suddenly, smoke began to fill the cockpit of Augarten's P-47. He had been hit.

"You're on fire!" one of the other pilots radioed to Augarten. Augarten's situation was critical. By now, the patrol had drifted further inland over German-occupied France, and Augarten needed to bail out. He opened the plane's canopy and dove over the side. The bailout did not go smoothly. Augarten had forgotten to take off his oxygen mask, and it hit him in the face. As he plummeted toward the ground, he groped for his parachute cord. It took a few moments, but he finally found it and pulled. Augarten landed in back of a French farmhouse.

As Augarten hit the ground, he had with him only the uniform on his back and an escape kit that contained some food and a little bit of money – but no gun. The farmer in whose field Augarten came down had seen the plane crash. The Frenchman ran out to give the pilot a pair of overalls, but, apparently fearing the Germans might come at any moment, quickly sent Augarten on his way. Augarten started walking and, after about a mile or so, came to another farmhouse. He knocked on the door, and a farmer answered. Augarten knew only a few phrases of French, and he used one then: "*Je suis American*" ("I'm an American.") The farmer talked with his wife, and the two decided to hide Augarten. But he still wasn't safe. German troops came by the farmhouse regularly, and each time Augarten hid in the attic while they searched the area.

After two weeks, Augarten felt he could no longer endanger his French hosts. He left early one evening and wandered through the countryside. He tried to work his way toward the front, hoping to sneak past the Germans and back to the American lines. As he walked, he was constantly on the lookout for German patrols. After hiking all night, he came upon another farmhouse, but this one looked strangely familiar. Augarten couldn't believe it – he had walked in a giant circle, and was right back where he started. He stayed for another week, but grew increasingly concerned about the harm to his hosts if the Germans found him. Augarten was also desperate to get back into action. He felt useless away from his unit, away from the war. There were railroad tracks a few hundred yards from the farm, and this time Augarten decided to follow the tracks toward the front line.

After walking for a while, he came upon some Frenchmen, and again identified himself as an American G.I. One of the men led Augarten to a ditch, where a group of British paratroopers who had been dropped off-course were already hiding. Augarten and the other soldiers stayed in the ditch for about a week. Each day, a Frenchman brought food. One day, however, he told the men he had seen Germans in the nearby fields. With danger so close by, he could not continue to help them. The men decided to break up into pairs and leave the area. Most decided to go to Spain, about five hundred miles away. But Augarten and one of the paratroopers decided to try to get through the front lines. Before going their separate ways, they divided up their weapons, and Augarten ended up with a pistol and a grenade.

That first night, Augarten and his partner encountered a group of German soldiers. From a distance, one of the Germans called out in Augarten's direction, "*Sind sie das, Karl?*" ("Is that you, Karl?"). There was no time to think. "*Ja,*" Augarten answered the soldier, using his scant knowledge of German to maximum effect, and walked away. Apparently convinced that he was another member of their unit, the Germans did not follow.

Augarten and the British paratrooper continued walking through the night. Several times, they crept past German soldiers sleeping in fox holes, as the two moved closer and closer to the front. As day broke, however, their luck finally ran out. They were walking down a road bordered on both sides by hedgerows when Augarten saw a German soldier a short distance away. "Halt!" the soldier shouted. "I'm going to give up," whispered Augarten's partner.

Augarten had other plans. He placed the grenade into his right hand, pulled the pin, and hurled it at the German. Augarten then scurried behind one of the hedgerows on the side of the road, finding shelter in a ditch. Chaos broke loose. The grenade exploded. The Germans began firing their machine guns wildly, raking the hedgerows. They were trying to get him to fire back and give away his position. Augarten kept still. The Germans stopped shooting and started to search the area. Finally, after about half an hour, they spotted him. This time, Augarten had no choice. He surrendered, and was taken prisoner along with the British paratrooper.

Augarten was relieved to discover that the Germans who captured him were not from the SS. Like all Jewish serviceman in the American military, his dogtags identified his religious faith with the letter "H," for "Hebrew." Augarten knew that, as a Jew, he would not have had much hope of surviving capture by the SS. But Augarten's captors were not interested in his religion. They took him and the paratrooper to an abandoned brick factory, where two captured Canadian pilots were also being held.

After three days, the prisoners were moved to a horse farm, which had been converted by the Germans to serve as a POW camp. The farm had a U-shaped building with nearly two dozen stables surrounding an open courtyard. In each stable, the Germans placed ten-to-fifteen Allied soldiers, separated by rank. Augarten, a second lieutenant, found himself in a stable with thirteen other officers.

Each morning, the Germans lined up the prisoners in the courtyard and counted them. Afterward, Augarten and the others were free to wander in and out of the stables, and talk to other prisoners. Soon after arriving at the farmhouse, Augarten met Gerald Gordon, a British paratrooper. Gordon worked in the farmhouse kitchen making food for the prisoners. Several days after the two men first met, Gordon smuggled a knife from the kitchen back into the stables and gave it to Augarten's group of officers. With the knife in their possession, the men began to discuss a possible escape attempt. Augarten wanted to go, as did Gordon, the two Canadian pilots from the brick factory, and two British officers. The rest decided to stay.

A few nights later, the six escapees gathered in Augarten's stall. Using the knife, they cut an opening in the stable's soft wood ceiling. One by one, each man climbed through to the attic above. After a short search of the attic, they found a window. They realized their plans had not gone unnoticed. Someone, probably the wife of the stable owner, had left a large dish of butter by the window. None of the six had eaten butter for weeks. The two British officers quickly dug in with their bare hands. Augarten and the others grew impatient. They wanted to move on as quickly as possible. The British finally finished eating, and the men huddled around the window. Looking out, they spied a guard making a pass every quarter hour. The window was about fifteen feet above the ground, and the men knew they risked injury if they tried jumping. Moving quickly, they fastened a rope from some extra clothes and, timing the guard's passes, lowered themselves to the ground.

The men went down in groups of two. Augarten watched as the two Canadian pilots lowered themselves down and ran across a street adjoining the stable. Augarten and Gordon went next. After sliding down to the ground, the two made their way across the street and into the woods. They hiked for a while, before running into a Frenchman who gave them some civilian clothes. But the two soon realized that the woods were slowing them down, and decided to try their luck on the roads instead. German tanks and trucks and refugees escaping the fighting choked the roads. Augarten and Gordon walked with the refugees, using them as cover.

Suddenly, Augarten heard a shout. "Halt!" He turned and saw two German SS officers motioning for him and Gordon to come over. Wearing French civilian clothing and carrying their uniforms in bundles under their arms, Augarten and Gordon walked over to the Germans. Augarten tried to remain calm, but he was gripped with fear. The SS officers began asking the men questions in German. Augarten responded in his broken French. Luckily, the Germans knew even less French than Augarten, and didn't realize the American barely spoke the language. The officers motioned for the two men to continue on their way.

The road became more and more clogged with Germans. Augarten and Gordon reluctantly decided it was too dangerous to continue walking out in the open. They found a farm and, after identifying themselves as

Some of the 101 pilots spend the day at the beach in Herzliya. *Standing, first and third from left:* Leon Frankel and Sid Antin. *Kneeling, first and second:* Bill Pomerantz and Giddy Lichtman. *(Courtesy of Red Finkel)*

American 101 pilots *(from left to right)* Giddy Lichtman, Bill Pomerantz, and Leon Frankel lean on an Me 109. The squadron logo is clearly visible on the left. *(Courtesy of Red Finkel)*

Many of the 101 pilots would crowd into one jeep for the ride from the Hayarkon Hotel to the airfield. *First, third, sixth, and seventh from left*: Rudy Augarten, Red Finkel, Leo Nomis and George Lichter. *(Courtesy of Red Finkel)*

Wayne Peake stands in front of an Me 109 that he has just ground-looped on take-off. *(Courtesy of Red Finkel)*

Members of Tiny Balkin's group await assignment: George Tzizik *(kneeling in front)*, Tiny Balkin *(seated, far right)*, George Baler *(standing, far left)*, and Mike Rubin *(kneeling on left)*. Notice Tzizik's wooden leg, slightly exposed below his right pant leg. *(Courtesy of Tiny Balkin)*

Tiny Balkin *(first from left)* with members of the Fourth Anti-Tank Squad. *(Courtesy of Tiny Balkin)*

Tiny Balkin. *(Courtesy of Tiny Balkin)*

American Indian Jesse Slade, a member of the Fourth Anti-Tank Squad. *(Courtesy of Tiny Balkin)*

The last group of Americans to sail on the *Mishmar Ha'Emek* at the San Jerome DP Camp before departure. Joe Becker *(second from left)*, Phil Balkin *(second from right)*, and Lee Silverman *(kneeling, center)* . *(Courtesy of Lee Silverman)*

Packed with refugees, the *Mishmar Ha'Emek* makes its final run to Palestine. *(Courtesy of Lee Silverman)*

On board the *Mishmar Ha'Emek*, Lee Silverman carries a mountain goat he has just slaughtered. Crete is visible to the right. *(Courtesy of Lee Silverman)*

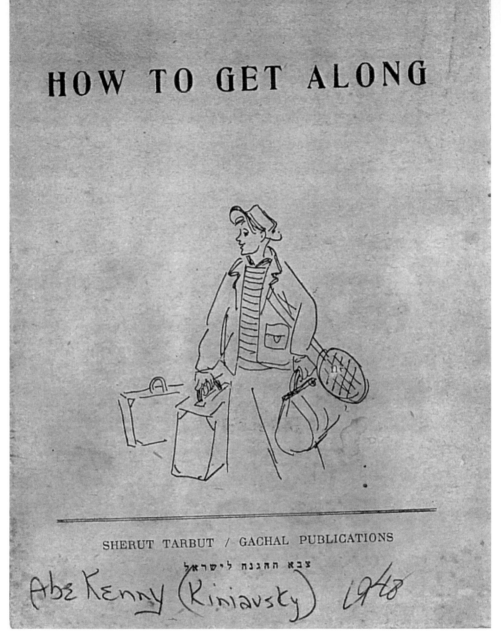

HOW TO GET ALONG

SHERUT TARBUT / GACHAL PUBLICATIONS

צבא ההגנה לישראל

Abe Kenny (Kiniavsky) 1948

An informational booklet published by the Israeli army to help foreign volunteers adapt. *(Courtesy of Abraham Kenny)*

Harold Schiffrin, a former editor of *Stars and Stripes*, was in charge of "Frontline," a military newspaper published for the English speaking foreign volunteers. *(Courtesy of Abraham Kenny)*

Joe Becker *(standing, third from left)* who came to fight despite a glass eye, joined Lester Gorn's *(standing, second from left)* Fourth Anti-Tank Squad. *(Courtesy of Tiny Balkin)*

Left: Eighteen-year-old Ralph Lowenstein, on his half-track. *(Courtesy of Ralph Lowenstein)* Right: A group of soldiers from the 79th Armored Battalion, on the day before the end of Operation Hiram. The building in the background is a former British police station on the Lebanese border. Ralph Lowenstein *(standing, first from left)* and Mort Levenson *(standing, second from right)*, shared a half-track. *(Courtesy of Ralph Lowenstein)*

TO CHRISTIAN
VOLUNTEERS

On behalf of the General Staff and of the Officers and Men of the Defence Army of Israel, I send you Christmas greetings and good wishes for a bright and happy year.

You, Christian volunteers in our Army, may be few in number, but you represent the many millions of non-Jews in many lands who, we are convinced are with us in our struggle for freedom and our battle for national independence. You are part of a noble tradition of men who have volunteered to fight for justice and righteousness which know no national boundaries. You are pioneers — pioneers in thought and action. To my knowledge you are the first Christians in history to take part in the field in Jewry's struggle for independence. You are certainly the first in history to celebrate Christmas on the soil of the State of Israel. I take this opportunity of thanking you for your help, expressing our appreciation of your courage and zeal and of your solidarity with our cause. You will be remembered in our annals.

A happy Christmas to you, and may the New Year bring peace and goodwill to all men.

YAAKOV DORI, Brigadier
Chief of the General Staff
Defence Army of Israel

A Christmas greeting from Chief of Staff Yaakov Dori to the Christian volunteers. *(Courtesy of Abraham Kenny)*

101 pilot John McElroy, Canada's eighth leading World War II ace with ten victories. *(Courtesy of Eddy Kaplansky)*

Canadian Jack Doyle *(right)* shot down four planes, to share squadron honors with Rudy Augarten. *(Courtesy of Eddy Kaplansky, Mike Finegood, Red Sturrey)*

101 pilot Denny Wilson flew Spitfires for Canada during World War II. *(Courtesy of Eddy Kaplansky)*

Former X-1 pilot Chalmers "Slick" Goodlin *(center)* was Israel's first test pilot. Canadian Lee Sinclair, a former RAF Wing Commander, stands above. *(Courtesy of Red Finkel)*

Phil Balkin (*second from right*) on his unit's half-track only days before he was killed. *(Courtesy of Tiny Balkin)*

Israeli casualties from the attack led by Phil Balkin's unit on Auja. One of the bodies may be that of Phil Balkin. *(Courtesy of Tiny Balkin)*

Lionel Druker, in winter battle gear, cuts a piece of bread with a butcher knife. (Courtesy of Lionel Druker)

Druker *(first from left)*, stands with his tank crew in the Sinai for the attack on Auja in December of 1948. *(Courtesy of Lionel Druker)*

Three AT-6's of 35 Flight fly in formation. *(Courtesy of Arieh Jacoby)*

Arabs surrendering en masse at Eilat, at the conclusion of Operation *Uvdah* ("Fact"). *(Courtesy of Lionel Druker)*

Lee Silverman *(first from right)* was one of the starting five players on the Israeli Air Force's championship basketball team. *(Courtesy of Lee Silverman)*

The outdoor basketball game, played against the U.S. Marines at the air force headquarters in Jaffa, was Israel's first international sporting event. *(Courtesy of Lee Silverman)*

Silverman *(fourth from left)* outscored the entire marine team. Note the marine uniforms. *(Courtesy of Lee Silverman)*

Allied soldiers, asked if they could stay. The owner was too fearful to allow them to stay in the house. However, he agreed to let Augarten and Gordon hide in a little shack on his property, about a half-mile away from the main house. They remained there for three weeks, receiving food twice a day from the farmer's young daughter, Madeline. Then, one day, Madeline told the two men that the Germans were growing suspicious. They were coming over to the house frequently, making it too dangerous for Augarten and Gordon to stay. The family directed the escapees to another area where some other soldiers were hiding.

A few miles away, Augarten and Gordon found a half-dozen black Senegalese troops in hiding. They had hooked up with members of the French underground. The group told the two that the Germans were retreating from the area. The Senagelese were thinking of more than simple escape from the retreating Germans. They were armed, and hoped to pick off some of the Germans. With Augarten and Gordon in tow, the Senagelese and their underground comrades positioned themselves along a road bounded on both sides by a ditch and a hedgerow. The men split up into two groups and hid behind the hedgerows. As dusk approached, a German soldier riding a motorcycle came speeding down the road. The men held their fire, and the motorcycle passed quickly and without incident. About five minutes later, the same motorcyclist came back from the opposite direction. This time, one of the men squeezed off a round. The shot missed, and the German sped off into the distance.

About an hour later, Augarten heard something coming up the road. He looked in the direction of the sound, and saw a group of soldiers marching alongside a tank. In the twilight, Augarten couldn't see the soldiers very well. All of a sudden, shots were fired from down the road toward the men and their tank. The tank stopped and the soldiers dove into the ditches sandwiched between the road and the hedgerows, only a few feet away from Augarten's group. Augarten held his breath, straining not to make any noise. Just then, one of the soldiers who had jumped into the ditch whispered loudly, "For Christ's sake, McCarthy, get off my foot!" Augarten couldn't believe his luck. "Are you Americans?" he asked the men. "Yes. Who are you?" came the reply. The soldiers took Augarten and the others to the company commander, who arranged for the group to be driven to Allied lines, about fifteen miles away. The American's two-month adventure through German-occupied France had finally come to an end.

Considering the ordeal Augarten had just been through, the army felt it appropriate to send him home instead of back into combat. But Augarten refused. He had pulled a lot of strings to get into the fighting in the first place, and had flown only ten missions before being shot down. Augarten formally requested permission to remain in Europe with his unit, and his request was granted. He telegrammed his parents to tell them he had survived, and went back to flying. During the remainder of his tour, Augarten flew over ninety missions. One of these stood out from the rest. During that flight, Augarten engaged several Messerschmitts, shooting down two. That feat earned him the Distinguished Flying Cross.

✡ ✡ ✡

After the war, the twenty-three-year-old Augarten returned to the States and began his university studies. He was studying International Relations at Harvard, as events were heating up in Palestine in early 1948. On the suggestion of a friend, Augarten attended a lecture at the Harvard Library given by a young Palestinian diplomat. Augarten thought the speaker was a skilled advocate for the Zionist cause. The speaker that day was Abba Eban, then a diplomat and representative of the new State of Israel and, much later, Israel's foreign minister.

After the lecture, Augarten told a friend active in a local Zionist group that he wanted to do something for his fellow Jews in Palestine. The friend gave him the address of someone to see in New York. On his spring vacation, Augarten visited the offices of Land and Labor for Palestine in Manhattan and told them about his background. At that time, the Haganah had been able to recruit only a handful of pilots, and they were very impressed with his war record. They asked if he could go to Palestine immediately. Augarten agreed, and went to tell his parents about his decision.

Augarten's parents were bitterly opposed to his returning to flying. The strain of having a son missing in action for more than two months had taken its toll. They were not prepared for Augarten to return to the dangers of combat. Deferring to his parents, Augarten decided not to do anything immediately. He returned to his studies at Harvard. As reports of the fighting in Palestine got worse, however, Augarten could not stay away any longer. He got back in touch with Land and Labor and arranged to fly out as soon as exams were over. To avoid another confrontation with his parents, he sent them a letter, timed to arrive after his departure. Augarten arrived in Israel shortly before the second truce, after receiving his Messerschmitt training in Czechoslovakia. His victory at the beginning of Operation Yoav was his first as a pilot in the Israeli Air Force, but it would not be his last.

On the same day that Augarten downed the Spit, the Israeli ground forces went into action as well. Army units assaulted the Egyptian fortresses at Iraq Suweidan and Iraq El Manshie, as well as Egyptian forces on nearby "Hill 113." The attack on Hill 113 was successful, and Tiny Balkin and other members of Lester Gorn's Fourth Anti-Tank unit were part of the force sent to occupy the captured hilltop. But the Egyptian strongholds at Iraq Suweidan and Iraq El Manshie repelled the Israeli attacks.

Facing strong Egyptian resistance, Israel's ground forces called on the air force to aid in the attack on Iraq Suweidan. U.S. Air Force veteran and 101 pilot Giddy Lichtman was in his room near the air base at Herzliya when he received a telephone call from the squadron's operations officer, ordering Lichtman to report immediately. Lichtman arrived at the base and received a briefing. A tank battle was in progress near the Egyptian fortress at Iraq Suweidan. Lichtman was ordered to attack the Egyptian troop concentrations with napalm. American Sid Antin would fly as Lichtman's wingman.

The ground crew loaded Lichtman's Me 109 for the attack. The air force had only recently added napalm to its arsenal, and this was the first mission the Me 109 would fly with that weapon. Lichtman and Antin took off and headed south, covering the short distance between the airfield and the target in less than twenty minutes. They came in at about 9,000 feet to look the area over. They got an eyeful. A mass of Egyptian soldiers and guns covered the top of the Monster on the Hill. Lichtman thought there must be two hundred people on the roof. The town itself was filled with tanks and other heavy equipment. A short distance away, Lichtman could see the tank battle raging between the Israeli and Egyptian forces.

With Antin flying above to provide top cover, Lichtman began his attack. He made a wide turn over the sea, and came in low. The Egyptian gunners picked Lichtman up immediately and opened fire. He saw the flash of the Egyptian guns and the troops running for cover, but the roar of the plane's engine prevented him from hearing any of the sounds of the battle. Lichtman dropped his load of napalm, and looked back to see a cloud of black smoke. He then opened up with his machine guns and cannon, knocking out a number of Egyptian tanks. Lichtman made two more passes through the town. The return fire was extremely heavy. As he watched the tracers streak past the cockpit, Lichtman felt like he was moving through a cloud of fire.

He headed south on his last pass through Iraq Suweidan, and then turned out over the sea. As he turned, he started to smell burning oil. Lichtman quickly checked his gauges. He could see the needle on the temperature gauge moving up. Lichtman's engine had been hit. His altitude was only about two hundred feet as he cut inland along the coast to head back toward the base. The plane was losing power. Adding to Lichtman's troubles, the engine started to spray oil, covering the canopy and blocking his vision. He cracked the canopy open to improve visibility, but it didn't help. The hot oil sprayed Lichtman in the face and goggles, keeping him mired in a kind of fog as his plane sputtered away from Iraq Suweidan.

Lichtman radioed Antin to tell him he couldn't gain altitude and was losing power. Neither pilot knew how far they were from the base. They agreed that Lichtman, who could at least see as far as Antin's plane, would fly as Antin's wingman in the hope that Antin could safely guide Lichtman back to Herzliya. Lichtman started to think about going down in Egyptian territory, and became concerned. All of the pilots had heard rumors that captured pilots were murdered and their bodies mutilated. According to some particularly gruesome stories Lichtman had heard, the Egyptians castrated their prisoners of war, sometimes stuffing the severed genitals into the mouth of the dead soldier. These images crowded their way into Lichtman's head. Still, he remained in control of the flight. He adjusted the fuel mixture to try to keep the engine temperature down. As the planes drew near the base, Lichtman was barely able to make out the strip. He dropped his gear in preparation for landing. Antin quickly radioed him to suggest coming in wheels-up – a more predictable way of bringing in a plane when there is a danger of a bad landing. Lichtman retracted his wheels and, unable to come around because of the loss of altitude, headed in the wrong direction down the concrete runway. The plane slid to a halt. Lichtman escaped without any injury and the plane suffered only minor damage. Both were back in the air a few days later.

Meanwhile, the fighting on the ground continued, with Israeli troops engaged in an assault on Egyptian forces in the Negev village of Huleiquat. The fighting was bloody. At one point, the Egyptians trained forty-millimeter cannons on the advancing Israeli soldiers, causing tremendous casualties. The Fourth Anti-Tank Squad was ordered to take its half-track to the battle to help evacuate the wounded. Tiny Balkin and a few other soldiers from the Fourth brought the Israeli casualties back to a makeshift hospital. Tiny waited outside as the doctors worked feverishly to treat the wounded soldiers. As he stood by, one of the doctors emerged from a tent with blood all over his clothing. The doctor, a new immigrant from Europe, was crying. *"Das ist ein schlachthaus"* ("This is a slaughterhouse"), he said in German. Despite the horrendous cost, Israeli persistence paid off. Huleiquat, another piece in the Negev puzzle, was taken early in the morning on October 20.

As Operation Yoav wore on, the bruising of the Israeli forces at the strategic hilltop village of Iraq Suweidan continued. The Egyptian troops were massed at the Monster on the Hill. At the ground force's request, the air force agreed to send two Beaufighters from the 103 Squadron to attack the heavily defended Monster on the Hill with napalm. But the air force did this without enthusiasm for what seemed to be a dangerous mission with little real chance of success. The high walls of the fortress protected a small compound, requiring the pilot either to drop his bombs from a safe height with impossible accuracy, or to come in so low as to expose his plane to fierce anti-aircraft fire from the fort's defenders. Only one day after bringing down the Egyptian Sea Fury without firing a shot, Len Fitchett was one of the two pilots chosen for this mission.

Fitchett, a non-Jew, had flown nightfighters with the Royal Canadian Air Force in World War II. He amassed an impressive war record. Fitchett had three and one-half kills to his credit. One earned him a small footnote in the history of World War II. In the Kiel corridor on April 27,

1945, Fitchett shot down the last German plane of the war. He had also experienced the other side of air combat. Fitchett had been shot down twice himself, once escaping enemy territory on foot with the help of the local underground.

While there was a strong feeling of camaraderie between all of Israel's flyers, Jews and non-Jews alike, some of the Jewish pilots privately regarded some of the non-Jews as mercenaries. For their part, some of the non-Jews did little to discourage the image. During a truce period, a U.N. inspector had asked one of the non-Jews why he had come to Israel. The pilot pulled a ten dollar bill out of his wallet, showed it to the inspector, and said, "Give me enough of these and I'll fly a broomstick to Tokyo." After the war, two former 101 pilots, Slick Goodlin and "Red" Constant, decided to have some fun with the issue. They printed up business cards for several of the foreign pilots. The card identified the bearer as a "Soldier of Fortune," a charter member of Local 88 of a fictitious company known as "Mercenaries, Inc." It also described the services the cardholder performed: "Planes Driven" "All Types" "Day or Night" "Wars Fought" – all at "Reasonable Rates."

Some of the Jewish pilots also fell under suspicion. One of Fitchett's squadron-mates was an assimilated Jew from the U.S. Something about Israel's struggle for independence had struck a chord within him. Without telling his family, he travelled to Israel to join the air force. He then wrote to his parents to tell them the news, looking forward to their proud response. The response he received was not the one he anticipated. His parents had heard that the Israeli Air Force had hired mercenaries. They wrote their son that it was a shame he had returned to his people just so he could make some money.

But nobody regarded Fitchett as a mercenary. He was quiet and well-mannered, and no man in the squadron had a bad word to say about him. Fitchett, as much as any of the Jews who came from abroad to fight for the Jewish state, had pure motives for joining Israel's struggle for independence. At the end of World War II, he visited several concentration camps in Germany, and the experience made a powerful impression on the young Canadian. To his parent's surprise, when John McElroy recruited him, he interrupted his university studies to join Israel's fledgling air force.

The Beaufighter was designed for a two-person air crew, and Fitchett had a British volunteer named Dov Sugarman as his navigator. But Fitchett's plane would carry a third passenger for the attack on the Monster on the Hill, American Stan Andrews. Andrews had started the war in the 101 Squadron with his friend Bob Vickman. Vickman's death during the Ten Days fighting had so affected Andrews that the air force grounded him, and made him the air force liaison to the U.N. truce supervision forces. For this work, Andrews used the assumed name Andre Stanek, an obvious play on Andrews' real name. Andrews, though, didn't want to spend the duration of the war restricted to ground duty. Without telling the general staff of the air force, he periodically hitched rides on bombing missions. Fitchett agreed to let Andrews come along for the Iraq Suweidan raid.

Late in the afternoon of October 20, Fitchett took off from Ramat David, the 103's air base, with a second Beaufighter piloted by South African Danny Rosin flying at his side. Fitchett and Rosin flew south toward Iraq Suweidan, with their bomb racks fully loaded. As they drew near to their target, the two descended until they were just above the ground, and then turned east toward the fortress. Both planes had to pull up to clear the its massive outer walls. The low approach worked, completely surprising the Monster on the Hill's defenders. Fitchett and Rosin dropped their bombs into the courtyard. Fitchett hit the target, and smoke filled the air. Although he didn't know it at the time, Rosin's bombs had failed to release, and stayed in their bomb racks.

After the planes cleared the fort, Rosin turned to head back to the base. As he turned, Rosin saw Fitchett's plane heading back toward the fort. Fitchett was going to make a second pass, as the now alert Egyptians filled the twilight with anti-aircraft fire. Fitchett's plane disappeared from Rosin's view as it entered the smoky darkness above the fort. Rosin returned to base, hoping to meet Fitchett there. Rosin landed and waited. The minutes passed, but still there was no sign of Fitchett.

The air force quickly dispatched a twin-engine Rapide to survey the area around Iraq Suweidan to find out what had happened to Fitchett's plane. The Rapide carried guns and ammunition to drop to Fitchett and the others. About thirty minutes after the attack, the Rapide crew spotted the bomber's wreckage, burning in the dark some ten miles from the fort. There was no sign of survivors.

Israel later learned that Fitchett managed to land the damaged plane. He and his two crewmates were able to get out alive. They could not, however, evade the nearby Egyptian troops. The Egyptians killed the three flyers, and mutilated their bodies. Like his best friend and fellow artist Bob Vickman, Stan Andrews would not live to tell the story of Israel's struggle for independence.

Still unable to break through at Iraq Suweidan, Israel's ground forces turned their attention toward the town of Beersheba, in the eastern portion of the Negev. Intercepted Egyptian communications suggested that Egypt was concentrating its forces in other parts of the Negev, away from Beersheba, leaving the town vulnerable to attack. Early in the morning of October 21, six days into Operation Yoav, Israel made its move. Following an artillery and mortar barrage, a platoon of half-tracks entered the town. George Baler and Mike Rubin, the "communists" whose determination to fight with an Israeli unit had landed them in the Palmach, were with the Negev Brigade as it helped provide the initial artillery barrage against the Egyptian forces in Beersheba. More Israeli armored vehicles arrived a few hours later, and soon most of Beersheba was in Israeli hands. All that remained was the police station, a British-built fortress no less impregnable than the Monster on the Hill. The Negev Brigade wheeled out a twenty-five-millimeter French cannon. The men aimed at the fortress, and fired four rounds. Although the shells caused little damage, the tactic worked. The Egyptians inside either surrendered or escaped further south. The capture of Beersheba was complete.

The Palmach suffered tremendous casualties during the war. The losses seemed to breed a stoic quality among Palmachniks that extended even to their families. Typically, when a Palmach soldier was killed, his mother would come to the unit a short time later to cook a meal for the men. There was also something of a wild-west atmosphere that Baler and Rubin found oddly appealing. While in Beersheba, some Palmachniks came up to Baler and told him he was to be formally inducted into the Palmach. They took him to a room and gave him a beer bottle to hold. Then, from about fifteen feet away, one of the men pulled out a rusty revolver and shot the neck off the bottle.

The day after the capture of Beersheba, Rubin, Baler and the other soldiers in Beersheba received a pleasant surprise. About a month earlier,

American conductor Leonard Bernstein had agreed to become the musical director of the Israeli Philharmonic for a two-month period. When Bernstein learned of Beersheba's capture, he and twenty-seven members of the Philharmonic climbed into two old buses and made their way south to the Negev town. They set up their instruments in an archeological excavation. The piano was placed on a rock stage, while the musicians sat on wooden benches or on the ground. The Philharmonic played works by Mozart, Beethoven, and Gershwin for the men who had taken Beersheba. It was the first symphony concert in the town's history. At its conclusion, Bernstein was made an honorary member of the Palmach.

The same day that Baler and Rubin were entering Beersheba, Rudy Augarten was again in the air over the Negev. This time, Augarten was in one of the squadron's new Spitfires. He was not alone on this flight. Canadian Jack Doyle flew the other Spit at Augarten's side. As the two patrolled, they spotted four Egyptian Spitfires. Veteran pilots, Doyle and Augarten turned to come out of the sun at the enemy planes. They each picked a target, coming in with their guns blazing. Augarten recorded his second kill of the war, Doyle his first. The two pilots also damaged the other two Egyptian planes before returning home.

As had become their trademark, the Egyptians showed no aggressiveness in the dogfight with the Israelis. Over time, the men of the 101 Squadron grew increasingly scornful of the "Gyppo" pilots. Once, several of the 101 pilots arranged for a dedication request to be sent to Radio Cairo from Europe. The request was for "Dance of the Sugar Plum Fairies," to be played in honor of the Royal Egyptian Air Force. The pilots were delighted when the station played the song and the unsuspecting Radio Cairo host read the dedication. On the few occasions when the Egyptians showed any fight at all, the pilots assumed Americans were flying those planes. This was based on an intelligence report that two American pilots, a forty-year-old pilot named Ellsworth and twenty-nine-year-old John Packard, had joined the Egyptian air force. The 101 pilots held a particular grudge against these two. When flying over Rafah, Slick Goodlin would taunt them over the radio: "Come on up, Packard! Come on up, Ellsworth! We're waiting for you!"

The air force had come a long way in a short period of time. When the war started, Tel Aviv's residents stood by helplessly as Egyptian planes bombed the city nearly every day, with no fear of encountering any Israeli opposition. In only a few months, with the arrival of fighter planes and foreign volunteers to help fly them, the Israeli Air Force had become the dominant air power in the region.

Although Israeli troops were still meeting stubborn resistance at Iraq Suweidan and Iraq El Manshie, the fighting in the rest of the Negev was going well. Israeli forces had ended the isolation of the Negev settlements, and had driven the Egyptian forces from much of the Negev. Most of the remaining Egyptian forces were trapped in the southwest corner of the Negev, in an area that was to become known as the Faluja pocket. Formerly the besiegers, the Egyptians would soon become the besieged.

At three p.m. on October 22, only one week after Operation Yoav began, another U.N.-sponsored truce went into effect, temporarily ending the fighting in the south. But it would not be long before the fighting would resume with the Egyptians.

18

OPERATION HIRAM

On the first day of the truce with Egypt, Paul Shulman woke to discover that two Egyptian warships had taken up positions opposite Tel Aviv. The Annapolis graduate had recently been promoted from chief of naval operations to commander of the navy. Dealing with the Egyptian ships was his responsibility.

One of the warships was the *Emir Farouk*, an enormous armored cruiser and the flagship of the Egyptian navy. The second vessel, considerably smaller than the *Farouk*, was a minesweeper. Shulman met with Ben Gurion and the army general staff to decide how to deal with the Egyptians, who were clearly trying to blockade Tel Aviv's port. Ben Gurion ordered Shulman to get rid of them. To confront the Egyptians, Shulman personally took command of a three-ship force that included the navy's most secret weapon.

Years earlier, during the days of Aliyah Bet, a Haganah agent in Italy had discovered the remains of a motorboat-size attack vessel of the type that had been used with great effect by Italian commandos during World War II. The assault boat was a kamikaze-type weapon. It was loaded with explosives, and piloted at speeds of up to thirty-two knots toward an enemy ship. At the last possible moment, the pilot would leap from the vessel to safety, while the boat continued on to its target. Even if the attack was successful, though, the pilot was extremely vulnerable to capture.

At one time, the Haganah considered carrying assault boats on Aliyah Bet ships, disguised as life boats. When the British challenged a refugee ship armed in this fashion, the assault boat could be lowered into the water and used to attack the British vessel. It was an idea that was soon abandoned. The Haganah never departed from its policy of keeping Aliyah Bet ships unarmed. When the war began, the navy purchased several of the boats in Italy, and hired a few former Italian commandos to help prepare the vessels and train Israeli crews.

Shulman's taskforce headed out to confront the Egyptians. One ship, the *Ma'oz*, was the mother ship for Israel's arsenal of assault boats. Like many of the vessels in Israel's tiny navy, the *Ma'oz* was a converted Aliyah Bet ship. It was the *Abril/Ben Hecht*, the same Irgun ship that David Gutmann sailed on more than two years earlier. The other two Israeli ships under Shulman's command were the two Canadian corvettes, the *Haganah* and *Wedgewood*.

The Israeli vessels pulled alongside the Egyptian ships. From the *Wedgewood*, Shulman called out to the Egyptians over the ship's loudspeaker: "Truce period or no truce period, if you don't get the hell out of here, I'm going to shoot!" The two Egyptian vessels moved out, sailing south toward Gaza. The Israeli ships followed, taking up positions in international waters opposite the Egyptians. An hour later, the Egyptian's shore batteries opened fire, and Shulman was forced to pull his ships further out to sea. He radioed Tel Aviv, asking for permission to attack the Egyptian ships in response. "No," came the emphatic response. Shulman radioed a second time, asking that his request be forwarded directly to Ben Gurion. A short time later, Shulman received a communication from the prime minister. "Paul, if you can sink them, shoot, if you can't, don't."

Shulman decided on a nighttime operation, using the assault boats. The *Ma'oz* sailed toward Gaza, positioning itself so that the Egyptian ships would be between it and the moon at the time of attack. That would increase visibility for the assault boat pilots. The other two ships sailed south of Gaza, to divert the attention of the Egyptians. Shortly after nine p.m., the *Ma'oz* crew lowered four small vessels into the water. There were three assault boats – one to attack the *Farouk*, a second to attack the minesweeper, and a third in reserve – and a small boat to retrieve the commandos after the attack.

It took nearly an hour for the attacking party to reach the Egyptian ships. The enemy vessels were silhouetted against the moonlit sky, and easily visible to the commando force. The assault boats positioned themselves for the final attack. At ten p.m. the two assault boats in the main force moved out. The pilot of the first vessel gunned his engine, sending his boat racing toward the *Farouk*. He armed his explosives. Then, at the last moment, he leapt from the assault boat. A few seconds later, he heard the explosion. In the moonlight, he could see the ship had been hit. Almost immediately, the second assault boat went into action. Although the second boat was supposed to attack the minesweeper, its pilot mistakenly believed his target was also the *Farouk*. He aimed his boat for the Egyptian flagship. The second boat scored a direct hit on the center of the huge warship. The *Farouk* erupted in flames. Within minutes, the *Farouk's* bow jutted up out of the water, and the vessel quickly sank. All of the assault boat commandos were safely retrieved from the water and returned to the *Ma'oz*.

The sinking of the *Farouk* would prove to be Israel's most dramatic naval victory in the War of Independence – and perhaps in any war since then. Some five hundred Egyptian sailors, many of whom were from the upper crust of Egyptian society, perished. Ben Gurion later believed that the sinking broke the back of the Egyptians, and hastened the end of the fighting with them. Ironically, though, the event received little publicity at the time. Israel was not anxious to draw attention to an attack that arguably violated the truce. The Egyptians, devastated by the magnitude of their loss, were also not interested in publicizing the Israeli assault. Word of the enormous loss found its way to the Egyptian public, despite the government's efforts to keep the incident quiet. It would be nearly a year before the Egyptian navy was able to recruit sailors into its ranks.

Other fallout from the raid affected Paul Shulman. King Farouk wrote to the U.S. State Department, complaining that an American citizen had sunk his navy's flagship. The U.S. government investigated the matter. A short while later, Shulman was asked to resign his reserve commission in the U.S. Navy.

✡ ✡ ✡

Israel's attention now turned north. Although the Seventh Brigade's capture of Nazareth had dealt a major blow to the Arab Liberation Army, Kaukji's fighters still maintained several strongholds in the Galilee, including the northern towns of Jish and Sasa. Because Kaukji had never felt himself bound by the U.N.-imposed truces, Israel was similarly unrestrained in its dealings with the Arab Liberation Army. Israel had planned to attack Kaukji's strongholds in September, during the second truce, and had even moved forces from the Seventh Brigade north for the operation. But the day it was to begin, the Stern Group assassinated U.N. Mediator Count Folke Bernadotte. Afraid that the assassination and the attack on Kaukji's forces would appear coordinated, Israel called off the operation.

On October 28, the IDF was ready to proceed with its campaign to rid the Galilee of the Arab Liberation Army. Code-named Operation Hiram, the assault involved the Seventh Brigade's 79th Battalion, as well as units from three other Israeli brigades. The 79th, which had been based in Safed, would attack Jish, travelling north for the assault. The army decided that the 79th would do so under cover of darkness. The night of October 28, a column of armored vehicles prepared to move out from Safed.

One of the vehicles in the column was driven by Ralph Lowenstein, an eighteen-year-old from Danville, Virginia. Dubbed the "*yeled*" ("kid") by the Israelis in the unit, Lowenstein was one of the youngest Americans to volunteer. His journey to Israel was unlike that of the other Americans who came to fight. He had been travelling in Europe during the summer of 1948, having just completed his freshman year at Columbia University. It was in France that he made the decision to go.

On July 24, 1948, Lowenstein sat in his room in the Hotel Montesquieu in Paris. He composed a letter to his parents, the most difficult one he ever had to write. "By the time you get this letter, I shall be in the tiny state of Israel," he began. Lowenstein knew the letter would come as a terrible shock, and he tried to explain his reasoning. "It has always been on my mind, that if I could go to Palestine and fight for my people I would. Mind you," he continued, "I said that it had always been on my mind, but this editorial which appeared in the obviously anti-Zionist *London Daily Express* made me swear to myself, that if ever I had the opportunity, I would go or call myself a coward if I didn't." He told of his efforts to locate the Paris embassy of the "Provisional State of Israel," and of his visit to a secret Haganah office, where he proved that he was Jewish by saying the Hebrew alphabet. In two days, he wrote, he would take a train to Marseilles, and from there a boat to Israel. "I realize that it will be difficult for you, and that hurts me more than anything else, but you must be brave," he continued. "I am neither brave nor adventurous, but I know that there is a job to do. When my job is done and I can return home with a clear conscience, I shall do so on the first plane or ship that can carry me."

The news jolted his parents, as Lowenstein feared it would. "From the minute we got your shocking first letter, telling of your enlistment, we were simply crushed. Dad and I have been heartbroken over it, we have no thought for anything else," Lowenstein's mother wrote. She poured out her anguish in a torrent of words. "I will never be reconciled to your being there - I will not stop grieving, nor will Dad, as long as you are there - and my soul is so seared with bitterness over the situation that I will hate everything connected with Israel and Zion as long as you are over there, and if you delay your return, I will hate them until the day I die, and Dad and I will sever all our connections with everything concerned with Zion, or Israel."

Lowenstein's parents asked others to write Ralph, hoping someone could convince him to return to America. They spoke to their rabbi, a German Jew named Max Kapustin, and he agreed to send a letter. But Rabbi Kapustin could not hide his admiration for Lowenstein's actions. "My first reaction was immense pride that one of my boys had mustered enough idealism and Jewish substance to feel that his place was with his people in a portentous hour of Jewish History. While my wife was crying and my own throat was choking I had a deep feeling of satisfaction because in all humility I felt that mine was a share in a great and noble thing which you had done." The rabbi would not ask Lowenstein to return, only to consider his situation carefully. "If, after conscientious deliberation and honest soul-searching you still feel that your place is in Israel now, then, I believe, I would not feel morally justified to call on you to come back. My blessings and my prayers would be with you, expressed in the ancient words of the Psalmist: 'Ride on in behalf of truth.'"

Ralph Lowenstein's parents were hardly the only ones to react negatively to their son's or daughter's decision to fight for Israel. While the Lowensteins tried to persuade their son to return to the U.S., other parents faked illnesses to lure their children home. But Lowenstein resisted his parents' entreaties. On October 28, he sat behind the wheel of one of the 79th's half-tracks, prepared to head north.

Riding with Lowenstein was Mort Levinson, one of the two Levinson brothers who had travelled to Israel with the Tiny Balkin group. Another of the drivers in the column was Norm Olin of Toronto. Olin had been a passenger on the *Marie Annick*, the small ship that arrived in Israel as the *Atlalena* lay burning opposite the shores of Tel Aviv.

The vehicles moved out, with their lights off to preserve the secrecy of the mission. The night was moonless, though, and it was nearly impossible for the drivers to follow the twists and turns of the dirt track that led north to Jish. The armored cars crept along, the drivers straining to keep their eyes on the road. In desperation, Lowenstein and Levinson decided that Levinson should sit on the hood of their half-track. From there, he would shout turning instructions back to Lowenstein. After several nerve-wracking hours, the column reached the jumping-off point outside of Jish, and the men went to catch a few hours of sleep before the start of the fighting.

Olin laid down to rest, but was startled to discover that he literally could not shut his eyes. The strain and tension of driving for several hours in complete darkness had locked his eyelids open. Desperate for relief, he went to the medical officer's tent. Many of the other drivers were already there, all experiencing the same problem. The officer laughed, and gave everyone eyedrops, immediately alleviating their suffering.

A few hours later, the assault on Jish began. By nightfall on October 30, two days after Operation Hiram began, every one of its objectives had been realized. Israeli forces captured Jish and Sasa, and drove the Arab Liberation Army across the border into Lebanon.

✡ ✡ ✡

The truce that began on October 22 did not bring quiet to Israel's front with Egypt. The warring parties continued to skirmish, and on November 9 Israeli ground forces finally captured the Monster on the Hill at Iraq Suweidan. At the same time, Israel's heavy and medium bombers continued to pummel the Egyptian troops concentrated at Faluja. The Hammer Squadron's three B-17's, with fighter escort from the 101 Squadron, bombed during daylight hours. The Egyptians learned to expect the arrival of the huge flying fortresses each afternoon at five p.m. "You could set your watch by it," navigator Jules Cuburnek recalled. Still, the Egyptians never sent up fighters to challenge the Israeli bombers. It was another measure of the strides made by Israel's air force in a matter of only months.

The B-17's faced a severe shortage of explosives during this period. But unwilling to stop the missions, the air force came up with a novel solution. Armorers took crates of empty soda bottles, and cut the bottoms off each bottle. These crates were dropped, intermingled with more traditional bombs. The rush of air through the openings of the bottles as they plummeted toward the earth caused a tremendous shriek, creating the illusion of firepower.

The bomb shortage was not the only problem to afflict the Hammer Squadron. The improvised bomb rack system installed in Czechoslovakia was not reliable. There were times when the bombardier would press the button to release the B-17's load of five-hundred-pound bombs, only to discover that one had hung up on the racks. It was too dangerous to land the B-17 with an armed bomb, so the crews devised a solution. When the bombardier was ready to release the bombs, he would signal another crewman standing next to the bomb bay. That crewman would watch to make sure that all of the bombs dropped. If one was hung-up, it was the crewman's job to kick it loose.

The 101 Squadron was also active during the third truce. For the second time since the war began, it relocated to a new fighter base, this one at Kastina. The desert base at Kastina was another former British airfield. Now, instead of moving farther away from the Egyptians for protection, they shifted further south to be nearer to the Egyptian lines. The new base was spartan, with two concrete strips, a small control tower and some ramshackle barracks. It was also remote. The squadron's swashbuckling pilots were now twenty miles from the Hayarkon Hotel, the Park Hotel, the Atom Bar, and the Gallei Yam – their favorite Tel Aviv hangouts. The men of the 101st had acquired a reputation in Tel Aviv. They drank and fought their way from one bar to another. They sported red baseball caps, a gift from Red Finkel's sister in New York. That piece of attire earned the 101 the nickname "The Red Squadron."

The fighter pilots didn't allow the distance from Tel Aviv to spoil their fun. If they couldn't walk to the Gallei Yam or the Atom Bar, they would drive – in stolen cars. There were always three or four cars on the grounds of the base, hot-wired by the pilots during trips to Tel Aviv. Even these were not always enough to accommodate the pilots. On one occasion, Wayne Peake found himself stranded in Tel Aviv. Everyone else had already returned to the base. Peake walked the streets, looking for transportation. He found a thirty-passenger bus and decided that it would do nicely. He climbed inside, crossed the ignition wires, and drove back to Kastina.

The 101 pilots' antics didn't stop with stolen cars. They once stole a boat and another time tried to take a camel. Sometimes, at night, Slick Goodlin and some of the other pilots, armed with forty-five's, would hunt the jackals that roamed the nearby fields. Other times, Jack Doyle or one of the others would borrow a Piper Cub and shout at the jackals from the air.

Their activities were the product of typical fighter pilot cockiness, magnified by the fact that the 101 was the only fighter squadron in the country. Their attitude was reinforced by the realization that the 101 had become an elite squadron. By the end of the war, with its all-star cast of pilots from the Allied air forces, some argue that it was the greatest squadron of the World War II era.

On November 11, Rudy Augarten left Kastina for a two-plane patrol near Egypt's El Arish air base. Augarten's wingman, a South African named Boris Senior, noticed an Egyptian Dakota lining up to land. He dove down to attack. "What are you doing? This is a truce," Augarten radioed to Senior. But by then it was too late, Senior had already fired on the Egyptian. The Dakota kept flying, though, and it was clear that Senior had missed. With his wingman having already fired his guns, Augarten felt the fallout would be no greater if the Dakota was brought down. He maneuvered behind the Dakota and fired. His bullets found their mark, and the Egyptian plane crashed just before the airfield.

One enemy plane continued to elude Israel's fighter squadron. For months, the contrails of a high-altitude reconnaissance plane had been visible in the daylight sky. But the Messerschmitts and Spitfires of the 101 Squadron were never able to climb fast enough to catch the spy plane. No one was sure of the nationality or type of the intruder's plane. Jack Doyle, for one, believed it was an Iraqi Mosquito. In August, the squadron added yet another fighter plane to its arsenal, one that would give the 101 a better chance of dealing with the spy plane. Al Schwimmer had managed to purchase two P-51 Mustangs, one of the front-line American fighters of the Second World War. Back in the U.S., Schwimmer had the planes dismantled and loaded into crates marked "irrigation equipment," and smuggled them out of the country to Israel. Jack Doyle was particularly amused by Schwimmer's subterfuge. "That's fine-looking irrigation machinery," he announced. "We can irrigate the Arabs with that."

The air force set a trap for the intruder. On November 20, Wayne Peake sat in one of the newly assembled Mustangs on one of the runways at Kastina. Peake, as a veteran P-51 pilot from the American air force, was the natural choice for the mission. In the north, at Ramat David, a spotter waited for the mystery plane to pass over. When he saw the contrails, he would radio the information to Kastina. Peake would then be scrambled after the intruder.

At around one p.m., the spotter saw the contrails, and radioed Kastina. Peake took off, and quickly climbed to 30,000 feet, the estimated altitude of the spy plane. The rest of the squadron stood on the tarmac below, following on a loudspeaker the radio communications between Peake and the control tower. Within minutes, they saw the intruder come into view. The tower radioed to Peake the order to shoot the plane down. But Peake couldn't find it. He had set his ambush too high. "He's right below you," the tower officer yelled to Peake. Peake found the plane. He got into position behind it and opened fire. Almost immediately, all four of the Mustang's guns jammed. A later check revealed that only forty-five rounds were fired. "My fucking guns are jammed," Peake shouted in frustration. Dejected, the rest of the squadron watched as the plane turned out to sea. But then, almost imperceptibly, the plane's vapor trail became thicker and darker. Moments later, the plane exploded, raining small bits of debris into the Mediterranean.

When Peake landed, everyone wanted to know what kind of plane he had just shot down. Peake thought it had been a four-engine bomber. After reviewing pictures of the different World War II bombers, he became convinced he had downed a Halifax. But the wreckage confirmed, to everyone's satisfaction but Peake's, that the plane had been a two-engine Mosquito. Peake's confusion was likely caused by oxygen deprivation at the high altitude, making his feat of shooting down the Mosquito with only forty-five rounds all the more remarkable. There was not enough wreckage to identify the plane's nationality. That would remain a mystery until January, following an even more dramatic encounter involving the 101 Squadron.

With the elimination of Kaukji's army, the capture of the Monster on the Hill, and the gradual settling in of the third truce, Israel's victory in the war began to look like a foregone conclusion. The panic that had marked the first few weeks of fighting, when Jerusalem was besieged and the Egyptian army was advancing on Tel Aviv, had long since receded. But as had been the case during the second truce, the period of inaction was harmful to Israel's effort to preserve harmony among its diverse band of soldiers. The source of the discord this time was concentrated in the ATC.

The problem began shortly after Operation Dust, when Israel took its first steps toward creating El Al, the country's first civilian airline. Periodically, the ATC's lone C-54 would be taken out of military service and quickly fitted for a civilian flight. The plane would be transformed inside and out: the spacious hold carpeted and lined with plush recliners, the desert camouflage paint removed, and a giant El Al logo placed on the fuselage. ATC crews flew those first flights. On September 31, 1948, Hal Auerbach, one of Schwimmer's early recruits, captained the very first El Al flight. Auerbach piloted the Constellation to Geneva to pick up Chaim Weizmann, Israel's first president. Weizmann was then an ailing man, and his physician feared for his well-being on a long flight in a plane without oxygen equipment. At the doctor's insistence, Auerbach kept the plane below 6,000 feet for the entire trip to Israel.

Weizmann's illness could not suppress his excitement at being a passenger on the first flight of Israel's fledgling carrier. He came up to the cockpit, where he spent ten minutes chatting with Auerbach. Auerbach had been given the Hebrew name Hillel Bahir for the flight, a ruse designed to conceal the fact that the C-54's air crew was non-Israeli. Weizmann couldn't help but comment on the fact that Auerbach and all the other "Israeli" crewmen spoke flawless English. "I'm happy you noticed that, Mr. President," responded Auerbach. "You see, sir, for this flight we chose all college graduates."

The El Al flights, unexpectedly, began to sew discord in the ATC. A rumor spread that the flights were conducted on a commercial basis, with paying passengers and commercial freight. The ATC crews, however, were not being paid on anything approaching a civilian scale. If the rumor were true, it meant that someone was reaping significant profits at the expense of the ATC crews.

It was not that anyone in the ATC opposed the creation of El Al. Indeed, many of the pilots hoped to fly for El Al once the war was over. For experienced pilots like Ray Kurtz and Norm Moonitz, post-war antisemitism in the U.S. had destroyed their dreams of becoming airline captains. A Jewish airline was, for them, a place of unlimited opportunity. But flying civilian flights on an essentially military pay scale was not what they had in mind.

While the ATC was digesting the El Al rumor, a bolt of lightning struck the unit. Throughout the war, the ATC had maintained a quasi-autonomous status. It was not technically part of the air force, and its members had never even been sworn into the IDF. In late November, though, they learned that the air force intended to formally absorb the ATC, which would become the 106th Air Transport Squadron. The crews would receive a choice. They could accept induction into the air force as officers for a one-year period, or leave the ATC's ranks.

The air crews were furious. They had been immensely proud of their contributions to Israel's emerging victory in the war. They were the ones who had flown in the desperately needed Czech arms, and who had paved the way for Operation Yoav with the daring nighttime flights over Egyptian lines into the Negev. Early on, the Israelis had exercised their authority over the ATC. All of the ATC's administrative staff was Israeli, despite the fact that none of these men had ever flown transport craft. The mostly American crews tolerated their often inefficient Israeli administrators, although they did not respect them. The idea that the transport squadron and its men were now to be forced to become part of the air force was received as a shocking expression of Israeli ingratitude for all the ATC had accomplished during the war. The American crewmen also feared the loss of citizenship that might result from accepting the air force plan and swearing an oath of allegiance to the IDF.

In a raucous meeting in the dining room of the Bristol Hotel, the ATC crewmen stated their opposition to the plan to Al Schwimmer. Schwimmer was torn. He sympathized with Israel's desire to formally absorb the ATC into the air force, to be able to more effectively exercise military discipline over its transport squadron. He recognized then what in hindsight would become clear to everyone: the ATC could not continue to exist outside of the air force. But he was also loyal to the men who sat before him, many of whom he had personally recruited. Schwimmer agreed to convey to air force commander Aharon Remez the ATC's opposition to the absorption plan.

Two days later, the group gathered again in the Bristol dining room, to hear the results of Schwimmer's communications with the air force. "They refuse to discuss it," Schwimmer announced. The men were furious. The air force's stubbornness only intensified their opposition. Harold Livingston, a young radio operator and an early Schwimmer recruit, proposed writing a letter to the air force. Signed by all of the air crews, the letter would state their opposition to the air force plan. Livingston's proposal was unanimously approved. The letter expressed the men's "disapproval" of the absorption plan, and expressed the signers' intention to remain "civilians employed by a civilian contract carrier." The forty-two assembled members of the ATC affixed their signatures. Again, Schwimmer was caught in the middle, but again he carried the message to the air force.

A few days later, the air force agreed to meet with the ATC to discuss the matter. Three representatives of the ATC – Livingston, Ray Kurtz, and Norm Moonitz – met with Remez and two members of his staff. Schwimmer also attended. The meeting did not go well. Remez was furious about the letter: "As far as I am concerned, you are no better than mercenaries. Worse, you are traitors! Jewish traitors! Betrayers of the Jews!" No changes would be made to the air force's plan. Later that day, following another gathering at the Bristol, the men prepared a second letter to the air force. It announced the unconditional rejection of absorption, and, more ominously, that all ATC operations would cease five days later, on December 9, 1948, unless the air force withdrew its absorption directive. Thus was born what would later come to be known as the "ATC Strike."

The strike never got started. Before the air force could respond to the ultimatum, Schwimmer, who had been away from Tel Aviv when the ATC made its strike threat, convened the group to discuss the matter. "I'm going to ask you to retract your letter, your ultimatum. I think it was a rash, ill-considered act," he declared. "If the ultimatum isn't withdrawn, it negates everything we came here to do." This time, Schwimmer's voice of moderation carried the day. The men voted unanimously to retract the strike threat, and an obviously pleased Al Schwimmer hurried from the meeting to personally take the good news to air force headquarters.

But the affair did not end there. The air force ordered every person who had signed the ultimatum to sign a formal retraction of that threat – or be immediately repatriated to his home country. Not surprisingly, the crewmen regarded it as an attempt to humiliate them. Schwimmer, who had so deftly maneuvered the group retraction and, he had believed, defused the crisis, pleaded with Remez not to go forward with it. Remez refused.

Despite their protestations, one by one the men signed the retractions. In the end, all but two signed – Harold Livingston and Norm Moonitz held out. The air force decided not to force the issue with Moonitz. He was simply too valuable for Israel to lose. But Livingston was another matter. Repeatedly, he was summoned to air force headquarters, and faced with a demand to sign the retraction. But the radio operator was adamant. The group had orally retracted the ultimatum and the written retraction was simply a humiliation to which he would not submit. In the end, Livingston made his point. Schwimmer intervened with Ben Gurion, who put an end to the matter once and for all. But the affair embittered Livingston, and he left the country a short while later.

The air force had initially timed the ATC absorption for January 1, 1949. Perhaps expecting that the plan would cause some turmoil, the air force knew that it would need the help of the ATC to bring over a second group of Spitfires from Czechoslovakia – an operation that had been scheduled for December. In the end, the plan leaked out before the Spits could be brought over, and the strike was averted in time to involve the C-46's in the ferry flights.

Sam Pomeranz, the aeronautical engineer and pilot who had successfully converted the first group of five Spitfires for the marathon flight to Israel, was also at the forefront of Velveeta II, the second such ferry flight. Velveeta II was much more ambitious than its predecessor. This operation, which would likely be the last time that both the Czechs and the Yugoslavians would cooperate with the Israelis in such an airlift, was scheduled to involve fifteen planes. Pomeranz, who was in charge of fitting the second group of planes with long range tanks and the necessary fuel system, would again lead the flight of planes on their long journey to the Middle East.

Pomeranz's work of readying the planes was assisted by George Lichter, a New Yorker who had flown P-47 Thunderbolts and P-51 Mustangs during World War II. Lichter's career in the Israeli Air Force began, as did that of most of the American fighter pilots, in Czechoslovakia. But unlike the others, Lichter did not continue on to Israel. Instead, he remained behind the Iron Curtain, for a thankless and far more dangerous job – that of training foreign volunteers and young Israelis on the unpredictable Me 109. Although the Czechs had originally contracted with the Israelis to provide that instruction, they had little appetite for the work. No one knew better than the Czechs just how dangerous their version of the Me 109 was. When they discovered early on that Lichter had a gift for instruction, they prevailed on him to take over.

To the young Israelis who came under his care, Lichter was an intimidating presence. Few of the Israelis had extensive experience with Lichter's brand of strict military discipline. They were used to the relative informality of the Haganah or Palmach. But Lichter introduced them to a distinctly American style of aircraft instruction. He insisted on absolute adherence to his commands, and did not hesitate to bark his disapproval at a careless recruit. Many of the young Israelis feared him, although they grudgingly admired his obvious skill as a pilot and instructor. Two of his Israeli students, Danny Shapira and Moti Hod, would later become the elite of Israel's air force. For many years, Shapira served as the air force's chief test pilot, and in 1966 became the first Westerner to fly a Soviet MiG-21, a plane that an Iraqi defector had flown to Israel. Hod later served as commander of the Israeli Air Force, a position he held during the Six Day War.

Lichter's skills were now directed to test flying each Spitfire as Pomeranz completed his modifications. By the middle of December, the planes were ready to go. To fly the modified planes, Israel sent twelve pilots to Czechoslovakia to join Pomeranz and Lichter. Although fifteen planes were available, Israel could only spare fourteen pilots. One of the fighters would have to remain behind. The group of pilots flown in from Israel included 101 veterans Bill Pomerantz (no relation to Sam); Red Finkel, who earlier in the war had spent several weeks in an Italian jail when the C-46 he was travelling on landed in Treviso; and Canadians John McElroy and Denny Wilson.

Another of the ferry pilots would be Caesar Dangott, a veteran U.S. Navy pilot. Dangott was a recent addition to the Israeli Air Force, and few knew his background. His name was clearly not Jewish, and everyone assumed that he must be another of the many non-Jews who had decided to fly for Israel. Shortly after Velveeta II, the commander of the 101 Squadron announced that the non-Jewish pilots would be given a short leave for Christmas. The non-Jews got up and walked out of the room, but Dangott remained. "That goes for you too, Caesar. You don't have to stay," the squadron commander told him. "But I'm Jewish," Dangott protested. It was the first confirmation for nearly everyone in the squadron that Dangott was a Jew.

In the months since Velveeta I, winter had arrived. The weather change significantly complicated the task of flying the planes over the Alps and into Israel. On December 18, Sam Pomeranz led an initial group of six Spitfires out of Czechoslovakia. The group was divided into two flights of three: one led by Pomeranz and one by Lichter. Pomeranz's flight included Bill Pomerantz, while Lichter's included John McElroy. Only the flight leaders carried radios – it was their responsibility to navigate the planes to Yugoslavia. From there, an ATC C-46 would lead the group on to Israel. The lack of radios required the other members of the flights to fly in tight formation. To avoid becoming lost, they had to maintain visual contact with their flight leader.

On the way over the mountains to Yugoslavia, the planes ran into a snowstorm. Pomeranz tried to lead the two flights over the storm, but at 14,000 feet they were still in the clouds. The planes, which lacked oxygen, could climb no higher. The men struggled to maintain visual contact, a task that was nearly impossible in the thick storm clouds. Finally, Pomeranz radioed to Lichter to take the other four planes back. Pomeranz would continue on alone to Yugoslavia. Although neither man knew it, by this time one Spitfire had already been lost. Bill Pomerantz had gotten separated from the others, and without a radio or navigational equipment was forced to crash land in Yugoslavia.

Lichter led the others back to Czechoslovakia, where everyone regrouped to try again. McElroy, for one, was not happy about the prior day's events. He had ferried a Spitfire to Malta during the Second World War, and he felt he had more experience than any of the others in this type of flying. McElroy was not prepared to again follow another pilot over the mountains to Yugoslavia. "Nobody's going to lead me this time," he announced. McElroy got his wish – he was given a flight of three to lead. As preparations were finalized for the flight, word arrived that one of the Spits on the earlier day's flight had crashed in the mountains. No one knew, however, which Pomerantz – Sam or Bill – had been flying that plane.

On December 19, the twelve remaining Spitfires took off for Yugoslavia. This time, all of the planes cleared the mountains safely, landing at the Yugoslavian air base of Podgorica. There the pilots discovered what had happened the day before. Bill Pomerantz had landed his plane safely. But Sam Pomeranz, the architect of the whole operation, had not. He died when his plane crashed into the mountains. McElroy believed that Sam Pomeranz blacked out as he continued to try to climb above the storm. His remains were later recovered, and given to Bill Pomerantz to bring back to Israel for burial.

On December 22, ten of the planes were ready to continue on to Israel. Two had developed mechanical problems and would have to be left behind. For this leg, two ATC C-46's had arrived from Israel to lead the way. The C-46's were along for more than just navigational assistance. Each also carried an emergency raft in case one of the pilots had to bail out over the sea during the 1,200 mile journey to Israel. After six hours of low-speed flying behind the lumbering transport planes, the ten remaining Spitfires landed safely in Israel. The timing was perfect. It was the first day of Operation Horev – Israel's final offensive against the Egyptians.

19

THE FINAL PUSH

With Operation Horev, Israel wanted to finish what it had begun in Operation Yoav – the establishment of control over all of the Negev. The leaders of the Jewish state again used Egyptian defiance of the U.N. truce terms to begin its offensive. Earlier, the U.N. Security Council had ordered the two countries to begin armistice talks. Israel had agreed unconditionally, but the Egyptians had refused, demanding that an entire brigade trapped in Faluja first be released. On December 22, Israel notified the U.N. that, because Egypt refused to begin armistice talks, Israel was free to take military action to expel the Egyptian forces.

The air force's bombers and fighters would again play a crucial support role in the second major drive against the Egyptians, striking at the Egyptian troops massed at the small Negev towns of Bir Asluj and Auja al-Hafir. The air force's role was to assist in the ground troops' assault on these towns, to strike at the Egyptian air base at El Arish, and to hit the troops based at Rafah, Gaza and Faluja. The three B-17's of the Hammer Squadron were back at work, daily bombing Egyptian positions.

For the 101 Squadron, Operation Horev would be the busiest period of the war. With the arrival of the Velveeta II Spits, the squadron was now flush with planes. In addition to the new Spitfires, the squadron also had two P-51 Mustangs and a handful of Me 109's. To the experienced World

War II flyers, it was startling to see at one base the three front-line fighters of World War II: the British Spitfire, the American Mustang, and the German Me 109. The Canadian pilots – Doyle, McElroy and Wilson – mostly stuck to the Spitfires. They were contemptuous of the Me 109, a plane that Doyle felt was "as useless as tits on a bull." Many of the squadron's other pilots grew accustomed to switching back and forth between the different planes.

Rudy Augarten was particularly adept at this, as his performance in the first four days of Operation Horev showed. On December 22, he climbed into a Spitfire in response to a report of Egyptian planes in the area, and damaged a Macchi that was about to land at the El Arish airfield. Two days later, he flew a P-51 Mustang on a fighter patrol. Later that same day, he escorted a bomber on an attack on the El Arish airfield, this time flying an Me 109. The next day, he was back in the Spitfire for a photo-reconnaissance mission over Egyptian positions. During the course of the war, he would shoot down four Egyptian planes, a total matched only by Jack Doyle. Augarten, who had flown a P-47 Thunderbolt during World War II, made his four kills from an Me 109, a P-51 Mustang and twice from a Spitfire. It was a remarkable display of flying skill.

The beginning of Operation Horev turned Tiny Balkin's thoughts to the danger of having two brothers fighting in the same war. He did not want both himself and Phil facing the dangers of combat, and the matter weighed heavily on his mind. Tiny also knew the situation was placing a great strain on his parents. Finally, he reached a decision. He would talk to his brother, and either he or Phil would have to go back. On Christmas day, he wrote to his mother, "One of us will be coming home."

✡ ✡ ✡

An early objective of Operation Horev was the Egyptian-held town of Auja el-Hafir, at the southern tip of the Negev. The attack was to be a coordinated affair, involving the air force, the tank corps, a commando battalion, the engineers, and an armored battalion. The armored battalion was the 89th, Phil Balkin's unit. The attack on Auja was set for December 26, the day after Christmas. The plan called for the engineers to prepare a road for the tanks and half-tracks, followed by a coordinated air and armored attack.

On the day of the attack, the engineer's work took longer than antici-pated, slowing by hours the arrival of the armor. The delay also destroyed the coordination between the air and ground attacks. Instead of aiding the ground assault, the air attack on Auja, which had gone off as originally scheduled, simply warned the Egyptians of the coming battle. When the ground troops arrived, the Egyptians were dug in and ready.

Phil Balkin was assigned to one of the battalion's half-tracks. His job was to load one of the vehicle's big machine guns. While he took his role seriously, he took much more pride in his own skill with a rifle. Phil was a crackshot. As a sixteen-year-old in California, Phil had frequented shoot-ing galleries, where he would challenge soldiers to a test of their shooting skill. The soldiers found Phil's challenge irresistible. "I'll tell you what, I'll even shoot left-handed," Phil would say. Of course, what the soldiers didn't realize was that Phil was a lefty.

Phil and the others were getting ready to move out with the rest of the 89th when the driver, South African Mike Isaacson, discovered the half-track wouldn't start. Isaacson got a push from another vehicle, and was able to get the half-track moving. Still, he didn't know the source of the engine trouble, and he worried the half-track might stall in combat. Isaacson told the men about his concern. He advised them that, under the circumstances, anyone who wanted to stay at the base could do so. But no matter what the others decided, he announced, he intended to go.

It was not a difficult decision for Phil and the other men. They were in this together. If Isaacson wasn't afraid, then neither were they. Phil climbed onto the half-track with the others, and they headed out. As they neared Auja, Phil's thoughts turned toward the coming battle. The South Africans had really taken him under their wing, and Phil was determined not to let them down. He settled into his position, checked his belts of ammo, and waited.

At the last minute, the army decided that the armored units would approach Auja from the main road to the northeast of town, rather than through the desert. This would speed up the assault and, assuming the attack went well, quickly free up some of the forces to attack nearby Abu Ageila. But Egyptian forces were strongest at this point. They unleashed withering machine gun and artillery fire on the attacking Israeli force. Phil's half-track entered the cauldron. Isaacson tried to maneuver the vehicle past an Egyptian gun position. Suddenly, the half-track stalled. They were sitting ducks. An Egyptian gunner sprayed the half-track with his heavy machine gun, as the men frantically tried to get the vehicle started again. Seconds ticked by, but the half-track wouldn't budge. Something had to be done quickly. Phil decided to take out the Egyptian gunner himself. He stood to get a better shot. As he did, an Egyptian round struck Phil in the head, and he fell back onto the half-track. Just then, the engine roared to life and Isaacson retreated beyond the range of the Egyptians. The crew rushed Phil to an aid station at Beersheba, but it was too late. He was already dead.

Tiny was with the Fourth at Iraq El Manshie when an officer called him over to tell him of his brother's death. Tiny was told that his fighting days were over. The army was pulling him out to avoid any danger that both brothers could be killed in battle. Tiny experienced a flurry of emotions. He was distraught over his brother's death, and the realization that his worst fear had come true made him sick to his stomach. His thoughts also turned to his parents, and the effect the loss would have on them. For a brief moment, Tiny was also sorry to leave the war, to leave the men of the Fourth whom he had grown to love and depend upon.

Phil Balkin's death was not in vain. The next day, the Egyptian forces at Auja surrendered. From there, Israeli ground troops advanced into the Sinai, for the first time taking the battle into Egyptian territory.

Israel still had to contend with the trapped Egyptian brigade at Faluja. The air force sent waves of bombers at the Egyptians, trying to pound them into submission. Often, 101 fighters escorted the bombers on these raids. On December 28, Jack Doyle flew one such mission. Doyle's wingman that day was Gordon Levett, a non-Jewish volunteer from Britain. Doyle flew a Spitfire, Levett a Messerschmitt. As the formation approached Faluja, Doyle and Levett saw eight Egyptian fighters below and to the east. Keeping an eye on the Egyptians, the 101 pilots stayed with the bombers until their run was completed. They then turned their attention to the four Spitfires and four Fiats, flying about four thousand feet below.

Because the radio frequencies of the Messerschmitt and the Spitfire were different, Doyle and Levett could not communicate with each other. Levett looked over to the flight leader. Doyle grinned, and pointed his index finger down at the gaggle of Egyptian fighters, his thumb forming the hammer of an imaginary gun. The Canadian dove, and Levett followed. Doyle struck first, shooting down a Fiat before the Egyptians even knew they were being attacked. As the Egyptians scattered, Doyle pursued a Spitfire, damaging it. Levett also claimed one Fiat downed and one Spitfire probably destroyed. With no other aircraft in sight, Doyle and Levett returned to base.

Later that same day, two 101 fighters flew another mission against the Egyptians. As the planes headed south, the flight leader saw a column of vehicles to the west of the Al Auja-Abu Ageila Road. Some of the vehicles bore Egyptian markings, and the two planes began a strafing run. The flight leader aborted the attack almost immediately, as soon as one of the vehicles ran up an Israeli flag. It turned out that the convoy was from Israel's Eighth Brigade. The Eighth had captured several Egyptian vehicles during the fighting, and added them to the column advancing against the Egyptians. No one in the Eighth thought to check, however, whether there were any markings on the roofs of the vehicles to indicate they were Egyptian.

Several days later, Lionel Druker and some other men from the Eighth Brigade were sitting in a Tel Aviv bar. Like the red-hatted pilots of the 101st, the Eighth Brigade tank crews also wore distinctive garb. In their case, it was a yellow scarf. 101 pilot Ezer Weizman – later a commander of the air force, defense minister, and president – noticed the scarves, and walked up to Druker's table. "I guess some of our guys shot at you the other day," he said flippantly. Druker's group did not like the pilot's tone, and a fight broke out. In the melee, Druker took a swing at the future president. A week or so later, Druker and Weizman met a second time. Weizman apologized for the prior incident, and the two shook hands. Over the years, Druker attended a number of Weizman's public speeches. Whenever Weizman spotted Druker in the audience, he invariably would announce: "Do you see that guy sitting over there? Thirty years ago he beat me up!"

Earlier in the war, the 101st had narrowly averted a potentially more devastating friendly-fire incident. There had been reports of an Egyptian battleship near the coast of Tel Aviv. The air force decided to send a B-17 to attack the ship. It was a precision-bombing mission, one for which the high-altitude plane was not designed. Willing to give it a try, pilot Al Raisin headed his aircraft to the area where the ship had been sighted. His navigator/bombardier for the flight was Jules Cuburnek, and Jack Goldstein was the radio operator. To the surprise of everyone on board, Raisin and Cuburnek found the Egyptian vessel. Cuburnek released the bombs. Predictably, they missed the target. But the bombs fell close enough to frighten the Egyptians, and the ship turned away from Israel's shores. Unfortunately, no one had alerted the 101st that a B-17 would be operating in the area.

Rudy Augarten was on a patrol when he noticed an unidentified plane flying near Tel Aviv. Augarten positioned himself behind the B-17 and prepared to shoot. At the last moment, he realized it was an Israeli plane. Augarten turned off and returned to base. Augarten's approach had not gone unnoticed by the bomber crew. The B-17's tail gunner had readied himself to shoot if Augarten had gotten any closer. Even though he knew the fighter plane was friendly, he was not willing to simply allow the B-17 to be shot down. "If it's going to be friendly fire, then I'd rather it be the other friend that gets shot down, instead of me," he told radio operator Jack Goldstein after the incident.

In addition to the B-17's and the medium bombers of the 103rd Squadron, Israel created yet another bombing force for the final campaign against the Egyptians. Israel had managed to purchase seven Harvard trainers in Canada, a plane more commonly known in the U.S. as the AT-6. Although the single engine, two-seater plane had been designed for instruction rather than combat, the air force converted the Harvards into makeshift dive bombers. Each was fitted to carry eight fifty-kilogram bombs, four on either side, and a single machine gun, mounted under the left wing. The bombs were released, two at a time, by flipping a series of four switches.

The planes were assigned to 35 Flight, a squadron commanded by American Ted Gibson. Gibson, the son of a Southern Baptist Minister, had flown dive bombers off aircraft carriers for the U.S. Navy during the Second World War. Pilots with experience on the Harvard were also assigned to 35 Flight – men like; 101 Squadron veteran Mitch Flint, another former navy pilot; and U.S. Air Force veteran Dick Dougherty. Gibson, an excellent instructor, trained the squadron's pilots on dive bombing techniques. The Harvards struck at Egyptian positions each day, from dawn to dusk. It was not uncommon for a pilot to fly four or five missions in a single day.

On December 29, Dougherty took off in a flight of three Harvards, escorted by two fighters from the 101 Squadron. The planes headed south toward the target area. As they neared the Egyptians, the Harvards climbed to ten thousand feet for the final approach, three abreast in a staggered formation. One at a time, Dougherty and the others rolled their planes over onto their backs and dived at an almost ninety-degree angle toward the enemy. As the planes hurtled toward the ground at three hundred knots, anti-aircraft and ground fire raced past. Dougherty flipped his four switches, releasing his bombs. Then, at three thousand feet, he and the other pilots pulled out of their dives, and began the return to the 35 Flight's base at Ekron.

But as Dougherty headed back, he noticed that one of his fifty-kilogram bombs had hung up. He flipped the switch again and tried to shake it loose, but it wouldn't budge. Dougherty had no choice. He would have to land the plane with the bomb still attached. He lined his plane up, and slowly made his approach, trying not to dislodge the bomb. With the plane just a few feet above the ground, disaster struck. The bomb came loose and exploded on the runway. The force of the blast and the spraying shrapnel caused the Harvard to cartwheel. The plane came to rest in a nearby potato field. Although it seemed that the explosion had damaged every part of the plane, the cockpit was remarkably intact. Dougherty walked away from the wrecked plane. Not surprisingly, he was haunted by the episode, as were other members of the squadron.

The dive bombing raids were terrifying enough for the pilots, even without the danger of having a bomb hang-up. There was the hail of enemy fire, the dive at speeds so fast that some pilots feared a wing might break off, and then a crushing five g turn out of the dive. But after each flight, the fear would subside and the men would return for the next one.

On December 30, Mitch Flint took off from Ekron in his Harvard for another mission against the Egyptians. Dougherty's experience from the day before was fresh in his mind as he dove on the Egyptians and threw his bomb switches. Flint pulled out of the dive safely and checked his wings. He couldn't believe it. One of his bombs had also hung up. Flint headed back to base, trying as Dougherty had to jettison the lone fifty-kilo bomb. But the bomb wouldn't shake loose and Flint, more frightened than he had been at any time in his life, made his final approach. As gingerly as he could, he guided the plane toward the runway, touching down softly. When the plane stopped, he ran to the wing to take the bomb off. He put his arms around the bomb and, as he did, it immediately fell from the wing. It was clear to Flint that, had the landing been any more forceful, the bomb surely would have come loose.

At the end of December, the second major ground offensive of Operation Horev began. Israel's targets this time included El Arish in the Sinai and Rafa in the southern part of the Gaza Strip. The tanks of the Eighth Brigade were slated to take part in the fighting. Lionel Druker, who had started with the Eighth before his transfer to the armored warfare school at Sarafand, had rejoined his old unit. During the third truce, some of his old platoon mates had asked him to return for the next offensive against the Egyptians. Druker agreed, and was back in his original Sherman and in position for a December 30 attack on El Arish.

Passing through the Sinai town of Abu Ageila, Druker's Sherman was part of the tank and commando force that raced ahead toward El Arish. Initially, the force advanced swiftly, reaching the El Arish airfield and capturing a Spitfire intact. But soon they fell under heavy enemy fire, and Druker's tank was hit. Druker radioed for another tank to rescue his crew, and ordered his men out of the tank. They took cover behind the stranded tank, until a second tank arrived several minutes later and they all clambered aboard. Within a few days, Druker had obtained a replacement tank, and was back on the front line.

As Israeli troops moved further into the Sinai, the British began to place enormous diplomatic pressure on Israel to withdraw to the international boundary. Britain advised Israel that, if it did not immediately pull its forces from the Sinai, Britain would intervene militarily on Egypt's side under the Anglo-Egyptian Treaty of 1936. Not wanting to draw the British into the fighting, Ben Gurion ordered the army to pull out of the Sinai by January 2, 1949. Operations would, however, continue on the Israeli side of the border and in the Gaza Strip.

By January 6, the situation on the battlefield had become extremely grim for the Egyptians. Except for the trapped brigade at Faluja, which faced constant Israeli bombardment, all of its forces had been expelled from territory allocated to Israel under the U.N. partition plan. Several of its strongholds in the northern part of the Sinai had also fallen, and the Israeli Army was poised to capture the town of Rafa. Finally recognizing the inevitable, the Egyptian government agreed to participate in armistice talks, and a cease-fire was scheduled to begin at four p.m. on January 7.

As was typical during the war, both sides tried to obtain whatever advantage they could in the hours before the fighting was to stop. The Eighth Brigade continued its pursuit of the Egyptians in the Gaza Strip. On the morning of January 7, the half-track in which George Baler was riding hit a mine. He was thrown clear of the vehicle, suffering in the process what would prove to be a minor head wound. The blow caused Baler temporary amnesia. His next memory was of several weeks later, when he woke to find himself on the *Marine Carp* travelling back to the United States, with a distraught Tiny Balkin at his side. The two men had travelled to Israel together months earlier and now, by a quirk of fate, were thrown together for a second, considerably sadder voyage home.

The air force was perhaps the busiest of all of Israel's forces in the hours before the cease-fire. On the morning of January 7, the Hammer Squadron's B-17's, the 35 Flight's dive bombers, and the 101 Squadron's fighters were all in the air. Jack Doyle flew two missions before the four o'clock deadline, on the second shooting down his fourth Egyptian plane of the war. But the real drama was yet to come.

With only a few hours left before the truce, 101 pilot John McElroy approached Slick Goodlin, the former X-1 test pilot. "I got a funny feeling there's a patrol in the area now, down around the El Arish-Auja area," announced McElroy. "Let's see if we can get a couple of airplanes and take off down there for one more patrol." McElroy and Goodlin went to the squadron engineering officer, to check if there were any serviceable planes. At first, the officer thought he had two Spitfires and one P-51. "Fine," said McElroy, "Slick and I will fly the Spitfires and get Lee here to take the P-51, and act as sort of a top cover for us, and we'll go down and see what we can find." Lee was Lee Sinclair, another non-Jewish Canadian volunteer and a former wing commander in the RAF. Soon, though, they learned the P-51 was not ready to fly. Only McElroy and Goodlin would be able to go.

They took off from Kastina, climbing to over 16,000 feet for the flight south. They didn't see anything for the first twenty-five minutes. But then, eight to ten miles off in the distance, McElroy noticed some smoke, and radioed the information to Goodlin. "Come on, we'll turn and have a look at this," McElroy instructed. As they moved in, McElroy saw an Israeli convoy that had obviously just been attacked. Some of the trucks in the column were on fire. The vehicles, as it turned out, were from the Eighth Brigade. Lionel Druker was in that column, astride his replacement Sherman. Off in the distance, McElroy noticed four Spitfires flying low over the column, apparently on another strafing run. "We've got some bogies out there," McElroy radioed to Goodlin.

Before McElroy and Goodlin could reach the scene, two of the Spits turned to the east, and two of the others dove out of sight. The 101 pilots were looking for the Spits when suddenly McElroy spotted two of them: "There's an enemy aircraft at twelve o'clock, right in front of us," he yelled to Goodlin. The two Spits were 3,000 feet below the 101 Squadron planes. "I'll take the one on the left and you take the one on the right," McElroy instructed. Both men dove, and started firing. McElroy hit his target from extremely close range. The shots struck the enemy's engine, cockpit and wings. The flying debris even hit McElroy's own plane, causing some minor damage. It all happened so fast that the enemy pilot never saw McElroy coming.

Goodlin's adversary put up more of a fight. He spotted Goodlin's Spit, and turned to engage the 101 pilot. The enemy fired, but at a bad angle. His bullets missed the mark. Goodlin managed to maneuver his plane into a position behind his opponent. The former X-1 pilot scored a direct hit on the Spit's engine. Goodlin watched as the pilot rolled his plane over and bailed out. McElroy noticed another Spitfire off to his right and slightly below his position. McElroy quickly glanced at the tail, to confirm that it was not a 101 Spit. It wasn't – the plane lacked the red and white stripes that the 101 used to designate its fighters. McElroy lined up behind the Spit and let fly with his machine guns and cannon from four hundred yards. He scored strikes down the fuselage and engine, and then broke off to find Goodlin. The two hooked up over the convoy, and headed back to base. The Eighth Brigade troops on the ground took care of the fourth Spit, bringing it down with their anti-aircraft guns.

During the dogfight, Goodlin noticed something McElroy had failed to see. The planes the two men had engaged were not Israeli, a fact that McElroy had been careful to confirm. But they were also not Egyptian. The Spits were British. The British had been flying reconnaissance flights over Israeli positions for weeks, often in formation with Egyptian fighters. McElroy and Goodlin passed over Kastina before landing, executing victory rolls to signal to those on the ground that they had scored on their mission. When they got out of their planes, Goodlin rushed over to McElroy. "Those were British Spitfires," he told the Canadian. "Oh no, you're crazy," McElroy responded. "The British wouldn't be down there, that's behind our line."

The 101 Squadron scrambled four more Spitfires to head south. One of the pilots in this group was Bill Schroeder, a former U.S. Navy pilot, and one of the Velveeta II ferry pilots. This would be Schroeder's first combat mission for Israel. The Israeli planes ran into a crowd of British fighters – four Spitfires and fifteen Tempests. In the ensuing melee, Schroeder brought down a Tempest, the fifth RAF loss of the day, all against no Israeli losses. A short while later, perhaps upset at having downed a British plane, Schroeder left the squadron and returned to the U.S. Schroeder's dispatch of the British plane on his only combat mission earned him the squadron nickname "Sudden Death."

Briefly, it looked as though a major international incident would result from the encounters between the Israeli and British planes. The British, who had still not recognized Israel and who continued to refer to the country as "Palestine," accused the Jews of unprovoked aggression against the RAF planes. Britain claimed its planes had been involved in peaceful monitoring flights, and even claimed initially that the Spitfires had not been armed. But Goodlin knew that his opponent had fired back, and the RAF pilots later confirmed that their weapons had been loaded. Britain and Israel quickly backed away from the confrontation. On the verge of winning its war with Egypt, Israel had no desire to draw England into the conflict. For its part, Britain's Labor government had been embarrassed by the whole affair, and came under attack in Parliament for needlessly placing RAF pilots in harm's way.

It was during a debate in the British Parliament on the January 7 incidents that another mystery was finally solved. The Labor government admitted, for the first time, that the Mosquito that Wayne Peake had shot down in November had also been a British plane.

John McElroy, who had begun his career as a fighter pilot with the RAF, felt badly when he learned that he had shot down British planes. He knew he had done the right thing. The planes were on the Israeli side of the border and had appeared to be attacking an Israeli convoy. But he would have preferred it if the planes had been Egyptian. Late into the night of January 7, he and the others discussed the day's events. At one point, someone suggested sending a telegram to Britain's 208 Squadron, to which the downed planes had belonged. The next day a telegram was prepared and sent, its text a mixture of apology and defiance: "Sorry about yesterday. You were on wrong side of fence. Come over and have a drink. You will meet many familiar faces."

There was another footnote to the encounter between the RAF and the 101 Squadron. Although nearly eight months had passed since Israel declared its independence, the British still held thousands of illegal Jewish immigrants in the Xylotymbou detention camps in Cyprus. That policy had infuriated Israel. But, with its hands full fighting the Arabs, Israel had not been able to do much in response to Britain's obviously vindictive measure. But with Israel's capture of two of the downed RAF pilots, it briefly considered detaining the two prisoners until the Jews on Cyprus were released. Ultimately, it gave up the idea and returned the two Brits unconditionally. Still, the affair drew attention to the situation on Cyprus and, by the end of the month, the British finally agreed to release all of the remaining detainees.

The cease-fire that went into effect January 7 held. On February 24, Egypt and Israel signed an armistice agreement, formally ending the fighting between them. Under the auspices of U.N. Special Envoy Ralph Bunche, Count Bernadotte's successor, Israel was negotiating agreements with Jordan, Lebanon and Syria. Bunche would later be awarded a Nobel Peace Prize for his efforts to negotiate a halt to the bloodshed. There was a need, however, for one more strategic operation.

A one-hundred-twenty-mile-long tract of desert stretching from Beersheba to the Gulf of Aqaba remained mostly uninhabited. With the fighting all but over, Jordan began quietly to infiltrate Arab Legion soldiers into the area in order to make a claim on the land during armistice negotiations. Although the area had been ignored by both sides during the war, the territory had great strategic significance for Israel. The desolate expanse could serve as a buffer against Jordan, and the sea port at its southernmost tip provided trade access with Africa and the Far East.

Israel desperately wanted to avoid another round of fighting. That meant taking the entire area without restarting the war. The operation to occupy the strategic sliver of land was code-named "Uvda" ("Fact"), a reference to the political objective of creating facts on the ground for the Jordanian negotiations. The plan called for two brigades to advance in secret from Beersheba. The Golani Brigade was to approach through the Arava, along the Jordanian border. Mike Rubin's and George Baler's Negev Brigade was ordered to advance through the valleys of the central Negev, closer to Egypt's border. If either brigade encountered enemy troops, its orders were to withdraw immediately. Supply and reinforcement of the two forces was the responsibility of the 106 Squadron – formerly the ATC.

Carrying thirty fully-equipped troops, fresh water, milk and other supplies in the cargo hold of the C-46, Slick Goodlin began the airlift segment of Operation Uvda from the Ekron air base on March 6, 1949. The test pilot had transferred to the transport squadron shortly after the fighting with the Egyptians had ended. For the next few weeks, the often overloaded C-46's continuously shuttled soldiers and equipment back and forth from Ekron to Avraham, a makeshift air strip thirty-five miles north of the Gulf of Aqaba.

On the last day of the airlift, American Percy "Pussy" Tolchinsky's left Ekron for the short flight south. Tolchinsky was a former B-25 pilot who had started his career in aviation at the Haganah course in Cream Ridge, New Jersey. Nine senior officials who wanted to get a first-hand look at Operation Uvda were also on board for the trip.

Tolchinsky landed at the Avraham airfield in less than an hour. After unloading, Pussy took on a load of cargo for the flight back to Ekron – five tons of land mines in wooden crates. Pussy headed the plane down the runway, with the original crew, passengers and the new cargo all on board. As the plane reached the end of the runway, it lurched into the air. Suddenly, there was a loud explosion as the right engine caught fire. Pussy tried to bring the plane back around for a landing, but it was losing altitude too quickly. He found an area that seemed suitable, and dropped the landing gear. At an altitude of about thirty feet, the plane stalled and fell onto its left wheel. The aircraft snapped to the left and stopped sharp. As the fire spread from the engine to the rest of the C-46, everyone scrambled to get off the plane and run for it. Within less than a minute, the first explosion shook the ground. In a matter of seconds the mines were exploding in full force, raining shrapnel over the entire area. Incredibly, no one was seriously injured.

While Pussy's C-46 burned, the few remaining Jordanian soldiers withdrew from the gulf area as the Negev and Golani Brigades approached. Without enemy resistance, the operation became a race to see which brigade could reach the Red Sea first. The honor went to the Negev Brigade. It took over an abandoned Jordanian police hut and raised a makeshift Israeli flag. The area formerly known to the Arabs as Um Rash Rash, where King Solomon had built ships to bring gold from Ophir nearly 2000 years earlier, was restored to its biblical name, Eilat.

Two hours after Rubin arrived with the Negev Brigade, the Golani Brigade reached Eilat and a victory celebration ensued. The sweltering heat encouraged everyone to jump into the Red Sea. Thousands of soldiers, men and women alike, peeled off their dusty uniforms and leapt naked into the water. It was, as Rubin recalled, "one of the largest naked bathing parties in history."

Operation Uvda was a complete success. With the capture of Eilat and the entire one hundred twenty miles leading to it from Beersheba, Israel had more than doubled its size without firing a shot. The cease-fire held and armistice agreements were quickly signed with the rest of Israel's Arab neighbors. Lebanon signed on March 23, just two weeks after Operation Uvda's completion. Jordan abandoned its claims to the area captured during Israel's final operation, and agreed to an armistice on April 3. Syria, the most stubborn of Israel's enemies, finally signed on July 20, 1949, ending Israel's longest and costliest war.

20

POST-WAR

In the spring of 1949, with the war over, most of the volunteers began to leave Israel. Many didn't wait even this long. The exodus began in January, after the success of Operation Horev had signaled an end to the fighting. Ralph Lowenstein was one of the early departures. The eighteen-year-old who had put aside his studies at Columbia University to fight for Israel managed to return to New York in time for the spring 1949 semester. When the rest of his class graduated two and one-half years later, Lowenstein, who added extra courses to catch up to the others, stood with them. He had managed to travel abroad, fight in another country's war, and still graduate from college on time.

Many stayed on for at least a few months, to help train young Israelis to fill the void created by the departing volunteers. This was particularly the case in the air force. In the 101 Squadron, Rudy Augarten, Caesar Dangott, Sid Antin and others remained in Israel to train the first class of Israeli fighter pilots. Augarten then returned to his studies at Harvard to complete his degree. He then came back to Israel, where he served for two years as the commander of the air base at Ramat David. When he resigned from the air force, he did so with the rank of lieutenant colonel. Jerry Renov, the "Flying Kippah" who had dropped a salami to his wife in besieged Jerusalem, also came back to Israel after a short stay in the U.S. to help train Israeli pilots. Slick Goodlin stayed on for a few months after the war, serving as the air force's first chief test pilot. The number of Americans in the air force after the war remained at such high levels that it was not until February 1, 1950, more than a year after the defeat of the Egyptians, that Hebrew replaced English as the required language for radio communication.

Outside of the air force, and within a relatively short period of time, some ninety percent of the American and Canadian volunteers had left Israel and returned home. A frequent topic of debate among foreign volunteers is whether Israel did enough to try to induce them to stay after the fighting was over. At the end of the war, Machal representatives Lee Harris and Akiva Skiddell approached Golda Meir, an influential member of Ben Gurion's government and a former American herself, to ask the government to make a special effort to persuade the American volunteers to remain in the country. "If you want these people to stay, some special effort has to be made," they pleaded. But Meir rejected their request. She pointed to the hundreds of thousands of new immigrants from Europe and the North African countries that Israel was struggling to absorb. "We can't start discriminating," she explained.

That is not to say that no effort was made to keep the foreign volunteers in the country. Israel offered a Hebrew language course, assistance in finding housing and, perhaps most important, loans for Machal soldiers who wished to start businesses in the country. Native American Jesse Slade, for one, took advantage of the loan program to start a cattle ranch in the Negev. But, in the end, it is not likely that even greater efforts on Israel's part would have made a difference. The overwhelming majority had come solely to lend a hand in the struggle for Jewish independence, with no intention of relocating permanently.

As the post-war quiet took hold in Israel, some signs of normalcy appeared. The air force even fielded a basketball team. Lee Silverman, a former member of UCLA's freshman team, was one of the early recruits. The air force team, with a starting five that included three Americans and a Canadian, won the national championship in the spring of 1949. A few months later, arrangements were made for the air force team to play a visiting squad from the U.S. Marines.

The game took place on an outdoor court in Jaffa. Soldiers crowded around the sidelines and stood on nearby balconies to get a glimpse of

Israel's first international sports event. Seated at center court was an American marine colonel and Aharon Remez, the commander of Israel's Air Force. In pre-game ceremonies, both teams lined up at center court and exchanged flags. There was an awkward silence during the ceremony. Israel's four North American players didn't speak, afraid their accents might give away their true nationalities.

It wasn't much of a game. The marines were each, in that service's finest tradition, big and strong. But they had no finesse for the game of basketball, which was reflected in the fatigue pants and boots each wore for the game. The Israeli squad quickly pulled ahead. But what the marines lacked in the finer skills of basketball, they made up by playing dirty. They pushed and shoved the much smaller Israeli players. Still determined to keep their identities secret, the North Americans kept their silence in the face of the marines' rough play.

But near the end of the game, which the Israeli team won 41 to 18, Silverman stood at center court when a huge Marine barreled into his back. Without thinking, Silverman whirled around and shouted, "You no good motherfucking son of a bitch!" Instantly, he realized his mistake. Silverman turned in time to see a bright red Aharon Remez and an open-mouthed marine colonel. After the game, all of the players attended a party. As soon as Silverman walked in, the entire marine team headed for him. "Only an American could swear like that!" one of them said. "I bet he was in the navy, too!" another one said of Silverman, who in fact had been in the U.S. Navy.

Within a few months of the game with the marines, Silverman left the air force and returned to California. Although he could not know it, he still had one more contribution to make.

American volunteers who returned to the States were relieved to discover there would be no repercussions as far as their citizenship was concerned from their efforts for Israel. Still, many of the returning soldiers were questioned by the authorities, and in some instances confronted with evidence of their having served in Israel's army. The experience was sufficiently unnerving to those who encountered it that several changed their names, hoping to avoid any future legal problems.

By no means, though, did all of the Americans who contributed to Israel's victory escape legal entanglements. Hank Greenspun's and Al

Schwimmer's escapades had hardly passed unnoticed. Schwimmer and Greenspun were charged with violating the Export Control Law, the Neutrality Act, and the Executive Order against shipment of aircraft and engines to the Middle East. Five other men were indicted with them, including Service Airways veterans Leo Gardner and Sam Lewis.

Lee Silverman arrived back in California shortly before the trial was scheduled to open in Los Angeles. He read a newspaper report about the upcoming trial of the "smuggling ring" with great interest. Almost all of the men had been in Israel with him, and one of the defendants, Leo Gardner, was a close friend. Silverman went down to the courthouse for the first day of trial, anxious to lend moral support to Gardner and the others. Silverman arrived during jury selection. He caught Gardner's eye and waved. Gardner, glad to see his old friend, came over to chat.

The prosecution was clearly determined to empanel a non-Jewish jury. It struck every prospective juror with a Jewish-sounding last name or accent. For their part, the lawyers for the defense sought to exclude those they feared might have anti-semitic beliefs. One question to prospective jurors approached this directly: "Do any of you hold any ideas or theories that there should be any distinction drawn of any kind between persons of the Jewish faith, race or creed and persons of other faiths, in connection with the enforcement of the laws of this country?" As Silverman and Gardner spoke, Silverman noticed that a new prospective juror was being questioned, a man named Marshall Chlavin. Chlavin was dark-skinned with sharp features. Silverman stared at the potential juror, convinced he had seen him before. He racked his brain for a few moments, trying to place Chlavin's face. Finally, he remembered.

Two years earlier, in November of 1947, Silverman had taken a public speaking class at UCLA. The U.N. passed the partition resolution on November 29th of that year, and a short while later Silverman's public speaking professor asked the students to give impromptu speeches on the subject. A woman stood up and spoke out strongly against the idea of a Jewish state. As she spoke, Silverman began to formulate a response. But before he had the chance to speak, a male student who Silverman didn't know caught the professor's attention. To Silverman's delight, that student delivered a stirring pro-Zionist speech.

Standing in the courtroom two years later, Silverman was certain that Marshall Chlavin was the student who had spoken some two years earlier. He told Gardner to immediately call over one of the lawyers. Attorney Bill Strong hurried over from the defense table, and Silverman related the story. Although Silverman couldn't offer any additional information about the potential juror – he didn't even know if Chlavin was Jewish – everyone agreed that there was reason enough to believe the man might be sympathetic. The defense managed to keep him on the jury. The final roster of jurors, however, suggested that the prosecution had mostly succeeded in empaneling a non-Jewish jury. Other than Chlavin, the other names on the final list of twelve jurors were Sprang, Hanlon, Howard, McGinley, Johnston, Scarborough, Carhart, Pearle, Ackerman, Irving, and Smock. The lead attorney for the defense, a former judge named Irving Pacht, was well aware that the jury was all or nearly-all non-Jewish, and tailored his arguments accordingly. In his closing statement, the Jewish lawyer declared: "You know, when I recently took a trip to Israel I visited the City of Nazareth, the birthplace of Jesus Christ, and it reminded me, and it reminds me now, of a rule of conduct He laid down which I have tried to follow in the course of my life, both as a lawyer and when I had the opportunity to serve in the judicial system. I tried to follow that rule. And that is, Do unto others as you would have others do unto you – the Golden Rule."

The trial lasted for more than three months. Intent on securing convictions, the prosecution even subpoenaed Nathan Liff, the elderly salvage yard owner who had befriended Greenspun. Herschel Champlin, one of the assistant U.S. attorneys prosecuting the case, examined him. An obviously uncomfortable Liff admitted giving the engines to Greenspun. "Mr. Greenspun approached me about some airplane engines which we bought from the War Assets, and he tried to buy it from me. And, after he told me for whom he is trying to buy these engines, I offered him the engines as a present," he testified. Liff was not happy to be in the courtroom, testifying against a man he admired. At one point during his testimony, he began to weep openly. Several of the jurors wept with him. Marshall Chlavin, however, showed no emotion. He stared in the direction of Greenspun and Schwimmer. Greenspun was troubled. "That's the guy who's going to hang us," he whispered to Schwimmer.

On February 2, 1950, after more than three months of trial, the case went to the jury. The deliberations took three days. Verdict in hand, the jurors returned to the courtroom. The defendants rose to hear the clerk of the court announce their fate. Four of the defendants, including Al Schwimmer and Leo Gardner, had been found guilty. Greenspun and the other two defendants had each been found not guilty. The verdict seemed to indicate some form of compromise on the part of the jurors.

After the clerk finished reading the verdicts of guilty and not guilty, he asked the judge whether he should read the rest of the form. "No, that is not part of the verdict," the judge instructed the clerk. Suddenly, Marshall Chlavin stood and addressed the judge. "I would like to have it read to the defendants, please." Irving Pacht, the lead defense attorney, now joined in, also asking for the rest of the verdict form to be read. The judge continued to resist. "As I indicated to the jury, punishment is not to be taken into consideration. This is a recommendation as to punishment. It is entirely my responsibility and has nothing to do with whether or not the jury has or has not found the defendants guilty or not guilty." Finally, though, he relented. The clerk read the rest of the form: "The jury unanimously recommends leniency on all guilty verdicts."

The judge ordered the clerk to poll the jury, asking each juror whether they agreed with the verdict. Chlavin acknowledged voting guilty, but insisted that the leniency plea was part of the decision. The judge was not moved. He ordered the judgment of guilty entered, disregarding the plea for leniency. He then dismissed the jury. Pacht was on his feet again: "Just a moment, before your Honor discharges the jury. I demand that you poll the jury again in light of Juror Chlavin's statement that that is not his verdict." After an extended argument, the judge agreed to a second polling. Again the clerk asked Chlavin whether he agreed with the verdict. "Not without leniency, sir – never," Chlavin announced. Concluding there was no unanimous verdict of guilty, the judge ordered the jury to resume deliberations.

The jurors were sequestered at a hotel near the courthouse. That first evening of the resumed deliberations, Chlavin was overwrought. His condition so worried the other jurors that just before midnight, the foreman sent a note to the judge: "We believe that Juror Chlavin is so emotionally upset that some official of the Court be designated to stay with him in his hotel room tonight."

The next day, the judge gave the jurors further instructions. He advised the jury that any recommendation of leniency would be "given most respectful consideration." A few hours later, the jury again returned verdicts of guilty against four of the defendants. Again, a plea for leniency was part of the verdict. Under that handwritten plea, all twelve jurors signed their names. Marshall Chlavin's signature was on the top of the list.

Chlavin's persistence paid off. The four men found guilty were each assessed $10,000 fines, which were paid by unnamed friends of Israel, and no jail sentences. Chlavin, the defendants were amused to learn, was Jewish, and in fact had been the commander of a Jewish war veterans post. Silverman's arrival in the courtroom during jury selection had been fortuitous.

There was, however, no Lee Silverman or Marshall Chlavin to rescue Charles Winters. Winters was the non-Jewish Miami businessman who sold three B-17's to Al Schwimmer, and then helped Schwimmer get the planes out of the U.S. Those three B-17's later formed Israel's entire heavy bomber squadron. In January of 1949, a federal judge sentenced Winters to eighteen months in prison for illegally exporting the planes. In the end, he would be the only American to go to prison for helping Israel.

Of all of the returning volunteers, perhaps none faced a more difficult reception than Tiny Balkin. After Phil's death, the army gave Tiny a ticket back to the States, and he returned to his family in California. When he arrived, he was devastated to learn his entire family blamed him for his younger brother's death. They believed that Phil went to Israel because of Tiny. In their minds, if Tiny had remained in California, Phil also would have stayed. They did not keep their feelings secret. One day, while walking down the street, Tiny ran into an old family friend. They exchanged greetings, and then the friend asked Tiny bluntly, "Are you satisfied? You killed your own brother!"

Tiny had his own pangs of conscience even without his family's accusations. Tiny now believed he was wrong to let Phil go to a different unit. He berated himself for not taking Phil into the Fourth. Tiny's guilt was overwhelming, and it cast a dark shadow over him. He married and raised a family, but he could not forget. Sometimes, he found himself flying into unexplained fits of rage. The decades passed, and still Tiny could not shake the burden of his brother's death.

Some forty years after the war, a seemingly minor incident helped Tiny finally overcome his feelings of responsibility. He attended a reunion of foreign veterans of the War of Independence. There, he found himself face to face with Mike Isaacson, the South African who drove the half-track that fateful day. The two men hugged, and began to cry. Tiny was shocked to learn that Isaacson too blamed himself for Phil's death. The South African believed his decision to go into battle even after the half-track had stalled cost Phil his life. Tiny comforted Isaacson, explaining that his brother's death wasn't anybody's fault. As he spoke to Isaacson, Tiny found himself for the first time understanding the injustice of blaming himself for what happened to his brother. The realization was long overdue. Finally, forty years after the war, Tiny was at peace with himself.

EPILOGUE

David Gutmann - Gutmann returned to the States, and enrolled in college. He obtained a Phd., and is a professor of education and psychiatry at Northwestern University.

Heavy Greaves - Heavy stayed in Israel for a few years after the war. He joined Israel's merchant marine, where he trained the first generation of Israeli merchant seamen. He left Israel in the early 1950's. At the end of his life, he worked as a Shabbos Goy.

David Starec - Starec remained in Israel after the war, Hebraicizing his last name to Kochavi. He became a university teacher. When we interviewed him for this book, Starec, who was already fluent in twelve languages and had a working knowledge of five more, was studying Chinese.

Paul Shulman - Shulman resigned from the navy in 1949, becoming a naval and maritime adviser to the prime minister. He later founded the National Engineering Company, which engaged in major civil engineering projects in Israel and throughout the world. Shulman settled in Haifa.

Herbert Hordes, Mike Rubin, and *George Baler* - These three settled in Israel after the war.

Ben Dunkelman - Dunkelman returned to Canada. He became president of Tip Top Tailors, a nationwide chain of clothing manufacturers. He also remained active in Jewish veterans' affairs.

Lionel Druker and *Arthur Goldberg* - Druker and Goldberg, fifty years after the war, remain the best of friends. They are also business partners. In 1951, they started Israel's first car rental agency. They later established a tour bus service. Their company, United Tours, continues to thrive.

Al Schwimmer - While Schwimmer escaped a prison term thanks to Marshall Chlavin, the felony conviction destroyed any chance he might have had for a career in aviation in the United States. He went back to Israel within a few years of the trial. There, he established Israel Aircraft Industries, Israel's largest employer, and for many years was its managing director. IAI's products have included the Kfir jet fighter and the Westwind line of commercial jets.

Sam Lewis - Lewis, who gave up his TWA captaincy at Schwimmer's request, became one of El Al's first captains. He continued to fly even after he passed El Al's mandatory retirement age for pilots, first for IAI and later as the private pilot for an Israeli tycoon.

Norm Moonitz - Moonitz flew for El Al for several years. He later flew for Lufthansa and for Trans International Airlines, based in Oakland.

Ray Kurtz - Kurtz lost his life in 1951, only two years after the war ended. He was ferrying a Mosquito bomber to Israel when his plane crashed near Greenland. His body was never recovered.

Harold Livingston - Moonitz's sidekick in Panama became a successful writer. Livingston has written more than a half dozen novels. He also wrote the screenplay for the first *Star Trek* movie, an effort that earned him an academy award nomination. His memoir of his experiences in Israel, *No Trophy No Sword*, appeared in hardcover in 1994. It is to be published in paperback under the title *Destination: Israel*.

Milton "Limey" Miller - The veteran of three armies who telegraphed Ben Gurion's Declaration of Independence to Jerusalem, became a hero after the war. Miller remained in military intelligence for more than twenty years. In a famous incident, he and another member of his unit intercepted a telephone call between Egypt's President Nasser and Jordan's King Hussein on the first day of the 1967 Six Day War. During that call, Nasser and Hussein agreed to blame Israel's destruction of the Egyptian air force on American and British planes – to deny Israel credit for its astounding victory and perhaps also to lure the Soviets into the war on the Arab side. Israel immediately released the transcript of the conversation Miller intercepted.

Lou Lenart - Lenart, the former Marine pilot who led the raid on the Egyptian forces advancing on Tel Aviv, has had a varied career. He was at one time the general manager of the San Diego Clippers of the National Basketball Association. He also co-produced *Iron Eagle*, a movie about air combat that starred Lou Gosset, Jr. He later moved back to Israel, where his youngest daughter joined the air force.

Gideon Lichtman - Lichtman returned to the U.S. after the war. He remained in the U.S. Air Force Reserve, and flew combat missions with his squadron in Korea.

Joe Weiner - Weiner returned to Canada, and rejoined the Canadian army.

Jerry Renov - The Flying Kippah had a passion for aviation that was never fully satisfied. After a few years back in the U.S., he rejoined the Israeli Air Force as a flight instructor. He devoted himself to learning to fly every type of aircraft possible, including hot air balloons, paraplanes, hang-gliders, amphibious planes, jets, and helicopters. His son became a pilot in the Israeli Air Force.

John McElroy - On his way back to Canada after the war, McElroy lost his flight log. That log contained the details of his downing of the two British Spits on January 7. McElroy was terrified that the log might fall into the hands of the authorities, and that he could be arrested for his actions against the nationals of a fellow member of the commonwealth. For a few years, he stayed in the United States. When it became clear there would be no repercussions for the dogfight with the Brits, he returned to Canada and rejoined the Royal Canadian Air Force.

Jack Doyle - Doyle also rejoined the Royal Canadian Air Force after the war.

Trygve Maseng - Maseng remained in Israel. For many years he was a pilot for Arkia, Israel's domestic air carrier. Dani Maseng, his son, is an accomplished musician, actor, and playwright who has starred in numerous Broadway productions.

Hank Greenspun - Greenspun returned to his family in Nevada. There he established a media empire that includes a cable TV station and the *Las Vegas Sun*.

Tiny Balkin - After a number of years back in the U.S., Balkin returned to Israel and settled on Kibbutz Barkayni.

Jesse Slade - Slade's cattle ranch in the Negev did not work out. He left Israel. Like Heavy Greaves, his last job was as a Shabbos Goy.

Rudy Augarten - Augarten left the Israeli Air Force in 1951 as a lieutenant colonel. He returned to school in the U.S. to study engineering. He went to work for Rockwell International, and was on the team that designed the command module and lunar lander for the first Apollo Mission.

Wayne Peake - The pilot who shot down the British Mosquito went back to the U.S., but never forgot Israel. Ill with cancer, his dying wish was to be buried in Israel.

Ted Gibson - The commander of 35 Flight joined El Al after the war. He was killed in a plane crash in 1951. When his father, a Southern Baptist minister, learned of his son's death, he said: "If my son had to die, it could not be for a better cause than the cause of the Jewish state."

Ralph Lowenstein - Lowenstein became a college professor, and served as dean of the college of journalism at the University of Florida for eighteen years.

Slick Goodlin - Goodlin remains active in aviation. The legendary test pilot is currently involved in developing a new type of aircraft.

APPENDIX

Interviews Conducted by the Authors

Samuel Alexander

Max Alper

Murray Aronoff

Harold Auerbach

Rudy Augarten

Shmuel B'ari

George Baler

Gideon "Tiny" Balkin

David Baum

Joe Becker

Raphael Ben-Yosef

Stanley Berger

Phil Bock

Sam Boshes

Zwi Brenner

Engee Caller

Alexander Caplan

Paul Chamberlain

Eli Cohen

Nat Cohen

Jules Cuburnek

Yochanan Dreyfus

Lionel Druker

Aaron Eden

Joe Eisen

Al Ellis

Irv Fellner

Aaron "Red" Finkel

Mitch Flint

Jack Fox

Leon Frankel

David Gen

Rabbi Abraham Goldberg

Arthur Goldberg

Dr. Moshe Goldberg

George Goldman

Jack Goldstein

Chalmers "Slick" Goodlin

Sam Gordon

Dr. David Gutmann

Professor Ruth Guttman

Sidney Halperin

Hillel Haramati

Eliahu Harris

Matityahu Harris

Moshe Hellner

Dr. Joe Herman

Herbert Hordes

Arieh Jacoby

David Kaplan

Abraham Kenny

Moshe Kidar

David Kochavi (Starec)

Nat Krotinger

Benny Kulbersh

Aaron Lebow

Lou Lenart

Mort Levenson

Aaron Levin

Betty Levin

Marlin Levin

Miriam Levin

Gideon "Giddy" Lichtman

William Lichtman

Shmaryahu Lieberman

Avi Livney

Maurice Lobe

Dr. Ralph Lowenstein

Dr. David Macarov

Aryeh Malkin

Dani Maseng

Mendy Mendelson

Chaim Meyers

Milton "Limy" Miller

Dov Mils

Norm Moonitz

Maier Naturman

Menachem Peretz

Zipporah Porath

Alisa Poskanzer

Leonard Prager

Al Raisin

Robert Reed

Leon "Lee" Reinharth

Bea Renov

Pinchas Rimon

Richard Rosenberg

Mayer "Mike" Rubin

Mordecai "Mort" Rubin

Rabbi Moses Sachs

Yechiel Sasson

Abraham Sengal

Leib Shanas

Abie Shefi

Manny Shell

Danny Shimshoni

Rose Shulman

Professor Hillel Shuval

Leon "Lee" Silverman

Smoky Simon

Benjamin Sklar

Art Sockol

Chaya Solomon

David Solomon

Yehuda Solter

Si Spiegelman

Phillip Strauss

Chaim Tal

Yaffa Tal

Josef Tunis

Saul Twicken

Joel Warner

Jack Yeriel

Shlomo Yurman

Charlie Zeevi

Nachum Ziv

Interviews Provided by Dr. David Bercuson

Rudy Augarten

Syd Cadloff

Murray Cappell

Eddie Chinsky

Danny Cravitt

Jack Doyle

Harold Freeman

Arthur Goldberg

Hyman Goldstein

Jack Goldstein

Lee Harris

Leo Heaps

Len Hyman

Yale Joffe

David Kaplansky

Eddy Kaplansky

Bill Katz

Harold Katz

Sam Lewis

Giddy Lichtman

John McElroy

Stan Miller

Harvey Nachman

Dr. W. H. Novick

Harold Orloff

David Panar

Aharon Remez

Danny Rosin

Boris Senior

Sydney Shulemson

Smoky Simon

Akiva Skiddel

Len Waldman

Joe Weiner

C.D. Wilson

Interviews Provided by the Diaspora Research Center

Jerry Renov

Paul Shulman

Interviews Provided by the Israeli Air Force Historical Branch

Trygve Maseng

Percy "Pussy" Tolchinsky

Brian Wiegel

Interviews Provided by American Veterans of Israel[1]

Max Alper	Benno Kate
Murray Aronoff	Harold Kates
Rudy Augarten	Harold Katz
Jerry "Tiny" Balkin	Frank Kettiver
Y.S. Belin	Nat Kroetinger
Art Bernstein	Joe Landau
Finke Bleviss	Marvin Lebow
Max Brown	Gideon "Giddy" Lichtman
Al Brownstein	Harold "Hal" Livingston
Engee Caller	Leo Majzels
Murray Cappell	Arieh Malkin
Alex Chapnick	John McElroy
Lenny Cohen	Jim McGunigal
Lionel Cowt	Nathan Miller
Freddie Dahms	Bill Millman
Bob Dawn	Nat Nadler
Lionel Druker	Abie Natan
Ben Dunkelman	Mickey Olfman
Al Ellis	Norm Olin
David Fendel	David Panar
Aaron "Red" Finkel	Rudolph Patzert
Charles Firestone	Wally Reiter
Mitch Flint	Pinchas Rimon
Ansel Garfin	Willie Rostoker
Al Gelmon	Abraham Segal
David Gen	Yehuda Sela
Arthur Goldberg	Akiva Skidell
Hy Goldstein	Red Sturrey
Myron Goldstein	Harvey Surilnikoff
Jerry Gross	Joe Villard
David Gutmann	Denny Wilson
Laz Kahan	

---

[1] Most of these interviews were conducted by Michel Finegood.

Interviews Provided by Dan Kurzman

Leonard Bernstein

Nahum Bernstein

Phil Bock

Moshe Brodetsky

Monroe Fien

Lee Harris

Zvi Shapiro

Paul Shulman

Rudolph Sonnenborn

BIBLIOGRAPHY

For basic historical information on the War of Independence, the authors have relied to a large extent on the existing literature about the war. This includes *The Edge of the Sword*, Netanel Lorch's comprehensive account of Israel's struggle for independence. We also acknowledge a debt of gratitude to Harold Livingston, whose memoir *No Trophy No Sword* was an invaluable source for information about the Air Transport Command, Harold Livingston's and Norm Moonitz's antics in Panama and Natal, the ATC strike, and the air force meeting following the Altalena incident.

Allon, Yigal. *Shield of David: The Story of Israel's Armed Forces*. New York: Random House, 1970.

Argaman, Josef. *It Was Top Secret*. Tel Aviv, 1994. (Hebrew)

Avinoam, Reuven (Ed.). *Such Were Our Fighters: Anthology of Writings By Soldiers Who Died for Israel*. New York: Herzl Press, 1965.

Banks, Lynne Reid. *Torn Country: An Oral History of the Israeli War of Independence*. New York: Franklin Watts, 1982.

Begin, Menachem. *The Revolt: The Story of the Irgun*. Tel Aviv: Hadar, 1964.

Bell, J. Bowyer. *Terror Out of Zion: The Violent and Deadly Shock Troops of Israeli Independence, 1929-1949*. New York: St. Martin's Press, 1977.

Ben-Ami, Yitshaq. *Years of Wrath, Days of Glory: Memoirs from the Irgun*. New York: Robert Speller & Sons, 1982.

Bercuson, David J. *The Secret Army*. Toronto: Lester & Opren Dennys Limited, 1983.

Berkman, Ted. *Cast a Giant Shadow*. New York: Doubleday, 1962.

Beurling, George F. and Roberts, Leslie. *Malta Spitfire: The Story of a Fighter Pilot*. New York: Farrar & Rinehart, Inc., 1943.

Black, Ian and Morris, Benny. *Israel's Secret Wars: A History of Israel's Intelligence Services*. New York: Grove Weidenfeld, 1991.

Boyington, Gregory "Pappy." *Baa Baa Black Sheep*. New York: Bantam Books, 1977.

Burstein, Samuel. *Rabbi with Wings: Story of a Pilot*. New York: Herzl Press, 1965.

Clark, Thurston. *By Blood and Fire: July 22, 1946: The Attack on Jerusalem's King David Hotel*. New York: G.P. Putnam's Sons, 1981.

Cohen, Eliezer and Lavi, Zvi. *The Sky is Not the Limit*. Jerusalem: Keterpress Enterprises, 1990.

Collins, Larry and Lapierre, Dominique. *O Jerusalem!* New York: Simon and Schuster, 1972.

Dahms, Evelyn M. *Goyim*. (Unpublished)

Dayan, Moshe. *Story of My Life*. London: Sphere Books Ltd., 1978.

Derogy, Jacques and Carmel, Hesi. *The Untold History of Israel*. New York: Grove Press,1979.

Dror, Yosef. *HaComando HaYami: Elav U'Memenu*. Israel: HaKibbutz Hameuchad, 1981. (Hebrew)

Dunkelman, Ben. *Dual Allegiance*. New York: Crown Publishers, Inc., 1976.

Eldar, Mike. *Flotilla 13: The Story of Israel's Navy Commandos*. Jerusalem: Keterpress Enterprises, 1993. (Hebrew)

Fenton, Denis. *Recollections and Reflections of Volunteers in the War of Independence*. (Unpublished)

Gelber, Yoav. *The Emergence of a Jewish Army*. Jerusalem: Yad Izhak Ben-Zvi Institute, 1986. (Hebrew)

Gitlin, Jan. *The Conquest of Acre Fortress*. Tel Aviv: Hadar Publishing, 1968.

Greenspun, Hank and Pelle, Alex. *Where I Stand: The Record of a Reckless Man*. New York: David McKay Company, 1966.

Hecht, Ben. *A Child of the Century*. New York: Simon and Schuster, 1954.

Heckelman, A. Joseph. *American Volunteers and Israel's War of Independence*. New York: KTAV Publishing House, Inc., 1974.

Hellman, Peter. *Heroes: Tales from the Israeli Wars*. New York: Henry Holt and Company, 1990.

Hochstein, Joseph M. and Greenfield, Murray S. *The Jews' Secret Fleet: The Untold Story of North American Volunteers Who Smashed the British Blockade*. Jerusalem: Gefen, 1986.

Holly, David C. *Exodus 1947*. Maryland: Naval Institute Press, 1995.

Hurewitz, J.C. *The Struggle for Palestine*. New York: Schocken, 1976.

Jane's Fighting Aircraft of World War II. New York: Crescent Books, 1995.

Kaplansky, Eddy. *The First Fliers: Aircrew Personnel in the War of Independence*. Jerusalem: Israel Defense Forces, The Air Force History Branch, 1993.

Katz, Samuel. *Days of Fire*. New York: Doubleday, 1968.

Katz, Samuel M. *Fire & Steel: Four Decades of Victory and Courage - The Story of the Most Awesome Tank Force in the World Today*. New York: Pocket Books, 1996.

Kimche, Jon. *The Secret Roads*. London: Secker, 1954.

Kurzman, Dan. *Genesis 1948: The First Arab-Israeli War*. New York: World Publishing Company, 1970.

Lapide, Pinchas E. *A Century of U.S. Aliya*. Jerusalem: Jerusalem Post Press, 1961.

Levett, Gordon. *Flying Under Two Flags: An Ex-RAF Pilot in Israel's War of Independence*. Portland: Frank Cass, 1994.

Livingston, Harold. *No Trophy No Sword: An American Volunteer in the Israeli Air Force During the 1948 War of Independence*. Chicago: Edition q, Inc., 1994.

Lorch, Netanel. *The Edge of the Sword*. New York: Putnam,1961.

Lorch, Netanel. *One Long War: Arab Versus Jew Since 1920*. Jerusalem: Keter, 1976.

Mardor, Munya. *Haganah*. New York: New American Library, 1966.

Milstein, Uri. *The History of the Israeli Paratroopers*. Tel Aviv: Shalgi, 1985. (Hebrew)

Naor, Dr. Mordechai (Editor). *The Hagana Lexicon.* Tel Aviv: Ministry of Defense, 1994. (Hebrew)

Nolan, Brian. *Hero: The Buzz Beurling Story.* Toronto: Lester & Opren Dennys Limited, 1981.

Nordeen, Lon. *Fighters Over Israel: The Story of the Israeli Air Force from the War of Independence to the Bekaa Valley.* New York: Orion Books, 1990.

O'Ballance, Edgar. *The Arab-Israeli War, 1948.* London: Faber, 1956.

Ondra, Winona Holler. *Lonesome & Coping.* Pennsylvania: Boyden, 1997.

Patzert, Rudolph W. *Running the Palestine Blockade: The Last Voyage of the Paducah.* Maryland: Naval Institute Press, 1994.

Perl, William R. *The Four-Front War: The Most Daring Rescue Operation of the Century.* New York: Crown Publishers, 1979.

Peyser, Joan. *Bernstein: A Biography.* New York: Ballantine Books, 1987.

Porath, Zipporah. *Letters from Jerusalem 1947-1948.* Jerusalem: Association of Americans and Canadians in Israel, 1987.

Postal, Bernard and Levy, Henry W. *And the Hills Shouted for Joy: The Day Israel Was Born.* New York: David McKay Company, Inc., 1973.

Raviv, Dan and Melman, Yossi. *Every Spy a Prince: The Complete History of Israel's Intelligence Community.* Boston: Houghton Mifflin, 1990.

Robinson, Donald (Ed.). *Under Fire: Israel's 20-Year Struggle for Survival.* New York: W. W. Norton & Company, Inc., 1968.

Sachar, Howard M. *A History of Israel: From the Rise of Zionism to Our Time.* New York: Alfred A. Knopf, 1981.

Safran, Nadav. *Israel the Embattled Ally.* Cambridge: The Belknap Press, 1981.

Schechtman, Joseph B. *The United States and the Jewish State Movement: The Crucial Decade: 1939-1949.* New York: Herzl Press, 1966.

Schiff, Ze'ev. *Tsahal B'Cheylo: Chayl Ha'avir.* Tel Aviv: Revivim, 1981. (Hebrew)

Shamir, Shlomo. *No Matter What – To Jerusalem.* Tel Aviv: Ministry of Defense, 1994. (Hebrew)

Shapira, Daniel. *Alone in the Sky.* Jerusalem: Keterpress Enterprises, 1994. (Hebrew)

Shmuelevitz, Matty. *The Red Days.* Tel Aviv: Ministry of Defense, 1978. (Hebrew)

Shores, Christopher and Williams, Clive. *Aces High: A Tribute to the Most Notable Fighter Pilots of the British and Commonwealth Forces in WWII.* London: Glubb Street, 1994.

Slater, Leonard. *The Pledge.* New York: Pocket Books, 1971.

Slater, Robert. *Great Jews in Sports.* New York: Jonathan David Publishers, 1992.

Spicehandler, Daniel. *Let My Right Hand Wither.* New York: Beechhurst Press, 1950.

Stone, I.F. *Underground to Palestine.* New York: Pantheon, 1978.

Sykes, Christopher. *Crossroads to Israel.* New York: World, 1965.

Szulc, Tad. *The Secret Alliance: The Extraordinary Story of the Rescue of the Jews Since World War II.* New York: Farrar, Straus and Giroux, 1991.

Tsur, Meron. *Moka Limon.* Tel Aviv: Ma'arive Book Guild, 1988. (Hebrew)

Walton, Frank E. *Once They Were Eagles: The Men of the Black Sheep Squadron.* Lexington: University Press of Kentucky, 1986.

Wyman, Mark. DP: *Europe's Displaced Persons, 1949-1951.* Philadelphia: The Balch Institute Press, 1989.

Yeager, Chuck and Janos, Leo. *Yeager: An Autobiography.* New York: Bantam Books, 1985.

Zaar, Isaac. *Rescue and Liberation: America's Part in the Birth of Israel.* New York: Bloch Publishying Company, 1954.

INDEX